THE BASIS OF MORALITY ACCORDING TO WILLIAM OCKHAM

by
Lucan Freppert, O.F.M.

FRANCISCAN HERALD PRESS
1434 West 51st Street
Chicago, Illinois 60609

THE BASIS OF MORALITY ACCORDING TO WILLIAM OCKHAM by Lucan Freppert, O.F.M. Copyright ©1988 by Franciscan Herald Press, 1434 West 51st Street, Chicago, Illinois 60609. All rights reserved.

Library of Congress Cataloging-in-Publication Data:

Freppert, Lucan.
    The basis of morality according to William Ockham / by Lucan Freppert.
      p.   cm.
    Bibliography: p.
    ISBN 0-8199-0918-1
    1. William, of Ockham, ca. 1285-ca. 1349—Ethics. 2. Ethics-History. 3. Christian ethics—History—Middle Ages, 600-1500. I. Title.
B765.O34F74   1988   87-34330
170'.92'4—dc19   CIP

Cover design by William Dichtl & Blane O'Neill, O.F.M.

MADE IN THE UNITED STATES OF AMERICA

ACKNOWLEDGEMENTS

I wish to express my deepest thanks and appreciation to the following:

To Fr. Allan B. Wolter, O.F.M., who directed the research for this work originally and did the most to prepare copy for publication;

To Dr. Girard Etzkorn and Mark Henninger, S.J., who not only gave encouragement but made the references' changes to correspond with the critical edition of Ockham;

To Dr. Marilyn McCord Adams, the moving spirit behind the plan to publish, who graciously contributed a valuable Preface.

Without the completely unselfish assistance given by these scholars this study would have remained buried, just another quaint and curious volume of forgotten lore.

Fr. Lucan Freppert
                                                    Quincy College
                                                    Quincy, Illinois

TABLE OF CONTENTS

PREFACE vii
CHAPTER I: INTRODUCTION 1
CHAPTER II: MORAL SCIENCE 15
CHAPTER III: THE HUMAN WILL AND RIGHT REASON 32
CHAPTER IV: GOD: THE OBJECTIVE NORM OF MORALITY 83
    1. Love God 85
    2. God Wills 97
    3. Will What He Wills 112
    4. Application to Special Problems 121
CHAPTER V: THE NATURE OF MORALITY 141
CHAPTER VI: CONCLUSION 171
BIBLIOGRAPHY 182
    Ancient and Medieval Works 183
    Ockham Literature 185
    General Works 190

PREFACE

In the summer 1982. I was doing some research on Ockham's ethics and had occasion to read the secondary literature on the subject published over the last twenty years. Ockham's notorious claims that God could command things contrary to right reason-- acts now called "adultery" and "theft" and even the hatred of God-- were approached from many angles. The More than Subtle Doctor was invidiously compared with Kant, likened to existentialists, and rendered into dontic logic. When I had all but finished my survey, Drs. Gedeon Gál, O.F.M., and Rega Wood of the Franciscan Institute called my attention to the doctoral dissertation of Lucan Freppert, O.F.M., entitled *The Basis of Morality According to William Ockham* (St. Bonaventure University, 1961). I devoured it with enthusiasm. Methodologically, Freppert eschewed anachronism, taking his cue for understanding Ockham's project from his immediate and prominent confrere Duns Scotus. Moreover, Freppert's booklength study was comprehensive, proceeding systematically from Ockham's understanding of moral science, to his treatment of the human will and right reason, through their relation to divine commands. Freppert's analysis of the texts was thorough and philosophically rigorous. Without agreeing to every detail, I found Freppert's work far and away the best piece on Ockham's ethics to date. I wondered why it had not been published in the Franciscan Institute's Philosophy Series back in the early sixties. How much ink and confusion could have been saved if only it had been! I opined to Dr. Girard Etzkorn, that it would be the definitive treatment of Ockham's ethics, if published now over twenty years later!

Inquiries revealed that plans to publish Freppert's dissertation, supervised by Allan B. Wolter, O.F.M. had been obstructed by historical contingencies having nothing to do with Freppert or his work. Consultation found Freppert willing to publish but unable (because of ill-health and other commitments) to return to the project. In fact, no content-changes appeared desirable. Since the dissertation had been submitted before the critical edition of Ockham had begun to appear, however, Freppert had used the incunabula edition of Ockham's Sentence Commentary. Freppert authorized changing the Ockham-references to volumes of the critical edition as a convenience to current readers, and this task was undertaken by Mark Henninger, S.J., Dr. Girard Etzkorn, and Allan B. Wolter, O.F.M.

Marilyn McCord Adams   University of California,
                                                 Los Angeles

CHAPTER I

INTRODUCTION

The forces which shape a man's life are indeed complex. Birth in a certain place and at a certain time provides the general setting where a particular man's development must take place. To escape this setting is difficult, often impossible. In a very real sense every man is a creature, though often far from a helpless slave, of his time. Although he may raise himself by his God-given faculties head and shoulders above the crowd, his feet, as it were, remain fixed to the ground. It is this contact with the existing world of men that impresses itself so forcibly on the whole life of every man. A man's intellectual life, too, develops in such a concrete setting. He may reject with his whole being all the prevailing philosophies of his time; nevertheless he can scarcely remain totally untouched by them. In fact, his very act of rejection may well be unconsciously inspired by a strong undercurrent that remains hidden but none the less forceful.

To assess accurately the complex influences which actually play a part in the formation of a man's life and character is always an arduous and hazardous task. The very complexity of these influences makes a completely detailed examination of them impossible. To isolate and subject to microscopic analysis any single cultural item runs the risk of distorting the cultural pattern as a whole. This risk is doubly great when the pattern itself is highly fluid. The danger lies in this: my stabilizing of the structure of the pattern freezes it in an unnatural state. We should by no means minimize the achievements of truly great historians or discount the valuable contributions they have made to our understanding of the people and the culture of ages which precede our own. We wish only to point out a fact that historians themselves are only too ready to acknowledge regarding the difficulties inherent in their work. These difficulties are magnified, no doubt, in those special periods of history which are characterized as "transitional." History's periods of transition have always been difficult and challenging objects of historical research.

CHAPTER I

In such a transitional period of history, at least in so far as the history of philosophy is concerned, lived William Ockham, the "Venerabilis Inceptor".[1] Small wonder, then, that in our own times of a developed historical research and improved methodology Ockham is still referred to as a "figure enigmatique."[2] Special commissions established for the purpose of passing judgment on the man and his works seemed unable to reach a definite conclusion.[3] And unlike other historical personages upon whom historians, coming upon the scene centuries later, with cold impartiality have been able to render a clear and final verdict, Ockham's trial continues. I choose the word "trial" intentionally; for that is what Ockham's case resembles in much of our contemporary literature. But while evidence is accumulated for the prosecution and the defense, it as yet seems insufficient for either an outright conviction or acquittal. We seem to be as helpless in our own days as the censuring boards of Ockham's time to reach a final decision. *Quot capita, tot sententiae.*

We do not feel that it is necessary to enumerate all the divergent labelings that Ockham's philosophy has acquired in the course of time. These have been admirably summarized elsewhere.[4] Suffice it to say that the labels have ranged from "conservative Augustinianism," freeing itself from the bonds of Aristotelian slavery, to "pure Aristotelianism," attempting to purge the accretions

---

[1] For the best treatments, concise yet complete, of the life of Ockham see P. Boehner (ed.) *The Tractatus de Successivis Attributed to William Ockham*, ("Franciscan Institute Publications; Philosophy Series," No. 1; St. Bonaventure, N.Y.: Franciscan Institute, 1944), pp. 1-15; L. Baudry, *Guillaume d'Occam. Sa vie, ses oeuvres, ses idees sociales et politiques*, tom. I: *L'homme et les oeuvres* ("Études de philosophie médiévale," XXXIX; Paris; Vrin, 1950). In a bibliographical footnote R. Guelluy presents a list of works on the life of Ockham: *Philosophie et théologie chez Guillaume d'Ockham* (Louvain: Nauwelaerts, 1947), pp. 1-2. Since the publication of Guelluy's book the following have also dealt with the life of Ockham: P. Boehner (ed.), *Ockham. Philosophical Writings* ("Nelson Philosophical Texts"; London: Nelson, 1957), pp. xi-xvi; F.Copleston, *A History of Philosophy*, Vol. III: *Ockham to Suarez* (Westminster: Newman, 1953), pp. 43-44; R. Höhn, "Wilhelm Ockham in München," *Franziskanische Studien*, XXXII (1950), pp. 142-155; J. Morrall, "Some Notes on a Recent Interpretation of William of Ockham's Political Philosophy," *Franciscan Studies* IX, (1949), pp. 335-369.

[2] R. Guelluy, *op. cit*, p. 13.

[3] P. Boehner (ed.), *The Tractatus de Successivis*, pp. 5-6.

[4] Cf. R. Guelluy, *op. cit*, pp. 13-21.

INTRODUCTION

of Augustinian-Platonic-Arabian influences.[5] Ockham has been called a nominalist and skeptic, an idealist and an agnostic on the one hand; on the other hand these titles have been denied and he has been defended as a realistic conceptualist.[6] As M. Menges notes, "Ockham has been accused of every theological, philosophical and political sin."[7]

Let us turn to the specific field of ethics. There is a scarcity of real studies on Ockham's ethics. As late as 1952 P. Boehner remarked that Ockham's psychology and ethics were hardly investigated as yet.[8] The situation has not changed much since that time, except that whereas P. Boehner refers only to an article by A. Garvens, we may also add the works of E. Bonke and E. Iserloh, which appeared at a later date than B. Boehner's article.[9] A Garvens pictured Ockham as destroying the entire basis of morality, extending his nominalism into the field of ethics, and, dedicated to a thorough-going voluntarism, ending in the dead-end of divine moral positivism.[10] E. Bonke, however, apparently thought that the criticisms of A. Garvens, as well as the criticisms of most of the

---

[5] Cf. L. Baudry (ed.), *Le Tractatus de principiis theologiae attribue a G. d'Occam* ("Études de philosphie médiévale," XXIII; Paris; Vrin, 1936), pp. 42-43; M. Menges, *The Concept of Univocity regarding the Predication of God and Creature according to William Ockham* ("Franciscan Institute Publications; Philosophy Series," No. 9; St. Bonaventure, N.Y.: Franciscan Institute, 1952), pp. 2-3; E. Moody, *The Logic of William of Ockham* (New York: Sheed and Ward, 1935), p. 9.

[6] Cf. A. Pegis, "Concerning William of Ockham," *Traditio*, II (1944), pp. 465-480; P. Boehner, "The Realistic Conceptualism of William Ockham," *Traditio*, IV (1946), pp. 307-335. See also M. Menges, *op. cit.*, pp. 178-180.

[7] M. Menges, *op. cit.*, p. 179.

[8] P. Boehner, "Der Stand der Ockham-Forschung," *Franziskanische Studien*, XXXIV (1952), pp. 30-31. A few years earlier the same author had written in "A Recent Presentation of Ockham's Philosophy," Franciscan Studies, IX (1949), p. 453: "Ockham's ethics is still little explored and probably less understood."

[9] A. Garvens, "Die Grundlagen der Ethik Wilhelms von Ockham," *Franziskanische Studien*, XXI (1934), pp. 243-273, 360-408; E. Bonke, "Doctrina nominalistica de fundamento ordinis moralis apud Gulielmum de Ockham et Gabrielem Biel," *Collectanae franciscana*, XIV (1944), pp. 57-83; E. Iserloh, *Gnade und Eucharistie in der philosophischen Theologie des Wilhelm von Ockham* (Wiesbaden: Steiner, 1956), pp. 44-79. See also J. Rubert y Candáu, "Los principios básicos de la etica en el ockhamismo y en la vía moderna de los siglos XIV y XV," *Verdad y vida*, XVIII (1960), pp. 97-116.

[10] A. Garvens, *op. cit., passim*.

CHAPTER I

general histories of philosophy which treat Ockham's ethics, are too severe in their condemnation of the "Venerabilis Inceptor."[11]

A more particularized question can be raised in the history of philosophy: how does Ockham fit into the Franciscan tradition? Assuming that there is something identifiable as a "Franciscan tradition," what place does Ockham occupy in it? Here again we have a wide divergency in viewpoints. Ockham may be pictured as standing off by himself, equally opposed to Thomism and Scotism, having no place in the Franciscan tradition.[12] On the other hand, Ockham may be considered as carrying on the tradition of St. Bonaventure and Duns Scotus, united in their mutual endeavors to combat unchristian errors of determinism and, in a more positive manner, attempting to uphold against the errors of necessitarianism the liberty and omnipotence of God, his free will in creating, and the complete contingency of the creature.[13] Or again, Duns Scotus may be to as Ockham's "principal adversary";[14] on the other hand, Ockham and Scotus are united in the Franciscan tradition through the ideal of "christian criticism," building a scientific philosophy committed to Aristotelian methodology, resisting the trend of Augustinian

---

[11] E. Bonke, op. cit., pp. 58-59.

[12] S. Belmond, "Deux penseurs franciscains: Pierre-Jean Olivi et Guillaume Occam," *Etudes franciscains*, XXV (1923), p. 197: "L'occamisme est donc un système autonome et ne peut en aucune façon faire partie intégrante du patrimoine doctrinale du grand ordre franciscain." See also F. Copleston, *op. cit.*, p. 46: "Though the philosophy of Scotus gave rise to certain of Ockham's problems and though certain of Scotus' views and tendencies were developed by Ockham, the latter constantly attacked the system of Scotus, particularly his realism; so that Ockhamism was a strong reaction to, rather than a development of, Scotism."

[13] L. Baudry (ed.), *Le Tractatus de principiis theologiae*, pp. 42-43: "En résumé, la philosophie de Guillaume d'Occam se présente comme un effort de la pensée chretiénne pour se libérer des entraves de l'aristotélisme. Par son souci d'affirmer la puissance et la liberté divines, de souligner l'action de Dieu en tout ce qui se produit, elle s'apparente, dans sa préoccupation fondamentale, à celle de saint Bonaventure et de Duns Scot. Certes, les différences sont profondes entre sa doctrine et celles de ces deux penseurs, il y a, en un grand nombre de points, une opposition radicale. Et cependant, en un sens, Guillaume reste de leur lignée." See also F. Copleston, *op. cit.*, p. 48; A. Maurer, "Scotism and Ockhamism," *History of Philosophical Systems*, ed. V. Ferm (New York: Philosophical Library, 1950), p. 221.

[14] M. De Wulf, *Histoire de la philosophie médiévale*, t. III (6. ed. rev.; Louvain: Institut supérieur de philosophie; Paris: Vrin, 1947), p. 30. For a criticism of De Wulf's statement that Ockham's principal adversary was Duns Scotus, see P. Boehner, "A Recent Presentation of Ockham's Philosophy," p. 444.

"wisdom philosophy" as exemplified in the writings of St. Bonaventure.[15]

These last remarks indicate that in examining the question of how Ockham fits into the Franciscan tradition, we find that the principal point under discussion usually turns out to be: what is the relation between Ockham and Duns Scotus, the reason apparently being that Scotus is held up as the embodiment, or at least the chief representative, of the elusive Franciscan tradition. Some indication of Ockham's connection with Duns Scotus has already been given above. In elaboration of this, it seems two theories have developed: either Ockham was in violent reaction to the teachings of Scotus; or he was a faithful disciple who accepted his master's principles, developed his doctrines and drew them to their logical conclusions. Again the extremes--reaction and acceptance are presented.[16]

With the appearance of the critical edition of Scotus and Ockham, it is becoming increasingly clear that Ockham is often "surreptitiously" indebted to Scotus in spite of the fact that he reacted explicitly to many of his positions.

It may be well to interject a note here that there does not seem to be any solid reason for believing that Ockham ever attended Scotus' lectures as a student or that the two Friars ever met.[17] But whether or not Ockham and Scotus were personally acquainted, it is true that Ockham's writings contain an abundance of

---

[15] P. Boehner, "The Spirit of Franciscan Philosophy," *Franciscan Studies*, II (1942), pp. 223, 226; F. Copleston, *op. cit.*, p. 46.

[16] These two views are brought out by L. Baudry, "A propos de la théorie Occamiste de la relation," *Archives d'histoire doctrinale et littéraire du moyen âge*, IX (1934), p. 203. See by the same author, "En lisant Jean le Chanoine," *Ibid.*, p. 193.

[17] B. Jansen, *Aufstieg zur Metaphysik heute und ehedem* (Freiburg: Herder, 1933), p. 206. See also C. K. Brampton (ed.), *The Imperatorium et Pontificum Potestate of William of Ockham* (Oxford: Blackwell, 1927), p. xiv. Here the editor states that "Ockham was a boy when Scotus died at Cologne." This statement, however, seems based on the assumption, scarcely true, that Ockham was born in the year 1300. Boehner has since given good reasons for saying that Ockham was born before the year 1290. See P. Boehner, *The Tractatus de Successivis*, pp. 3-4. This would make Ockham a "boy" of eighteen years of age or more at the time of Scotus' death in the year 1308--and certainly old enough to have been a student of Scotus. See also in this connection F. Ueberweg and B. Geyer, *Grundriss der Geschichte der Philosophie*, II. *Die patristische und scholastische Philosophie* (Basel, 1951), p. 572: "...die Annahme, dass Ockham ein Schüler des Duns Scotus gewesen sie, dass er den Titel Magister der Theologie geführt, dass er in Paris studiert und dort als Lehrer gewirkt habe, muss als unbegründet fallen gelassen werden."

CHAPTER I

criticism directed at his religious confrere.[18] There is no doubt whatever that Ockham criticized Scotus on frequent occasions; but the main point at present is the spirit of his criticism. And in answer to this question both P. Boehner and E. Moody have argued the point with convincing reasons that Ockham's criticisms "where they bear on the teachings of Duns Scotus...come nearer to being interpretations or discussions of doctrine, than critical attacks."[19] The question of why Ockham criticized Scotus is certainly not a new question. For instance M. O'Fihely, better known as Maurice a Portu (d. 1513), a master at Padua in 1491, raised the question in his commentary on *De primo principio* of Duns Scotus.[20] And he, perhaps, came nearest the truth when he said that although no one is ever safe from criticism by a member of the Friars Minor, not even (or especially?) a fellow-Friar, Ockham's concentrated attacks on Scotus were due largely to the admiration he had for the doctrine of the Subtle Doctor.[21]

---

[18] P. Boehner, "A Recent Presentation of Ockham's Philosophy," p. 444: "The statement that Scotus was the main adversary for Ockham can be correctly or incorrectly construed. It is true that none of the great scholastics has been more criticized by Ockham than Scotus. One has but to read the Venerable Inceptor's writing in order to find overwhelming evidence for it..."

[19] E. Moody, "Ockham and Aegidius of Rome," *Franciscan Studies*, IX (1949), p. 442; P. Boehner, "A Recent Presentation of Ockham's Philosophy," p. 444: "Ockham admires Scotus and he has learned much from him, in spite of his differences. We could say that Ockham has developed his own philosophy and theology in constant critical discussion with Scotus. He has performed a true "crisis," a discrimination, discarding many Scotistic doctrines, but also retaining an equal if not a greater number of them."

[20] See E. Longpré, "Maurice du Port," *Dictionnaire de théologie catholique*, t. Xa (Paris: Letouzey et Ané, 1928), col. 404-405.

[21] See the commentary on *De primo rerum omnium principio* in *Joannis Duns Scoti opera omnia*, tom. IV, ed. Vivès (Paris: 1891), p. 762: "Nescio enim, quo zelo ductus Guillelmus Occham...conatus est totum processum doctoris in hoc capitulo, et sequenti perturbare: aut quia Anglicus, et iste Scotus, qui raro concordat: aut quia subtilem et ingeniosum impugnando, similis apparere voluit: aut quia forte Fidem Christianam magnificando, voluit omni ista esse credita...Forte etiam non in vituperium Doctoris, quem suum, et religionis, et subtilem plerumque nominat, scripsit, sed rigore Minorum, qui nemini parcunt, synteresi et conscientia sibi appropriatis, motis, cunctos ingenii elevatione, et indagine, salve pace aliorum dixerim, transcendentes, usus est: sed quomodocumque fuerit, aurum purgavit quoties in fornace examinans rigorosi verba Scotica commovit...Aestimo breviter, quod vere ille doctissimus, atque Catholicus, admirative potius quam assertive contra huius Doctoris doctrinam aliquando insurgit: licet, ut verum fateat, equo albo, sua disputatio abundavit."

INTRODUCTION

In the field of ethics it seems that basically Ockham followed the general viewpoint of Scotus.[22] The common interpretation is that while St. Thomas held an immutable natural law expressed, for example, in the absolute commands of the Decalogue, Scotus reserved the characteristic of "absolute" to only the first two commandments, denying that the last eight had any immutable validity. It was left to Ockham, then, to extend Scotus' rejection of the immutability of the commandments also to the first two commands. All the commandments were looked upon as positive, alterable decrees of almighty God.[23] In the field of morality Ockham would appear as a somewhat blind follower of Duns Scotus, merely depending upon him in theory and at times drawing his master's ideas to their logical conclusions.

Although there does seem to be a certain amount of validity and merit in outlining the relation between Thomas-Scotus-Ockham in the light of their consideration of the absolute character of the Decalogue, there is present, too, the danger of understanding this outline in such a way that the whole problem is oversimplified. This is especially true in so far as the realtion between Scotus and Ockham is concerned. To imply that Ockham accepted *in toto* all of Scotus' ethics and merely employed Scotus' principles to complete the destruction of Christian morality as expressed in the Decalogue, is certainly a misunderstanding of Ockham's viewpoint and Scotus' as well.[24]

---

[22] Cf. E. Hochstetter, "Viator mundi," *Franziskanische Studien*, XXXII (1950), pp. 10-11.

[23] *Ibid.*, pp. 13-14: "Die einzelnen Gebote, die unserem Wollen die Richtung geben sollen, sind niedergelegt im Dekalog. Sittlich richtig ist also etwas nur deshalb, weil es von Gott geboten ist. So hatte es schon Hugo von St. Victor gelehrt...und so auch Duns Scotus, von dem Ockham hierin abhängig ist. Auch dass diese Gebote keine absolute Gültigkeit besitzen, sondern positiv sind, hatte schon Duns von den letzten acht Geboten behauptet, während Ockham auch die ersten beiden miteinbezieht." See also F. Ueberweg and B. Geyer, *op. cit.*, p. 582: "In der Ethik wandelt Ockham in den Bahnen des Duns Scotus, geht aber viel weiter als dieser, insofern er das gesamte Sittengesetz, alle Gebote des Dekalogs lediglich in dem Willen gottes begründet sein lässt, so dass die jederzeit und beliebig geändert werden können." Cf. H. Meyer, *Geschichte der abendländischen Weltanschaunng*. III. *Die Weltanschauung des Mittelalters* (Würzburg, 1948), p. 318; F. Copleston, *op. cit.*, p. 104; A. Maurer, *op. cit.*, pp. 217, 221-222; G. Stratenwerth, *Die Naturrechtslehre des Joannes Duns Scotus* (Göttingen: Vanderhoeck and Ruprecht, 1951), pp. 115-116; S. Tornay, *Ockham: Studies and Selections* (La Salle, Ill.: Open Court, 1938), p. 74.

[24] Cf. S. Tornay, *op. cit.*, p. 75.

CHAPTER I

There can be no doubt that a more balanced view could be obtained in the interpretation of the ethical theories of Scotus and Ockham if either of them had constructed in detail what could legitimately be called an "ethical system." The trouble is, they did not. Such a system is no doubt implicit, at least in its foundations, in their works; but attempts to construct an ethical system according to Scotus or Ockham is very liable to be unduly influenced by the particular viewpoint of the interpreter. This danger is more likely to be present for the interpreter of Ockham than for Scotus. It is indeed uncommon to find in Ockham's writings a whole question devoted entirely to the discussion of an ethical problem; and this is true in spite of the fact that Ockham has written more on ethics than is perhaps generally realized. On the other hand, however, to say that Ockham has not constructed a system of ethics, is not the same as saying that he is "unsystematic" in the sense of being self-contradictory or abounding in irreconcilable statements. Ockham always impresses the reader as a careful writer who weighs thoughtfully the implications of his statements, constantly keeping in mind the principles upon which they are based. If we allow, as it seems we must, for some evolution or development in his thought, his writings reveal an inner consistency which it would be difficult to equal, much less surpass, in any commentary on his writings.

In the past students of the works of Ockham were plagued, not only with the ordinary difficulties in understanding the style of language and thought of a representative of a period of history remote from our own, but with questions of the authenticity of the works attributed to Ockham and the reliability of the available texts. Fortunately with the appearance of the 17 volume critical edition of Ockham's philosophical and theological works by the Franciscan Institute of St. Bonaventure University, we were able to bypass these special difficulties; the last of the *Opera philosophica* (volume VII) in this edition contains the various doubtful and spurious works that in the course of history were formerly attributed to Ockham.

In the examination of Ockham's basic ethical theory we will make use extensively of his *Commentary on the Sentences*. Properly speaking this work is divided into two parts; the commentary on the last three books comes to us only as a *Reportatio*, that is, the original lecture of a master or bachelor as copied down by one of his students or a scribe; the commentary on the first book, however, is an *Ordinatio*, that is, the author's own revision of his original lectures before final publication. In the *Opera theologica* of the Franciscan Institute edition the *Ordinatio* is contained

INTRODUCTION

in volumes I-IV under the title: *Scriptum in librum primum Sententiarum Ordinatio* (1967-1979) whereas the shorter *Reportatio* is reproduced in volumes V-VII (1981-1984) as *Quaestiones in librum secundum, tertium, et quartum Sententiarum (Reportatio)*.

Already in 1952 the late Philotheus Boehner called attention to the fact that certain questions included in the 1495 Lyons edition of the *Reportatio* did not belong fundamentally to the original "report" and nevertheless they appeared to have a certain unity among themselves. They comprise qq. 3, 8, and 25 in Bk. II and qq. 5, 12-15 in Bk. III together with certain "doubts" added at the end of Bk. IV. The editors of the critical edition have confirmed Boehner's early judgment that these questions do not belong strictly to the commentary on the *Sentences*, but were unable to determine precisely the occasion when they were written or disputed. To these questions found in the Lyons edition they added another important question not found there entitled "De connexione virtutum," and published the collection under the title *Quaestiones variae* as Volume VIII (1984).

There are still some areas of doubt and dispute regarding the relative chronology of the philosophical works of Ockham; but the chronological dispute is mainly in regard to works that are not very pertinent in so far as Ockham's ethics is concerned.[25] The only point we wish to make in connection with the chronology of Ockham's works is that it must be remembered that the *Ordinatio*, that is, the commentary on the first book of the *Sentences*, was revised after the writing of the *Reportatio*, the commentary on the last three books of the *Sentences*.[26] The foreign elements in the

---

[25] See for example, the disagreement between P. Boehner and L. Baudry in P. Boehner, "The Relative Date of Ockham's Commentary on the Sentences," *Franciscan Studies* (1951), pp. 307ff.

[26] *Ibid.*, p. 307. P. Boehner has shown that "Ockham went over his work (the *Ordinatio*) at least twice..." See "The Text Tradition of Ockham's Ordinatio," *The New Scholasticism*, XVI (1942), pp. 203-241. P Boehner is in substantial agreement with K. Michalski's earlier studies on the text of the *Ordinatio*: "Die vielfachen Redaktionen einiger Kommentar zu Petrus Lombardus," *Miscellanea Ehrle*, I (1924), p. 260; and "Le criticisme et le scepticisme dans la Philosophie du XIVe siècle," *Bulletin...Cracovie* (1926), pp. 43-45. See also P. Boehner, "Ockham's Philosophy in the Light of Recent Research," p. 24: "There is clear evidence for at least two redactions (of the *Ordinatio*). Of the first redaction we know one complete ms., one abbreviation, and one ms. which shows the additions of the second redaction usually on the margin." A. Maier places the first redaction of the *Ordinatio* between the years 1317-1319; the second redaction between 1320-1323. See her article, "Zu einigen Problemen der Ockhamforschung," *Archivum franciscanum historicum*, XLVI (1953), pp. 161-194.

CHAPTER I

Reportatio, however, seem to be later additions and were most probably written at the time of the *Quodlibeta VII*, which are subsequent to both the *Reportatio* and the *Ordinatio*.[27] To put the matter briefly, the sequence of the works of Ockham which contain his ethical theory appears to be: *Reportatio, Ordinatio, Quodlibeta* and additions to the *Reportatio*, that is, the foreign elements in the Lyons edition.

We have deliberately omitted making any mention of the so-called "political works" of Ockham. In commenting on the political works of Ockham modern authors take widely different viewpoints. Some see in Ockham's writings an almost complete dividing line between those which are philosophical and those which are political. This is perhaps the more traditional view.[28] On the other side there are those, principally G. Lagarde, who emphasize the unity between Ockham's philosophical and political writings. Ockham's political views are considered as the natural consequents and development of his philosophical principles.[29] But in any case, we do

---

[27] P. Boehner, "The Notitia Intuitiva of Non-existents," pp. 242-243.

[28] J. Morrall, "Ockham's Political Philosophy," *Franciscan Studies*, IX (1949), p. 338: "It is only in writers influenced by the Neo-Thomist interpretation that we meet with the idea that Ockham's polemical position was a necessary result of his philosophy. Previous ages seem to have considered it no absurdity to make an important distinction between the two aspects of Ockham's intellectual activity. It is, in fact, a distinction that Ockham himself would have accepted. In his Oxford philosophical works he makes clear again and again that the difference between philosophy and theology is radical and total...This point cannot be emphasized too strongly when Ockham's 'political' treatises are in question; for these writings are theological through and through. Ockham approaches politics by way of ecclesiology; revelation, not reason, has the last word in this sphere."

[29] G. Lagarde, *La naissance de l'esprit laïque au déclin du moyen âge*, V. *Bases de depart de l'ockhamisme* (Presses Universitaires de France, 1946), p. 10: "L'oeuvre d'Ockham révèle une unité interne profonde...Pensées par une personnalité unique, usant de la même méthode et de la même langue, les deux parties de l'oeuvre d'Ockham ont exercé sur l'orientation de la pensée contemporaine une influence similaire." In this connection see also R. Scholz, *Wilhelm Ockham als politischer Denker und sein Breviloquium de principatu tyrannico* ("Schriften des Reichsinstituts für ältere deutsche Geschichtskunde": Leipzig, 1944), p. 11: "Es mag als ein gewisser Widerspruch ersheinen, über Ockham als Politiker und über seine Staatslehre zu schreiben; denn Ockham war kein Politiker, wenn er auch an der Politik sehr lebhaft teilnahm, und er hat seine Staatslehre geschrieben oder neu entwickelt. Ockham war Theologe, und was er schrieb, hangt mit seiner Theologie zusammen, das heisst in seiner Zeit allerdings auch mit seiner Philosophie. Denn die scholastische Theologie seiner Zeit ist eben Philosophie, ist Weltanschauung." L. Baudry remarks--and this view seems more balanced and nearer to the truth--in "Le Philosophie et le Politique dans Guillaume d'Ockham," *Archives d'histoire doctrinale et littéraire du moyen âge*, XII (1939), pp. 209-210: "Guillaume n'a pas déduit son systeme social et politique de sa

INTRODUCTION

not hesitate in maintaining that Ockham's political writings are not important in so far as a construction of his basic philosophical theory of ethics is concerned. And it is, of course, Ockham's philosophical theory of ethics that is of prime interest to this study. So even if we should grant the close connection between Ockham's philosophical writings and his later political writings, the latter remain rather in a special field of application of philosophical and theological principles.[30] Nor is Ockham interested in the field of political theory itself.[31] In fact it would seem more reasonable to label these writings "polemical" rather than "political."[32]

In the political writings references do occur, of course, to ethical questions; but these references are more incidental in character rather than directly concerned with ethical problems as such. There is this difference, too, that since the political writings are frankly polemical in character, Ockham makes free use of an appeal to the people approach (*argumentum ad populum*). In so far as ethics is concerned he relies on the generally accepted ter-

---

philosophie comme on déduit la conclusion des prémisses dans un syllogisme...Mais on ne saurait conclure de là que le philosophe et le polémiste sont en quelque sorte disjoints dans sa personne. L'hypothèse est à priori invraisemblable...nous devons nous attendre à voir sa philosophie pénétrer et peut-etre dominer ses vues sociales et politiques." See the same author's, *Guillaume d'Occam. Sa vie, ses oeuvres, ses idées sociales et politiques*, tom. I: *L'homme et les oeuvres*, p. 11 (note 5).

[30] See F. Copleston, *op. cit.*, pp. 46-47: "It might appear that there is a radical discrepancy between Ockham the cold logician and academic philosopher and Ockham the impassioned political and ecclesiastical controversialist. But such a supposition is unnecessary...the difference in tone between his philosophical and polemical works is due rather to a difference in the field of application of his principles than to any unreconciled contradiction in the character of the man...it seems to me an exaggeration to imply that Ockham the logician and Ockham the politician were almost different personalities..."

[31] J. Sikes et al. (eds.), *Gulielmi de Ockham. Opera politica*, Vol. I (Manchester University, 1940), p. vii: "The tendency of much modern study of Ockham has been to emphasize how largely his interests were theological; what he had to say about politics appears very much a by-product of his master preoccupation." P. Boehner (ed.), *Ockham. Philosophical Writings*, p. 1: "[Ockham's] interest was not so much focused on political theories in general, as on the special problem of the relation between State and Church, or, more concretely, the relation between the Papacy and the Roman Empire of his days." F. Copleston, *op. cit.*, p. 111: "It would be a mistake to suppose that Ockham was a political philosopher in the sense of a man who reflects systematically on the nature of political society, sovereignty and government. Ockham's political writings are not written to provide an abstract political theory; they were immediately occasioned by contemporary disputes involving the Holy See..."

[32] Sikes et al. (eds.), *op. cit.*, p. vii: "The works here presented could indeed more properly be called polemical than political; not until the last two books of the *Contra Benedictum* do we find Ockham engaging directly in political discussions."

CHAPTER I

minology and system of the scholastic notion of natural law in his argumentation. In his philosophical writings, on the other hand, Ockham carefully avoids any mention or use of the system of natural law ethics. It is this difference in viewpoint which led to the decision to consider Ockham's basic ethical theory from the standpoint of his philosophical works alone.[33]

There are two works--not by Ockham but extremely helpful for an understanding of him--that deserve explicit mention here. The first is *De principiis theologiae,* edited by L. Baudry in 1936. According to L. Baudry, the author of *De principiis theologiae* was a contemporary of Ockham whose intimate knowledge of the doctrines of Ockhamism is well presented in a synthesis of Ockham's theology.[34] The synthesis is achieved in terms of two principles of theology: 1) that God can make all that which it is not contradictory to make (divine omnipotence); 2) that beings should not be multiplied without necessity (Law of parsimony, Ockham's razor).[35]

The other important work to be mentioned here is later in origin. It is the *Collectorium* of Gabriel Biel (d. 1495). E. Gilson mentions that the *De principiis theologiae* is more useful to consult for an understanding of Ockham, since it is a more faithful account of his doctrines. G. Biel, a more original thinker, often disagrees with Ockham, although even when disagreeing he usually does so along genuinely Ockhamistic lines.[36]

Useful as these and other secondary sources, both medieval and modern, may be for a sound reconstruction of Ockham's basic

---

[33] J. Kölmel, "Das Naturrecht bei Wilehlm Ockham," *Franziskanische Studien,* XXV (1935), pp.39-85.

[34] L. Baudry (ed.), *Le Tractatus de principiis theologiae,* pp. 15-16: "Le rédacteur du *Tractatus de principiis theologiae* n'est pas G. d'Occam, mais un personnage anonyme du milieu du XIVe siècle cherchant à s'assimiler sa doctrine et à en saisir les idées fondamentales. Ce personnage a été contemporain de Guillaume, peut-être l'a-t-il connu et vécu dans son intimité; en tout cas, la conformation du traité le prouve, il avait une connaissance etendue et precise de ses oeuvres. Cela suffit pour conférer au *Tractatus de principiis theologiae* une grande importance historique."

[35] *Ibid.,* pp. 18-19: "Pour l'auteur du *Tractatus* deux principes dominent la philosophie de Guillaume d'Occam. Le premier: Dieu peut faire tout ce qui peut être fait sans contradiction, est tout simplement l'énoncé du dogme de la toutepuissance divine. Le deuxième définit les conditions de la preuve: il ne faut pas multiplier les choses sans necessite..." See E. Gilson, *History of Christian Philosophy in the Middle Ages* (New York: Random House, 1955), p. 792.

[36] E. Gilson, *op.cit.,* p. 499.

INTRODUCTION

theory of ethics and for a correct interpretation of his writings, especially passages whose uncertain wording leaves us in some doubt regarding their meaning, our chief reliance must still be on the words of Ockham himself.

Since the words of Ockham relative to his ethical theory are widely scattered throughout his writings, that is, the *Commentary on the Sentences* and the *Quodlibeta*, we have endeavored to order the study of these passages according to a single, central question: What is the norm of morality? We find that in answer to this question two norms are proposed: a subjective and proximate norm consisting in man's right use of his reason and will; an objective and ultimate norm consisting in the will of God. More accurately, these two norms together form a twofold norm of morality. By relating the human act to this twofold norm we will finally be able to judge its morality and the degree or kind of morality which is involved.

According to the above brief statement of Ockham's basic theory of ethics, I have devoted a chapter to the study of each of these topics. One chapter to the study of the human will and right reason as determinants of the morality of an act; a second chapter on the relation of the human act to the will of God; a third chapter on the determination of the morality of the human act consequent upon its relation to Ockham's twofold norm of morality. These three chapters, consequently, will provide us with the substance of Ockham's basic theory of ethics.

In analyzing the role which man's will and right reason play in the morality of the human act we are dealing, more precisely, with conditions which are necessarily required for any act to be morally good or morally evil. The act must be elicited freely; it must be performed in accord with right reason if it is to be called a morally good act, against right reason if it is to be a morally evil act. In so far as the will of man is concerned we must find out what freedom means for Ockham and, more importantly as far as ethics is concerned, study his conclusion that only an act of the will can be moral. The role of right reason can be seen more clearly in terms of that kind of prudence which is required and sufficient for the performance of a morally good act. This leads to a determination of what is meant by the statement that "the act must be elicited in conformity with right reason."

The human will and right reason are only the proximate norms of morality. Man's will and reason are not, as are God's, always and everywhere, by their very nature, "right" will and "right" reason. The creature needs an outside norm according to which he can and

CHAPTER I

must order his actions. This norm, ultimate in nature, is for Ockham the will of God. Obedience to the will of God is cast in terms of the love of God. Of primary importance, consequently, is the meaning of this love of God expressed in action. Put in the form of a dictum, the ultimate norm of morality can be expressed: Love God and do what he wills. An examination of this formula will constitute the major part of the chapter on the will of God as the ultimate norm of morality. In the concluding section of the same chapter various problems involved in the application of this formula, problems which represent the extremes to which Ockham's theory of ethics can be drawn, will be presented for solution.

A third chapter on the foundation of morality, the relation of the moral act to the norm proposed by Ockham, will seek to distinguish the different types of morality which can be found in the human act. Here the focus of attention is on the distinguishing features of the necessary virtuous act as contrasted with the contingent virtuous act. Negatively, this raises the further question: In what does the malice of an act consist? Basically, this chapter is but an application of the principles of the two preceding chapters on the norm of morality.

In the conclusion we will seek to form a general statement conceived as characterizing Ockham's theory of ethics. For this purpose, however, we have thought it useful and, in fact, necessary to include an introductory chapter to the study of Ockham's ethics. The introductory chapter presents Ockham's viewpoint regarding moral science and its connection with other closely related notions. We begin this study, then, with Ockham's notion of moral science and how it is to be distinguished from other sciences.

In concluding this introduction to the study of Ockham's basic ethical theory, we cannot but help recall a remark made by Montesquieu in his Preface to *The Spirit of Laws*. "If this work meets with success," he says, "I shall owe it chiefly to the grandeur and majesty of the subject." In this spirit we could say that if this work meets with any degree of favorable criticism at all, it is due rather to the genius and the expression of that genius on the part of William Ockham. I wish I could appeal to some compensating accomplishment on my own part as Montesquieu does ("I also am a painter"). But such, alas--or perhaps fortunately--is not the case.

CHAPTER II

MORAL SCIENCE

In treating the meaning of "moral science" Ockham's main interest lies not in a discussion of its nature and method, but rather in offering several distinctions and in determining how the notion of moral science is to be distinguished from certain other closely related topics. Except for a very brief question in the *Quodlibeta*, whether a demonstrative science of morals is possible, we must glean out material from widely scattered sources in Ockham's writings. He did not treat the subject of the nature of moral science systematically nor subject it to an examination in detail. He does give us some indication, however, of his views concerning the notion of moral science in general, prudence, practical science and praxis, the ways in which these are related to one another and the mutual influence they exert. We will examine each of these notions in the succeeding paragraphs. Our purpose in this chapter is not to give a complete or detailed description and explanation of the above topics--to do so would be beyond the scope and intent of this study--but to select those elements which are of greater importance in view of their applicability within the general framework of Ockham's fundamental theory of ethics.

Ockham briefly defines "the moral" as comprising those human acts which fall under the power of our will.[1] In a more strict sense, for a human act there are the added qualifications that it be elicited by the will according to the natural dictates or right reason and any other circumstances that are required.[2] Although

---

[1] *Quodl.* II, 14: "...dico quod 'morale' accipitur large pro actibus humanis qui subiacent voluntati absolute." (OTh IX, 176). *In I Sent.*, prolog. q. 12: "...[scientia moralis] est praecise de moribus qui sunt in potestate nostra..." (OTh I, 359). For a lengthy treatment of this question see A. Garvens, "Die Grundlagen der Ethik Wilhelms von Ockham," *Franziskanische Studien*, XXI (1934), pp. 245ff.

[2] Ockham, *Quodl.* II, 14: "Aliter accipitur ['morale'] magis stricte pro moribus sive actibus subiectis potestati voluntatis secundum naturale dictamen rationis et secundum alias circumstantias." (OTh IX, 177).

CHAPTER II

these qualifications certainly indicate the normative aspect of moral science and may well have a special meaning for Ockham, as we shall see later on, he does not pause to give an explanation of his definitions but immediately sets out to distinguish positive moral science from non-positive moral science. The first of these is that part of moral science which contains the human and divine laws obliging us to do or avoid those things that are good or evil only in so far as and because they are prescribed or prohibited by a legitimate superior.[3] This part of moral science is the science of the jurists, the science of jurisprudence. Positive moral science is not itself a demonstrative science, although it often uses and is regulated by the principles of the non-positive, demonstrative part of morals. But the positive part of moral science is not demonstrative itself, because the jurists base their arguments on, and apply the principles of, human positive laws. Human positive laws, in turn, are not based on strictly evident or rational propositions.[4] This seems to be the generally accepted view among Neo-scholastics; and in our own times Mortimer Adler, speaking before the University of Notre Dame Natural Law Institute, gave succinct expression to the same idea in the following terms:

> Rules of positive law are strictly opinion. I am using the word 'opinion,' in the strict sense, as applied to propositions to which the intellect assents only when it is moved to assent by the will...Positive law is promulgated through extrinsic and official promulgation, and then only through dogmatic statement, not through rational proof.[5]

The non-positive part of moral science, on the other hand, does not derive its principles from the precepts of a legitimate superior. It directs human actions by means of principles which

---

[3] *Ibid.*: "Scientia moralis positiva est illa quae continet leges humanas et divinas, quae obligant ad prosequendum vel fugiendum illa quae nec sunt bona nec mala nisi quia sunt prohibita vel imperata a superiore, cuius est

[4] *Ibid.*: "...dico quod moralis scientia positiva, cuiusmodi est scientia iuristarum, non est scientia demonstrativa, quamvis sit a scientia demonstrativa ut in pluribus regulata; quia rationes iuristarum fundantur super leges humanas positivas, quae non accipiunt propositiones evidenter notas."

[5] M. Adler, "The Doctrine of Natural Law in Philosophy," *University of Notre Dame Natural Law Institute Proceedings*, I (1947), pp. 77-81. See also H. McKinnen, "Natural Law and Positive Law," *Ibid.*, pp. 85-103.

are either self-evident or known through experience.[6] Notice, particularly, that in both the definition of positive moral science as well as that of non-positive moral science the normative aspect of moral science is brought out. The first definition speaks of "the human and divine laws obliging us" and the second speaks of "the principles which direct human actions." Morals as a non-positive science is a demonstrative science. For any body of knowledge which deduces its conclusions syllogistically from principles that are either self-evident or known from experience is a demonstrative science. And non-positive moral science does just that.[7] Its superiority over positive moral science appears both from its characteristic of demonstrability and from the fact that positive moral science uses, and is regulated by, the principles of the non-positive, demonstrative part of morals. However, in this connection we should also keep in mind that while the ordinances of positive law are derivable from the principles of practical reason, they are determinations of, not deductions from, these principles.[8]

There are two ways of acquiring knowledge in the non-positive moral science. Either the principles are self-evident (per se nota) or they are known by experience. Although all self-evident knowledge is evident knowledge; not all evident knowledge is self-evident. A proposition is said to be self-evident if it is known through the knowledge, intuitive or abstractive, of the terms of the proposition itself.[9] But on the other hand, intuitive cognition of

---

[6] Ockham, *Quodl.*, II, 14: "Scientia moralis non positiva est illa quae sine omni praecepto superioris dirigit actus humanos; sicut principia per se nota vel nota per experientiam sic dirigunt..." (OTh IX, 177). Cf. E. Hochstetter, "Viator mundi," *Franziskanische Studien*, XXXII (1950), p. 9; and the same author's "Ockham-Forschung in Italien," *Zeitschrift für philosophische Forschung*, I (1947), p. 575.

[7] Ockham, *Quodl.*, II, 14: "Sed disciplina moralis non positiva est scientia demonstrativa. Probo, quia notitia deducens conclusiones syllogistice ex principiis per se notis vel per experientiam scitis est demonstrativa; huiusmodi est disciplina moralis, igitur etc." (OTh IX, 177). *Ibid*: "Ad principale dico quod de illis quae subiacent voluntati, possunt formari propositiones verae et per se notae, quae multas conclusiones possunt demonstrare." (OTh IX, 178).

[8] See M. Adler, *op. cit.*, p. 77.

[9] Ockham, *In I Sent.*, prolog., q. 1: "...propositio per se nota est illa quae scitur evidenter ex quacumque notitia terminorum ipsius propositionis, sive abstractiva sive intuitiva." (OTh I, 6). Cf. *Ibid.*, q. 2 (OTh I, 81-82). Ockham outlines more precisely and completely the conditions required for a *per se nota* proposition in I *Sent.*, 3, 4: "...ad hoc quod propositio sit per se nota oportet quod quaecumque notitia terminorum, sive sit perfecta sive imperfecta, sive confusa sive distincta, -- dummodo illi idem termini qui prius apprehendantur et non alii --, sive abstractiva sive intuitiva,

CHAPTER II

the terms of a contingent proposition is sufficient and necessary to cause evident knowledge of such a proposition.[10] There are many principles in moral philosophy which are self-evident. As examples of these Ockham mentions the following: the will must act in accord with right reason; every evil can and must be avoided.[11] Practical conclusions can, of course, also be drawn from these principles, as in the following way: good should be done to a benefactor; someone who saves our life is a benefactor; therefore good should be done to the person who saves our life.[12] Experience, too, may be a source of knowledge. In fact, some knowledge is of such a nature that it can be acquired only through experience. The universal proposition, for example, that every person who is angry should be placated by flattering language, is one whose truth

---

sit sufficiens cum formatione propositionis ad causandum notitiam evidentem illius propositionis." (OTh II, 439). Cf. L. Baudry, *Lexique philosophique de Guillaume d'Ockham* (Paris: Lethielleux, 1958), p. 179.

[10] S. Day, *Intuitive Cognition. A Key to the Significance of the Later Scholastics* ("Franciscan Institute Publications; Philosophy Series," No. 4; St. Bonaventure, N.Y.: Franciscan Institute, 1947), pp. 147-148: "...although a *propositio per se nota* is an evident proposition, not every evident proposition is a *propositio per se nota*. Any knowledge whatsoever of the terms of a *propositio per se nota* is sufficient to cause evident knowledge of the proposition. But a special kind of knowledge of the terms of a contingent proposition is necessary to cause evident knowledge of that proposition. Specifically, *intuitive* cognition of the terms of a *propositio per se nota* is sufficient to cause evident knowledge of the proposition. But a special kind of knowledge of the terms of a contingent proposition is necessary to cause evident knowledge of that proposition. Specifically, *intuitive* cognition of the terms of a contingent proposition is necessary if we are to have evident knowledge of such a proposition; whereas even *abstractive* cognition of the terms of a *propositio per se nota* is sufficient to cause evident knowledge of such a proposition." Ockham defines evident knowledge in *I Sent.*, prol., 1: "...dico quod notitia evidens est cognitio alicuius veri complexi, ex notitia terminorum incomplexa immediate vel mediate nata sufficienter causari. Ita scilicet quod quando notitia incomplexa aliquorum terminorum sive sint termini illius propositionis sive alterius sive diversarum propositionum in quocumque intellectu habente talem notitiam sufficienter causat vel est nata causare mediate vel immediate notitiam complexi, tunc illus complexum evidenter cognoscitur." (OTh I, 5-6). Cf. L. Baudry, *op. cit.*, p. 92; R. Guelluy, *Philosophie et théologie chez Guillaume d'Ockham* (Louvain: Nauwelaerts, 1947), pp. 80-81.

[11] Ockham, *Quodl.*, II, 14: "...multa sunt principia per se nota in morali philosophia; puta quod voluntas debet se conformare rectae rationi, omne malum vituperabile est fugiendum, et huiusmodi." (OTh IX, 177-78).

[12] *Quaest. Variae*, q. 6: "Scientia moralis accipitur dupliciter. Uno modo pro omni scientifica notitia quae evidenter potest haberi per doctrinam. Et haec procedit ex principiis per se notis, ut quod benefactori est benefaciendum; quilibet liberans a morte est benefactor; igitur tali est benefaciendum." (OTh VIII, 281-2). See L. Baudry, *op. cit.*, p. 241.

can be attained only by a process of induction from the facts obtained experientially that this man and that man etc. should be placated in such a way.[13]

Knowledge in the field of morals can be acquired through experience, but it is not always necessary that it be acquired in that way. A student of moral philosophy could acquire knowledge of the principles which are self-evident without relying on any experience either on his own part or on the part of others. And he could, with this limited knowledge, direct his actions perfectly. But such is the case only in the realm of pure possibility. As a matter of fact, it would be practically impossible or could be done only with the greatest difficulty, since a student of this kind would have knowledge of only the more universal principles and be completely lacking in prudence.[14] For by definition prudence in the proper sense of the term is knowledge acquired through experience.

The question then arises: How does knowledge in the science of morals differ from the habit of prudence? To put the answer in general terms, we may say that moral science is distinct from the habit of prudence in so far as the former deals with the less universal principles, not as known by a process of deduction from general propositions but as known through experience.[15] The dis-

---

[13] *Quaest. Variae*, q. 6: "Alio modo (scientia moralis) accipitur pro notitia scientifica evidente, quae solum habetur et haberi potest per experientiam et nullo modo per doctrinam. Verbi gratia haec: 'quilibet iracundus ex tali occasione per pulchra verba est liniendus et mitigandus' non potest evidenter sciri nisi per experientiam notitiam evidentem de multis propositionibus singularibus, puta, quod iste sic sit mitigandus et ille et sic de singulis." (OTh VIII, 281-2). See E. Gilson, *History of Christian Philosophy in the Middle Ages* (New York: Random House, 1955), p. 790.

[14] Ockham, *In I Sent.*, prolog., 11 (OTh, 320).

[15] *Ibid.*: "Sed quomodo tunc distinguuntur scientia moralis et prudentia. Dico quod distinguuntur sicut habitus magis universalis et minus universalis. Quia scientia est de magis universalibus et prudentia de minus universalibus quae cognoscuntur praecise per experientiam et non per deductionem ex magis universalibus." (OTh I, 321). Cf. also *Quaest. Variae*, q. 7 (OTh VIII, 330-2). See also R. Guelluy, *op. cit.*, p. 304: "Toute connaissance normative doit-elle s'identifer avec la prudence, ou bien faut-il faire une différence entre celle-ci et l'éthiqué? La question donne à Ockham l'occasion de s'expliquer sur les connaissances que l'expérience est seule a donner. Après avoir noté que l'exercice peut donner lieu à un *habitus* organique qui facilité certaines actions plus qu'un *habitus* intellectuel...notre auteur applique à la science pratique ce qu'il nous a répété à plusieurs reprises en parlant de la science en général: certaines vérités indémontrables vont de soi, mais il en est que l'expérience seule peut faire connaître. Bien souvent, ajoute-t-il, le savant con-

CHAPTER II

tinction between moral knowledge and the habit of prudence can be more accurately determined through an analysis of the different senses in which the term "prudence" is accepted. Ockham mentions that there are four ways in which the term "prudence" is used:[16]

a) In the widest sense (as used by St. Augustine in the *First Book of De libero arbitrio*)[17] prudence signifies knowledge which directs, either immediately or mediately, any human act. In this sense evident knowledge of universal propositions, whether acquired by deduction from principles which are self-evident or by induction from facts known through experience, pertains to pru-

---

naît les unes et les autres mieux que le praticien. C'est ainsi que l'éthique comporte des connaissances plus générales que la prudence."

[16] This question is treated in *Quaest. Variae*, q. 7: "Prudentia accipitur quadrupliciter. Uno modo accipitur pro omni notitia directiva respectu cuiuscumque agibilis mediate vel immediate; sicut accipit Augustinus prudentiam, I *De libero arbitrio*. Et isto modo tam notitia evidens alicuius universalis propositionis quae evidenter cognoscitur per doctrinam, quia procedit ex propositionibus per se notis, quae notitia scientifica proprie est scientia moralis, quam notitia evidens propositionis universalis quae solum evidenter cognoscitur per experientiam, quae notitia est etiam scientia moralis, est prudentia. Exemplum primi: 'omni benefactori est benefaciendum'; exemplum secundi: 'quilibet iracundus per pulchra verba est leniendus.'--Alio modo, accipitur pro notitia evidenti immediate directiva circa aliquid agibile particulare, et hoc pro notitia alicuius propositionis particularis, quae evidenter sequitur ex universali propositione per se nota tamquam maiori et per doctrinam. Exemplum: 'isti est sic benefaciendum,' quae sequitur evidenter ex ista: 'omni benefactori' etc.--Tertio modo, accipitur pro notitia immediate directiva accepta per experientiam solum respectu alicuius agibilis. Exemplum: 'iste iracundus est leniendus per pulchra verba.' Et haec notitia est solum per experientiam accepta respectu alicuius propositionis particularis cognitae per experientiam; et haec videtur esse prudentia proprie dicta secundum intentionem Philosophi, prout distinguitur a scientia morali.-- Quarto modo, accipitur pro aliquo aggregato ex omni notitia immediate directiva, sive habeatur per doctrinam sive per experientiam, circa omnia opera humana requisita ad bene vivere simpliciter. Et isto modo prudentia non est una notitia tantum, sed includit tot notitias quot sunt virtutes morales requisitae ad simpliciter bene vivere, quia quaelibet virtus moralis habet propriam prudentiam et notitiam directivam.-- Quod probatur, quia prudentia est notitia complexa; nunc autem ubi est alius et aliud sit complexum, ibi est alia et alia notitia, cum igitur aliud et aliud sit complexum, cuius notitia est immediate directiva respectu operationis unius virtutis et alterius, igitur est alia et alia prudentia." (OTh VIII, 330-1). Ockham also gives a twofold division of prudence *Ibid.* , q. 6: "Prudentia accipitur dupliciter: uno modo proprie pro notitia evidenti alicuius propositionis singularis, quae solum habetur mediante experientia...Alio modo accipitur communiter pro notitia evidenti alicuius universalis practice quae solum evidenter cognoscitur per experientiam." (OTh VIII, 282). See also L. Baudry (ed.), *Le Tractatus de principiis theologiae attribué à G. d'Occam* ("Etudes de philosophie médiévale," XXIII; Paris: Vrin, 1936) p. 74; G. Biel, *Repertorium generale...Gabrielis Biel super quatuor libros Sententiarum* (Tuebingen, 1527), *I Sent.* prol., ll, H, J; A. Garvens, *op. cit.*, pp. 379-380.

[17] St. Augustine, *De libero arbitrio*, I, c. 13. n. 27 (PL 32, 1235).

dence. Such knowledge also pertains to moral science, however, as we have spoken of it above. So prudence taken in this wide sense is not distinct from the knowledge contained in moral science. As examples of this type of prudence Ockham mentions "Good should be done to those who do good" (a principle which is self-evident) and "Angry people should be placated by soft words" (a universal proposition known by experience).

b) In a more restricted sense prudence refers only to knowledge of a particular proposition which is an evident conclusion deduced from a self-evident general proposition. And, furthermore, this evident knowledge is immediately directive in respect to some particular action to be performed. But this is using prudence in an improper sense. An example of this is that "Good should be done to this person." This is a particular proposition deduced from the general, self-evident proposition "Good should be done to those who do good." But since moral science also uses self-evident propositions, that is, general propositions and the conclusions drawn from them, it is not distinct from the type of prudence mentioned in this paragraph.

c) In the proper sense prudence refers only to knowledge of a particular proposition with the added provision that it be known through experience alone. This knowledge, likewise, is immediately directive in respect to some particular action to be performed. It is this type of prudence that, according to Aristotle, is distinct from moral science.[18] "This angry man should be placated by soft words" is an example of such knowledge, knowledge of a particular proposition acquired only by experience.

d) Also in an improper sense prudence signifies the sum total of directive knowledge, known either deductively or from experience, regarding those actions which are necessary for man to perform in leading a good life. Although the term "prudence" is used to refer to the sum total of such knowledge, actually prudence in this sense is multiple because each moral virtue has its own proper directive knowledge. Consequently, there are as many distinct acts or habits of prudence as there are distinct propositions that are known. For prudence is complex knowledge, that is, knowledge of propositions; and where there are distinct propositions, there are also distinct acts by which these propositions are known. But there are distinct propositions which direct the various human acts required for leading a good life. Therefore, there are dis-

---

[18] Aristotle, *Ethica Nicomachea*, VII, cc. 5-9 (1140a24-1142a16).

tinct acts or habits of prudence corresponding to the propositions.[19]

Prudence in the proper sense, listed third in the series above, is distinct from moral science. Prudence as knowledge acquired through experience obviously is different from that part of moral knowledge derived from self-evident principles; and prudence as knowledge of particular propositions is distinct from moral knowledge gained from experience in so far as the latter refers to universal propositions.[20] However, not every particular proposition which is known through experience can be called prudence. A merely factual or categorical proposition, such as "This man is good," is a particular proposition which is known only by experience, but it has no connection whatsoever with prudence because it lacks the added conditions that the knowledge be directive and dictative of some action to be performed.[21] These conditions are an indispensable aid for distinguishing prudence from those practical sciences, such as logic or grammar, which are not dictative and are not directive at least in the same sense that prudence is called directive.[22]

The practical sciences fall into two general classes: those that are dictative and those which are only ostensive in character.[23] The dictative practical sciences either demand that some-

---

[19] Ockham, *In III Sent.*, 12: "Et quot sunt complexa distincta circa quae potest esse prudentia, tot sunt habitus distincti et actus similiter." (OTh VI, 419).

[20] *Quaest. Variae*, q. 6: "[Scientia moralis] adhuc distinguitur a prudentia proprie dicta, quia haec prudentia est circa singularia, alia [scientia moralis] circa universalia. Et sic patet quomodo scientia moralis et prudentia distinguuntur. (OTh VIII, 282-3). See A. Garvens, *op. cit.*, pp. 380-82.

[21] Ockham, *Quaest. Variae*, q. 6: "...aliquis potest habere...notitiam evidentem alicuius propositionis contingent sumptae sub propositione universali. Et hoc per experientiam, puta quod iste est benefactor...cuius notitia non est prudentia, quia non est directiva." (OTh VIII, 283). Cf. also *In I Sent.*, 35, 6 (OTh IV, 510-12); *In III Sent.*, 12 (OTh VI, 419-20).

[22] Ockham, *In I Sent.*, 35, 6: "...logica, rhetorica, grammatica et artes mechanicae sunt simpliciter practicae, et tamen non sunt dictativae. Sed dictamen de exercitio istarum notitiarum practicarum non pertinet ad istas artes, sed ad prudentiam pertinet." (OTh IV, 509-10). Cf. also *In I Sent.*, prolog., 11 (OTh I, 316-17); *In III Sent.*, 12 (OTh VI, 419-20). See also L. Baudry (ed.), *Tractatus de principiis theologiae*, p. 73; G. Biel, *op. cit.*, I Sent., prol., 11, J.

[23] This and the following is taken from *In I Sent.*, prolog., 11: "Potest tamen distingui de practica, quia quaedam est dictativa et quaedam tantum ostensiva. Prima est illa qua determinate dictatur aliquid esse faciendum vel non faciendum; et sic lo-

thing be done or require that something be avoided. Aristotle speaks of the dictative practical sciences in the sixth book of the *Nicomachean Ethics* and the third book of *De anima*.[24] The dictative practical sciences include neither logic, rhetoric, or any of the mechanical arts. The mechanical arts do not demand, for example, that a house should be built. Such a demand would pertain to prudence. The ostensive practical sciences only tell us how something is to be done in the right way. The art of architecture would require that a house be built out of a certain kind of wood or stone, with such and such a foundation, walls and roof, and so on. But it would not demand that the house be built, for this pertains to prudence. Logic and the other arts are only ostensive, and not dictative, in this same way.

There is, however, a distinction to be drawn between dictative and directive. In defining the various types of prudence Ockham spoke of them in terms of their directive influence.[25] However, as is evident from other texts dealing with prudence, it is really the dictative element which is important in prudence, especially when it comes to the distinction between prudence and the arts.[26] It is really the dictative element which characterizes prudence. for while the arts are not dictative, they are directive in respect to something done by us. The term "directive" can be used in reference to both prudence and the arts, however, if it is remembered that prudence directs that an act be done, while the arts direct how it is to be done. However, I prefer for the present to use the supple-

---

quitur Philosophus VI *Ethicorum* et III *De anima*. Et isto modo nec logica nec grammatica nec rhetorica est practica, nec etiam ars quaecumque mechanica, quia nulla istarum dictat aliquid esse faciendum vel fugiendum, sicut ars mechanica non dictat quod domus est facienda, sed hoc pertinet ad prudentiam qua scitur quando est facienda et quando non...Secunda notitia practica est tantum ostensiva, quia non dictat aliquid fugiendum aut prosequendum, sed tantum ostendit opus quomodo fieri potest...si intellectus dictet....Sicut ars aedificatoria ostendit quod domus componitur ex lignis et lapidibus et ex fundamento tali et talibus parietibus et tali tecto, et sic de aliis, et non dictat quod domus est facienda nec quando est facienda, sed ad prudentiam pertinet dictare quod tali tempore est facienda, vel sic est agendum vel sic. Et eodem modo logica et aliae artes sunt tantum ostensivae et non dictativae." (OTh I, 316-17).

[24] Aristotle, *Ethica Nicomachea*, VI, c. 1 (1138b 18-29); *De anima*, III, c. 9 (432b 26-29).

[25] See note 16 of this chapter.

[26] Ockham, *In I Sent.*, prolog., 11: "...logica et aliae artes sunt tantum ostensivae et non dictativae. Sunt tamen directivae..." (OTh I, 317). Cf. *In III Sent.*, 12 (OTh VI, 419-20).

CHAPTER II

mentary term "dictative" to specify more clearly the peculiar directive influence of prudence. Architecture will not demand that a house be built; but if it is to be built, it should be constructed according to the specifications and directives of the architect[27] While not dictative in nature, the arts are still directive and practical.

However, moral virtue does not pertain to the practical arts but is connected with prudence.[28] Perhaps this idea can be explained more clearly by an examination of the notion of "praxis" as it is used by Ockham. For praxis, too, has a necessary connection with moral virtue. In terms of its connection with practical knowledge, praxis can be defined as any operation directed by practical knowledge; or, in other words, it is any operation which is the object of practical knowledge.[29] In the widest sense, then, praxis is the operation of any power, whether that power be free or not. More strictly, it is any operation which falls under the power of the will.[30] It is this latter definition which will be of particular interest here.

In the more strict sense praxis may include such acts as volition, cognition, exterior acts, since any of these may be under the will's power.[31] Similarly, any act of the sensitive faculties may

---

[27] *In III Sent.*, 12: "Sed quae est tunc differentia inter artem et prudentiam? Respondeo: prudentia dictat de aliquo operabili a nobis, sed ars non. Sed quomodo est ars practica? Dico quod est practica quia dirigit in praxi vel in aliquo operabili a nobis, licet non dictet de praxi elicienda. Exemplum: ars faciendi domum non dictat quod domus sit facienda, sed quod domus debet componi ex lignis et lapidibus sic vel sic dispositis. Et ita dirigit quatenus, si domus fiat, dirigit facientem ut sic vel sic faciat." (OTh VI, 420).

[28] *In I Sent.*, 35, 6: "...tales [artes] non sunt dictativae, et tamen vere sunt practicae..." (OTh IV, 510). *Ibid.:* "...virtuose agere non pertinet ad artem, sed ad prudentiam. Similiter virtus moralis, secundum Aristotelem, VI *Ethicorum*, numquam est sine prudentia; igitur nec actus virtuosus sine actu prudentiae."

[29] *In I Sent.*, prolog., 10: "Virtus moralis non adquiritur sine praxi..." (OTh I, 277); *Ibid.:* "...omnis operatio cuius notitia directiva est practica est praxis. Vel sic: omnis operatio quae est praxis..." (OTh I, 279).

[30] *In I Sent.*, prolog., 10: "Primo modo praxis idem est quod operatio cuiuscumque virtutis, sive liberae sive naturalis...Tertio modo accipitur praxis strictius. Et praxis isto modo dicta idem est quod operatio exsistens in nostra potestate." (OTh I, 287-88). Cf. *In I Sent.*, prolog., 10 (OTh I, 292); *In I Sent.*, 35, 6 (OTh VI, 512-13, 517). See also G. Biel, *op. cit.*, I Sent., prol., 10, D.

[31] Ockham, *In I Sent.*, prolog, 10: "...omnis operatio quae est in potestate nostra est praxis. Et ideo cum tam cognitio quam volitio quam alii actus exteriores sint in potestate nostra, sequitur quod quilibet istorum vere poterit dici praxis." (OTh I,

be called praxis if it is commanded (actus imperatus) by the will.[32] Praxis, of course, can exist without any operation on the part of the sensitive faculties. For instance, moral virtue could exist in the will and be called true praxis without any corresponding act by the sensitive faculties.[33] Taking praxis in the meaning we are considering, we would hold this consequence as valid: "Intellection is commanded by the will, therefore it is praxis." But it would not be valid to say: "Intellection is commanded by the will, therefore it is practical." The first consequence is true, because it follows validly that if something is commanded by the will, it is praxis. For acts of the sensitive faculties are not called praxis unless they are commanded by the will. Therefore, if the will would command an intellection in the same way as it commands acts of the sensitive faculties, the intellection would be called praxis with as much right as an act of the sensitive faculties. Or to put this in another way: when the commanding act (actus imperans) is praxis, the commanded act is also praxis. But note again that it does not follow validly that if an intellection is commanded, it is practical. Pure speculation, which can hardly be called practical in any sense, can be commanded by the will. In this case speculation is not practical, but it is true praxis.[34]

---

292); *Ibid.*: "...praxis...est omnis operatio exsistens in potestate voluntatis....Et isto modo praxis dicitur vel potest dici tam de actione voluntatis quam de operatione intellectus quam etiam de operatione exteriori." (OTh I, 294). Cf. *Ibid.* (OTh I, 281ff.); *Quaest. disp. de fine in Quaest. Variae* (OTh VIII, 144-8). See also E. Bonke, "Doctrina nominalistica de fundamento ordinis moralis apud Gulielmum de Ockham et Gabrielem Biel," *Collectanaea franciscana*, XIV (1944), p. 63.

[32] Ockham, *In I Sent.*, prolog., 10: "...actus potentiae sensitivae non dicitur praxis nisi quia imperatur a voluntate..." (OTh I, 284).

[33] *Ibid.*: "...virtus moralis potest esse in voluntate sine operatione potentiae sensitivae; igitur praxis potest esse sine omni operatione potentiae sensitivae." (OTh I, 277).

[34] *Ibid.*: "Praeterea, quod dicitur quod non sequitur intellectio est imperata a valuntate, ergo est praxis; sed sequitur: ergo est practica,' hoc non est verum, quia bene sequitur 'est imperata a voluntate, ergo est praxis.' quia...actus potentiae sensitivae non dicitur praxis nisi quia imperatur a voluntate, ergo eadem ratione si aeque perfecte imperetur ipsa intellectio, ipsa aequaliter dicetur praxis. Confirmatur: quia quando actus imperans est praxis, actus imperatus est etiam praxis. Similiter, non sequitur 'intellectio est imperata, ergo est practica,' quia pura speculatio, quae nullo modo potest esse practica, potest esse imperata a voluntate, et tamen non potest esse practica." (OTh I, 284-85). *In I Sent.*, 35, 6: "Quod autem talis speculatio sit vere praxis, patet. Quia omnis operatio secundum electionem hominis est vere praxis; sed talis operatio potest esse secundum electionem hominis; igitur vere potest esse praxis." (OTh VI, 518).

CHAPTER II

The above remarks indicate the important difference between praxis and a practical act. Praxis is any operation in the control of the will; a practical act, on the other hand, is one which has praxis for its object, at least its partial object. Or in other words, the object of a practical act is some operation which is under the control of the will. Now there are many acts which are under the control of the will themselves but which do not have praxis as their partial or complete object. For example, the acts of contemplating God, of geometrical or metaphysical speculation, are all in our will's power. But they are not thereby practical, although they are true praxes. Therefore, this consequence does not follow validly: "Every operation falling under the power of the will is praxis, therefore geometry is practical." but it would follow that every operation falling under the power of the will is praxis, therefore some of the operations in geometry, for instance, those which I can elicit contingently, are true praxes even though these acts are not practical. Such speculation, however, which does not fall under the power of the will is not true praxis.[35]

In what does praxis primarily consist? It should be noted that primarily praxis is an act of the will itself. For primarily volition falls under the power of the will, and, in fact, no other act which we perform falls under the power of the will except mediately through an act of volition. Therefore, no other act should be called praxis primarily.[36] Expressing this same idea in a different way, Ockham argues that any act which is in the power of the will is either speculative, practical, or praxis. An act of the will is in

---

[35] *In I Sent.*, 35, 6: "...sciendum est quod differentia est inter actum practicum et praxim. Nam praxis est operatio exsistens in potestate voluntatis....Sed actus practicus est ille qui habet pro obiecto -- saltem partiali -- praxim vel aliquod operabile contingenter a voluntate. Nam multi sunt actus intelligendi exsistentes in nostra potestate qui non habent praxim nec aliquid operabile a nobis pro obiecto partiali. Sicut actus considerandi geometricalia, et similiter actus considerandi Deum, et actus speculandi metaphysicalia sunt in potestate nostra, et...practici non sunt, sed tamen vere sunt praxes....Ad secundum dico quod non sequitur 'omnis operatio exsistens in potestate voluntatis est praxis, igitur ego possum facere quod geometria erit practica,' sed sequitur quod ego possum facere quod aliquis actus geometriae -- puta ille quem possum contingenter elicere -- sit vere praxis, quamvis non possit ille actus esse practicus. Ad aliud dico quod manifestum est quod aliqua speculatio non est praxis, quia manifestum est quod speculatio divina non est praxis, quia illa non est in potestate voluntatis." (OTh IV, 517-19). Cf. *Ibid.* (OTh IV, 512-13).

[36] *In I Sent.*, prolog., 10: "Tamen praxis primo dicitur de actu voluntatis, cum ipsa sit primo in potestate nostra, et nulla alia sit in potestate nostra nisi mediante ea, et ideo nulla alia dicetur praxis primo." (OTh I, 292). Cf. *In I Sent.*, 35, 6 (OTh IV, 514). See E. Bonke, *op. cit.*, p. 63.

the power of the will; it is not speculative or practical, because only acts of the intellect can be called speculative or practical. Consequently, the act of the will is praxis.[37]

If the will, then, freely and contingently elicits an operation, that operation is called praxis. If, however, God would conserve such an operation without any continued act of causation on the part of the will, then this operation would cease to be true praxis, because it would no longer fall under the power of the human will.[38]

The last remarks suggest that some brief statements be made about the questions of praxis on the part of God. We must bear in mind that when we speak of an act of the will as praxis primarily we are speaking precisely of a will which elicits its acts after the manner of a created will, wherein the acts of the will are distinct from the will itself. However, the divine will is not such a will.[39] Since the will of God cannot be called praxis in the primary sense, so neither can an act of his will be called praxis. When we speak of divine volition, however, we may give different meanings to the term. It can mean, first, the divine will itself, which is really identical with the divine essence. In this meaning of divine volition we do not call volition praxis, because it cannot be understood as something which is "in the power of the will"; for this volition exists by the same necssity as the will of God itself, since it is in every way the will itself. But if by divine volition we mean something like "to will a creature to exist" or "to will to reward a creature," then we are not speaking of the divine will precisely, but we are at the same time signifying a creature and are using the term "divine volition" in the same way as the terms "creation" or "conservation." Such a divine volition is, obviously,

---

[37] Ockham, *In I Sent.*, prolog., 10: "Praeterea, omnis actus qui est in potestate nostra est speculativus vel practicus vel praxis; sed operatio voluntatis est in potestate nostra, et non est speculativa nec practica, quia istae sunt condiciones actuum intellectus; igitur est praxis." (OTh I, 279).

[38] *Ibid.*: "...si voluntas libere et contingenter aliquam operationem eliciat, tunc illa operatio dicitur praxis; et si post Deus illam eandem continaret sine omni causatione vel conservatione voluntatis respectu illius, tunc vere diceretur non praxis, quia non esset in sua potestate." (OTh I, 294).

[39] *In I Sent.*, 35, 6: "...dico quod quando dictum est prius quod actus voluntatis est primo praxis, ibi, non fiebat sermo nisi de voluntate habente actum elicitum receptum in se in sua potestate....Sed sic non est de voluntate divina, quia ipse actus ibi non est receptus in voluntate, sed est ipsa voluntas indistinctus ab ea re et ratione." (OTh IV, 514--15). Cf. *Ibid.*, 10, 1 (OTh III, 329).

CHAPTER II

in the power of the God, who creates, conserves, or rewards contingently.[40] Creation, conservation, reward and similar works of God can be called praxes, for they are dependent on the will of God. It may then be noted, also, that God's knowledge which corresponds to these praxes can be called practical in a true sense.[41] For that knowledge is practical which has praxis as at least its partial object.[42]

Moral science is one of the practical sciences. Its knowledge is practical, directive and dictative, knowledge. As such it must have praxis for the total or at least the partial object of this direction and prescription. Especially if we recall Ockham's definition of the "moral" as comprising those human acts which fall under the power of the will,[43] and the more strict definition of praxis as an operation which falls under the power of the will,[44] do we see the connection more clearly between moral science and praxis. As a practical science morals has a directive influence on praxis, and as a dictative practical science it commands that praxis be done or omitted. Nor is this directive-dictative influence only mediate and remote. We might be tempted to think that since moral science deals with only the more universal principles, its influence is remote and is exercised only mediately through the more particular principles of prudence. This, as a matter of fact, was the opinion

---

[40] *In I Sent.*, 35, 6: "Et ideo sicut ipsamet voluntas non potest esse primo praxis, ita nec ipsa actus volendi potest esse praxis....Ad aliud dico quod volitio divina diversimode accipitur. Uno modo pro ipso actu exsistente realiter eodem cum divina essentia. Et ista volitio divina non est praxis, quia non est in potestate voluntatis, sed tanta necessitate est ista volitio quanta est ipsa voluntas, quia est omnibus modis ipsa voluntas. Aliter accipitur volitio divina ut sit idem quod velle creaturam esse, vel remunerare vel huiusmodi. Et sic non praecise dicit voluntatem divinam sed etiam connotat creaturam in esse reali. Et sic est idem quod creatio vel conservatio vel aliquid huiusmodi, et sic est in potestate sua, sicut contingenter creat, conservat et huiusmodi." (OTh IV, 515-16). Cf. *Ibid.* (OTh IV, 512-13). See also E. Bonke, *op. cit.*, p. 63; P. Vignaux, "La puissance divine," *Dictionnaire de théologie catholique* (Paris: Letouzey et Ané, 1926), t. IX, col. 763.

[41] *In I Sent.*, 35, 6: "... in potestate voluntatis divinae est producere creaturam contingenter, et omnia alia facere circa creaturas est in potestate voluntatis divinae. Ideo ista productio potest aliquo modo dici praxis, quia scilicet contingenter est a voluntate divina, et per consequens notitia sibi correspondens vere practica dici potest." (OTh IV, 512--512). Cf. *Ibid.* (OTh IV, 509--512, 514--17, 520--22).

[42] See note 35 of this chapter.

[43] Ockham, *Quodl.* II, 14 (OTh IX, 176); *In I Sent.*, prolog., 12 (OTh I, 359).

[44] See note 30 of this chapter.

of Duns Scotus; Ockham disagrees and criticizes the opinion.[45] Thus according to Ockham, it would be wrong to say that every particular principle is more immediate in directing a praxis than a universal principle. As an example he mentions what he considers to be a parallel case, the syllogism. Here the universal major and the particular minor are both partial causes of the knowledge of the conclusion of the syllogism. Neither the major nor the minor cause more or less, before or after; both cause immediately, and equally so, the conclusion that is attained.[46]

Moral science may be taken in the above sense as a purely practical science. Its propositions are moral and normative, signifying that something must be done or not be done. But traditional moral science, such as that handed down by Aristotle, includes many propositions that are not practical but are purely speculative. Such a moral science would be really a part of a science, since many practical conclusions depend on and follow from the speculative principles.[47] It would certainly be a mistake to call such speculative principles "practical" on the grounds that they are principles from which practical conclusions necessary for a good life are drawn. The practical principles or conclusions are immediately directive in living the good life, but it does not follow that the cause of this practical knowledge must also be called practical. If this were the case, then all knowledge could be considered as dealing with moral goodness or at least with some action to be performed. All knowledge would be practical. If the remote speculative principles were to be called practical, then geometry

---

[45] Ockham, *Quaest. Variae*, 6: "...non bene assignat Ioannes differentiam in primo inter scientiam moralem et prudentiam in hoc quod scientia moralis est de universalibus et dirigit remote et mediate solum, prudentia est de particularibus et dirigit immediate et propinque. Tum quia supponit quod scientia moralis non dirigit nisi mediante prudentia, quod falsum est..." (OTh VIII, 283).

[46] *Ibid.*: "...notitia maioris universalis et minoris particularis aeque dirigunt in praxim sequentem, quia ambae istae notitiae sunt duae causae partiales respectu notitiae particularis conclusionis...ita quod neutra notitia prius causat quam alia, sed ambae aeque immediate causant illam notitiam..." (OTh VIII, 284).

[47] *In I Sent.*, prolog., 12: "...una pars scientia moralis est simpliciter speculativa et alia simpliciter practica. Et ratio est quia...multae conclusiones practicae dependent ex principiis speculabilibus et sciuntur per ea, et ideo volens tradere notitiam talium conclusionum pracicarum oportet quod utatur principiis speculabilibus ex quibus conclusiones illae sequuntur. Et propter hoc in scientia morali tradita a philosophis et a Sanctis inveniuntur multae veritates simpliciter speculativae, sed vocant eam scientiam moralem quia conclusiones practicae morales sunt ultima adquisita in illa scientia." (OTh I, 360).

CHAPTER II

could be considered a practical science, since its principles are used by architects in their work of construction. Furthermore, none would admit that if practical conclusions would be directed towards pure speculation, then these practical principles should be called speculative. For instance, we know from experience that gluttony, incontinence and anger are obstacles to contemplation and that the opposite virtues are an aid to contemplation. Yet we do not call these practical virtues "speculative." So, by the same reasoning, we should not call speculative truths "practical" just because they are used in order to derive from them practical principles which are immediately directive of some action to be performed. Consequently, the fact that practical principles are derived from speculative propositions or not, is not the point which settles the issue. Knowledge is called "speculative" or "practical" depending on the object, total or partial, that each has. Practical knowledge is that knowledge which has praxis as at least a partial object.[48]

I have attempted in this preliminary chapter to explain Ockham's notion of moral science in general. The notion of moral science can be understood more clearly, I believe, by comparing it with various related topics: prudence, practical science, and praxis. Moral science, directing and prescribing human acts which fall under the power of the will, is definitely related to prudence. Prudence differs from moral science in so far as the former is concerned properly with only particular propositions known solely through experience. Prudence does not comprise every particular proposition so known, but only those which are expressed in normative form. As Ockham puts it, prudence deals with particular propositions which are directive-dictative of an action to be performed. Prudence, together with the merely ostensive propositions, would belong to the general class of practical science. Closely connected with practical science, as an operation at least directed, if not demanded, by it is praxis. Praxis in the more strict sense

---

[48]*Ibid.*: "...illa notitia quae est ut boni fiamus...est practica. Si autem sit causa alicuius notitiae immediate dirigens nos circa aliquid quo sumus moraliter boni, non oportet, quia isto modo quaelibet notitia potest se habere ad bonitatem moralem vel saltem ad aliquod opus...non oportet quod sit practicum, quia isto modo geometria ordinatur ad opus. Unde geometria isto modo multum dirigit latomos in operationibus suis...quantumcumque aliqua practica ordinetur ad speculationem, non propter hoc dicetur speculativa nec e converso. Ideo dico quod ordinari ad aliam notitiam vel non ordinari nihil facit, sed considerandum est obiectum et totale et partiale et secundum hoc dicenda est notitia speculativa vel practica." (OTh I, 360--62).

of the term is an operation which falls under the power of the will. Acts in the power of the will, however, are the object of moral science. Therefore, praxis, if it is directed-dictated, is the object of moral science. Moral science, then, at least in so far as it is a practical science, deals with praxes, directing those actions which fall under the control of the will. As a directive practical science morals also demands these actions to take place. Morality, accordingly, is concerned only with those actions which are in our power; and primarily it is concerned with only those actions which are elicited by the will, for no other act falls under the power of the will except mediately through an act of the will. Therefore, no other act should be called praxis primarily, nor should it be called moral primarily.[49] The will occupies the supreme and the key position. In a sense the realm of morality is an exclusive domain of the will. In the words of St. Augustine: "The will is in all things; everything is will."[50]

Ockham states that moral science is certain, useful, and evident.[51] In fact, moral science is more certain than many other sciences and it is useful and evident to a high degree. But if moral science is to be considered certain, useful, and evident, it must be built on firm foundations. What in particular, is the basis for the dictative character of moral science? Why and how are free acts, acts in the power of the human will, demanded? What is the nature and norm and conditions of a moral act? These are some of the questions we will attempt to answer in the light of Ockham's teaching in the following chapters.

---

[49] See note 36 of this chapter.

[50] St. Augustine, *De civitate Dei*, XIV, 6: "Voluntas est quippe in omnibus, immo omnes nihil quam voluntas esse." See S. Tornay, *Ockham. Studies and Selections* (LaSalle, Ill.: Open Court, 1938), p. 64: "The Augustinian principle of the all-pervasiveness of the will is for him [Ockham] too the fundamental principle. Consequently, the problem of ethics is synonymous with the problem of the will." See O. Suk, "The Connection of Virtues according to Ockham," *Franciscan Studies*, X (1950), p. 112.

[51] Ockham, *Quod.* II, 14: "...ista scientia est certior multis aliis...ista scientia est multum subtilis, utilis, et evidens." (OTh IX, 178). See E. Gilson, *op. cit.*, p. 497: "It is worthy to note, however, that the science which Ockham considers as one of the safest and best established we may acquire naturally is ethics."

CHAPTER III

THE HUMAN WILL
AND
RIGHT REASON

Moral science is properly concerned only with acts which are in our power, acts over which we have control. Such acts constitute the material object of the science. Formally they are considered in the science of ethics under the aspect of their moral rightness or wrongness. In the science of psychology these same acts are considered according to their physical nature or entitatively; in ethics their moral quality is the object of study. Only an act in our power can be the object of morality. Since an act is not in our power unless it is a free act, it follows that good and evil, in so far as these terms are accepted with a moral connotation, cannot be predicated of any act that is not free.[1] Consequently, the whole moral order rests on and presupposes human liberty. The agent's moral responsibility and, correlatively, the act's moral imputability with all its consequences, demand that the agent has acted freely and has performed an act which was under the control of his will.[2] This does not in any way force us into a Kantian identification of liberty and morality. The two notions, liberty and morality, remain distinct; the latter merely presupposes the former as a necessary condition.[3]

---

[1] In terms of *praxis* this may be expressed in the following way: *praxis*, too, can be virtuous or evil. For *praxis* is in the power of our will, therefore it implies a free act. Cf. *In I Sent.*, 35, 6 (OTh IV, 517).

[2] In this connection we may quote the words of St. Thomas Aquinas in the *Summa theologica* (Paris: Vivès, 1871), I, 2, q. 18, a. 9: "Moralitas necessario praesupponit libertatem, quia actus, qui non procedit a ratione deliberativa, non est proprie loquendo moralis."

[3] See, for example M. Cronin, *The Science of Ethics*, Vol. I: *General Ethics* (New York: Benziger, 1909), p. 201: "What is the relation of freedom to moral goodness? Are they, as Kant asserts, one thing? Is the free will the morally good will, and, *vice versa*, is the morally good will the free will? Our answer is that they are not identical; that freedom is only one of the pre-conditions of moral goodness, but that it is not moral goodness itself..." The author goes on to add a further clarification in the footnote: "This question is important, since many modern Ethicians--for instance, Fichte and Hegel--take the identification of the two conceptions, freedom and moral goodness, as the starting points of their Ethical systems. For this assumption they indebted to Kant."..Further information on the identification by

THE HUMAN WILL AND RIGHT REASON

Human freedom is the first condition that must be present before we can even begin speaking of a good act in the moral order. Freedom must also be present, of course, for any morally evil act. But there is also a second condition required. The second condition is that the free act must be elicited by the will in conformity with the dictates of right reason (if it is to be a good act) or contrary to the dictates of right reason (if it is to be an evil act). These two conditions, I believe, were at least implicitly embodied in the treatment of moral science in general in the preceding chapter. Recall especially Ockham's definition of moral science as that science which has for its object human acts that are in the power of the will and are elicited according to the dictates of right reason.[4] However, in the present chapter we will investigate in greater detail and more explicitly these two conditions for a morally good act, namely: first, that the act is willed freely; secondly, that it is willed according to the dictates of right reason.

Since moral science, by definition, treats those acts which are free, the possibility and actual existence of human freedom or liberty is presupposed for the science. The fact of man's liberty is a generally accepted presupposition for any of the Scholastics' ethics; it can be considered as such for Ockham's ethics also. This liberty in the moral sphere is not to be understood in the sense of moral liberty consisting in an immunity from moral obligations. On the contrary, while man is bound morally because of his obligations, he is still physically free, though not morally, to fulfill these obligations or not. The freedom of which we wish to speak may be termed a physical liberty, an immunity from any internal necessity and external compulsion to act or not to act. Essentially, though not completely, it consists in the freedom of contradiction or the freedom of exercise, by which the will, undetermined by anything other than itself, chooses to act or not to act. Ockham describes this liberty in the following terms. Liberty, he says, is the power by which I am able to place different acts indifferently and contingently, so that I can cause or not cause a certain effect without any difference or change taking place in the conditions existing outside of the will itself that would account for either the causing or the not

---

Kant of freedom and moral goodness may be gathered in J. Collins, *A History of Modern European Philosophy* (New York: Macmillan, 1941), pp. 281 ff. The latter author remarks that according to Kant "the will can be regarded as free when, and only when, it acts in accordance with the moral law of duty..." See also J. Donat, *Summa philosophiae christianae*, tom. VII: *Ethica generalis* (ed. 7a; Barcelona: Herder, 1944), pp. 195-202.

[4] *Quodl.*, II, 14. (OTh IX, 176-177). See chapter II, pp. 21-22.

causing of the effect.[5] To posit an act indifferently or contingently means, according to Ockham, that the will is in absolute possession of itself, so that the will is able not to act, even if all the necessary requirements to an act are given in a particular case.[6] Understanding freedom in this sense, Ockham's basic argument to prove its existence is grounded in experience. We know from our own conscious experience that we are free; for we experience the fact that no matter how our reason dictates that something is to be done or not to be done, our will can still act or not act. We can suppose that an object is known by our intellect and presented to our will and that all the other conditions requisite for an act of willing are present. Now in this case, if the will at first refrains from acting, and then later--while the condition outside the will itself remain unchanged--the will does act, then the only explanation for the will's acting in the one case and its not acting in the other case would be its liberty. To assign any other reason or set of reasons in explanation of why the will acts or does not act would necessarily involve the presupposition that this reason or set of reasons exist (or do not exist) at one time and do not exist (or exist) later. Otherwise an existing reason or set of reasons would cause the act at one time and fail to cause the act at another time. But this variation, causing the will to act in one case and not in another, could only happen or take place if there were some variation in the reasons or conditions themselves--that is, if we would exclude the will's freedom and self-determination. In other words, the conditions for action would have to vary, correspondingly, with the variations in the actions. But this change in the conditions outside of the will is excluded in the above supposed case. But such supposed cases actually do occur, as we know from experience. Therefore, the will must be endowed with liberty.[7]

---

[5] *Quodl.*, I, 16: "...voco libertatem potestatem qua possum indiffernter et contingenter diversa ponere, ita quod possum eumdem effectum causare et non causare, nulla diversitate existente alibi extra illam potentiam." (OTh IX, 87). Cf. P. Boehner, "Ockham's Tractatus de praedestinatione et de praescientia Dei et de futuris contingentibus and its Main Problems," *Proceedings of the American Catholic Philosophical Association*, XVI (1941), p. 181; A. Garvens, "Die Grundlagen der Ethik Wilhelms von Ockham," *Franziskanische Studien*, XXI (1934), p. 257.

[6] Ockham, *In I Sent.*, 38, unica: "Praeter istos modos adhuc est unus modus quo potest voluntas creata cessare ab actu causandi, scilicet se sola, quantumcumque nullum praedictorum desit, sed omnia sint posita. Et hoc, et non aliud, est voluntatem contingenter causare." (OTh IV, 581). Cf. P. Boehner, *op. cit.*, p. 181: "Therefore according to Ockham liberty is not only the power of free choice which would presuppose the choice between two objects, but ultimately the power of self determination or the dominion of the will over its own act."

[7] Ockham, *Quodl.* I, 16: "Voco libertatem potestatem qua possumus indifferenter et contingenter diversa ponere, ita quod possum eumdem effectum causare nulla diversitate exis-

THE HUMAN WILL AND RIGHT REASON

This is the liberty of indifference by which the will, free from internal necessity and external compulsion, determines itself to act or not to act. To use a different termionology, it is the liberty of election or free choice by which the will freely chooses to act or not to act. The will is also able to choose the morally good or the morally evil; it is capable of choosing between contraries--the freedom of contrariety. Against any debasing theory that holds an essential corruption of human nature through original sin--thus crippling man to the extent of making him incapable by nature of any good acts--Ockham strongly insists that the human will by its very nature is endowed with, and has not lost, the power to choose good or to choose evil. "Our will is such that it can act rightly or wrongly," that is, choose the morally good or the morally evil.8 Man debases himself by sin; sin is primarily an abuse of the power of the human free will. In this Ockham is opposed to what was later to be a fundamental doctrine of Luther and his followers, namely, the complete corruption of human nature "owing to the continuance of original sin and the inextinguishable tinder of concupiscence."9 The human will is certainly not conceived by Ockham as helplessly enslaved to sin, possessing no power for righteousness, unable to choose what is good in the sight of God. In fact, in Luther's mind at least, Ockham's insistence on the freedom of the will and its power of performing good acts was "the extreme Scholastic position" against which Luther argued with characteristic scorn and ridicule.10

The human will is endowed with liberty, and in virtue of its liberty it may perform free acts. The free acts a man may perform are either interior or exterior acts. Interior acts are of two kinds: either they are immediately under the control of the will, therefore immediately free acts; or they are only mediately free by virtue of a relation to the im-

---

tente alibi extra illam potentiam... Non potest probari per aliquam rationem, quia omnis ratio hoc probans accipiet aeque ignotum cum conclusione vel ignotius. Potest tamen evidenter cognosci per experientiam, per hoc quod homo experitur quod quantumcumque ratio dictet aliquid, potest tamen voluntas hoc velle vel non velle vel nolle." (OTh IX, 87-8); *In I Sent.*, 1, 6: "Nec est causa alia quaerenda nisi quia natura illarum causarum partialium est talis.--Sed unde constat nobis quod natura illarum est talis? Hoc est per experientiam: quia experimur quod libere et contingenter ante volitionem efficacem sanitatis possumus appetere potionem amaram vel non appetere, non autem stante illa volitione cum firma opinione aliter non posse consequi." (OTh I, 499).

[8] *Quaest. Variae*, q. 8: "Voluntas nostra est huiusmodi quod potest recte et non recte agere." (OTh VIII, 410); cf. also *In I Sent.*, prol., q. 10 (OTh I, 292-3; *ibid.*, 10, 11 (OTh III, 342): *Quodl.* III, 19 (OTh IX, 275-81).

[9] H. Grisar, *Luther*, Vol. I, trans. E. Lamond (St. Louis: Herder, 1913), p. 200.

[10] *Ibid.*, pp. 130 ff.

mediately free acts.[11] Perhaps we can translate this division into the more modern Neo-Scholastic terminology. Although the terms are not unanimously agreed upon, we may take the discussion of human acts in the moral theology textbook of Noldin-Schmitt as sufficiently representative for our purposes here.[12] We can retain Ockham's primary division of acts into those which are exterior and those which are interior. Exterior acts are those which are performed by a bodily action, for instance the act of walking, seeing, talking. Interior acts are those of the internal powers of the soul, for instance the act of thinking, knowing, willing. Both the exterior and the interior acts may be either elicited or commanded (imperate). An act is elicited in so far as it immediately proceeds from a faculty. An act is commanded in so far as it comes under the power of the will mediately. Primarily an elicited act refers to an act immediately proceeding from the will. Although acts of other faculties may rightly be termed elicited in reference to that power which produces them, for instance an act of knowing in so far as it proceeds immediately from the intellect, or an act of seeing in relation to the sense organs of sight, in the field of morals the acts of faculties other than the faculty of the will are termed imperate or commanded acts. The reason for this is obvious; moral science is only interested in these acts under the aspect of their freedom, the aspect of their relation to the will. So the acts of any faculty, internal or external, other than an act of the will are considered as commanded acts. However, an act of the will, too, may be considered under the aspect of an imperate act. This would be true in those cases in which the will would command its own acts. For example, the will could command that it make an act of loving God. We will speak later on of the morality of such commanded acts of the will. Here we wish to refer only to their possibility.

In the light of the observations made above, it seems that we can apply the term "elicited act" to the type of act Ockham has referred to and designated as "immediately in the power of the will." On the other hand a commanded act is one which also falls under the power of the will,

---

[11] Ockham, *In IV Sent.*, q. 16: "Duplex est actio conveniens homini: exterior et interior... Operatio interior duplex est: una quae immediate est in potestate voluntatis, sicut volitio; alia, quae non est in potestate voluntatis nisi mediante primo actu." (OTh VII, 358). Confer *In I Sent.*, prolog., 4 (OTh I, 156-57). See also E. Bonke, "Doctrina nominalistica de fundamento ordinis moralis apud Gulielmum de Ockham et Gabrielem Biel," *Collectanea franciscana* XIV (1944), p. 63.

[12] H. Noldin and A. Schmitt, *Summa theologiae moralis*, t. I: *De principiis* (ed. 27a; Innsbruck-Leipzig: Rauch, 1940), pp. 46-47: "Actus humani alii sunt eliciti, alii imperati: *eliciti* dicuntur, qui a voluntate procedunt et in ipsa perficiuntur ut actus amoris, odii, desiderii; *imperati* dicuntur, qui ex imperio voluntatis ab alia potentia, sive interna...sive externa...exercentur."

THE HUMAN WILL AND RIGHT REASON

but only mediately. Now regarding the elicited act, the will has freedom in this way: given everything sufficient and necessarily required for such an act (the object is known and God wishes to concur with the human will in causing the act), then the will by its own liberty, without any other thing determining it, can choose to elicit or not elicit the act. The will is self-determining in reference to these acts. They are elicited freely and contingently. Regarding the mediately free acts, we cannot say that they are free at all unless they fall under the command of the will. They are free mediately, however, since they come under the will's power in virtue of the immediately free act in which the will elicits the command that brings the commanded act into being. the commanded acts, consequently, do not proceed immediately from any self-determining power, but they proceed mediately through a determination of the will.[13]

Whenever there is a commanded act, then, there are actually two distinct acts. The first, the elicited act, commanding (actus elicitus imperans); the second, the commanded act itself (actus imperatus ab elicito). Although these can be said to compose only one act morally, they are physically distinct. According to Ockham this distinction must also be kept in mind when we speak about the morality of these acts. For since it is only the act which is in the power of the will immediately that can be truly moral, commanded acts cannot be termed moral or immoral of themselves but only in relation to an act which is under the control of the will immediately. Consequently, commanded acts of the will are said to be moral or virtuous only by extrinsic denomination. That is to say, they are called moral or virtuous, not by reason of something intrinsic to the acts themselves, but because of something external to them, namely, the elicited act immediately in the power of the will.

It is worth while observing here that when we speak of an act's being in the power of the will, so that the will acts freely, we do not understand this to mean that such an act cannot possibly be impeded. No Christian has to, or can, concede such a viewpoint. Ockham mentions that Aristotle had to concede it, because he did not hold that God immediately causes anything in his creatures. But the Christian, who must hold that

---

[13] Ockham, *In IV Sent.*, q. 16: "Operatio interior duplex est: una, quae immediate est in potestate voluntatis...alia, quae non est in potestate voluntatis nisi mediante primo actu, et ideo primo actu destructo ille actus non est in potestate animae, sicut intellectio. Et ideo unum actum elicit anima libere et contingenter, et alium naturaliter. Loquendo de primo actu, posito omni sufficienti et necessario requisito ad talem actum, puta ad actum voluntatis, si obiectum cognoscatur et Deus velit concurrere cum voluntate ad causandum, quando placet voluntati, potest voluntas ex sua libertate sine omni alia determinatione actuali vel habituali actum illum eius obiectum elicere vel non elicere. Et ideo respectu illius actus non oportet in aliquo quod determinetur voluntas nisi a seipsa." (OTh VII, 358-59). See A. Garvens, *op. cit.*, pp. 256-57.

CHAPTER III

God concurs in every action immediately, has to hold, consequently, that if God does not cooperate with the human will, the creature cannot elicit any act, because a necessarily required partial cause of the act is lacking. So when we say that an act is in the power of the will, we really mean that there is no created being which can impede this act; we do not mean that it cannot be impeded by almighty God in any or in every case in which he would choose not to cooperate with the human will in producing a particular act.[14]

Moral science, as we have seen, deals with acts which are under the control of the will. The connection between moral science and the will can be further elaborated by a consideration of two related topics which are in need of further discussion and explanation. In the first place, only an act of the will is virtuous or evil; and secondly, any act not immediately in the power of the will is not moral of itself, but it receives its morality by extrinsic denomination. In other words, the mediately free act depends for its morality on an act which is immediately in the power of the will. There is a further question that arises in this connection: Is there any act which is moral of itself, intrinsically and necessarily? This last question will be investigated later. Here we are interested in the first two statements as expressed above: only an act of the will is virtuous or evil; any act immediately not in the power of the will is moral only by extrinsic denomination.

Only an act of the will is virtuous or evil. Ockham's treatment of morally good and evil acts, especially in connection with those acts which we have termed "commanded acts," so emphasizes the role of the will in causing these acts that he comes to the conclusion that only an act of the will is virtuous or vicious.[15] Only an act of the will is virtuous, because only an act of the will, strictly speaking, can be called praiseworthy or worthy of blame. Therefore, it alone is virtuous. This

---

[14] Ockham, *In III Sent.*, 7: "Et quando dicitur quod actus voluntatis est in potestate voluntatis, si intelligitur sic quod non possit impediri, hoc nullus christianus debet concedere; licet Philosophus habeat eam concedere qui non ponit Deum immediate aliquid causare in istis inferioribus. Sed christianus, qui habet ponere quod Deus concurrit in omni actione immediate, habet ponere quod Deo non coagente cum voluntate, voluntas nullum actum elicit, quia deficit causa partialis necessario requisita. Sed tamen actus voluntatis sic est in potestate voluntatis quod per nullum creatum potest actus suus simpliciter impediri." (OTh VI, 206).

[15] *In III Sent.*, 11: "...solus actus voluntatis est bonus vel malus moraliter." (OTh VI, 375). See also *In I Sent.*, prolog., 10 (OTh I, 292). The same holds for meritorious acts, e.g. *In III Sent.*, 9: "...actus meritorius necessario requirit activitatem voluntatis." (OTh VI, 281-82). See E. Iserloh, *Gnade und Eucharistie in der philosophischen Theologie des Wilhelm von Ockham* (Wiesbaden: Steiner, 1956), p. 47: "Ein menschlicher Akt ist nur soweit moralisch gut...als der so verstandene freie Wille bei ihm aktuell mitgewirkt hat; eine Moralität im notwendigen Akt lässt Ockham nicht gelten. Alles andere ist moralisch indifferent."

is, of course, not an original viewpoint. In confirmation of his view Ockham appeals to St. Augustine and Aristotle. Aristotle says that no act is really blameworthy unless it is in our control. "No one sins by being blind from birth...but if he is blind through his own fault then he would be worthy of blame."[16] And St. Augustine is referred to as an authority in support of the opinion that a sin is so voluntary that unless it is voluntary it would not be a sin.[17] Or again, Ockham argues that that act which is first and principally virtuous is an act of the will. This is evident because only such an act is praiseworthy or blameworthy. But according to the teaching of the Fathers of the Church no act is praiseworthy or blameworthy unless it is rendered so by either a good or a bad intention. But intention is an act of the will. And, also, St. Anselm states that only the will is punished because only the will sins.[18] Probably Ockham had in mind the following statement from St. Anselm's work, *De conceptu virginali et de originali peccato*:

> Whatever is done, should be imputed to the will. But if this is so, one may wonder why the body and its senses are punished for something the will has done. But such an objection is not valid, because only the will is punished. For something is not a punishment for a person unless it is contrary

---

[16] Ockham, *In III Sent.*, 11: "...quia solus actus voluntatis est laudabilis vel vituperabilis; igitur solus ille est virtuosus....Confirmatur per Philosophum, III *Ethicorum*, ubi dicit quod nullus actus est vituperbilis nisi sit in potestate nostra. Nullus enim culpat caecum natum quia est caecus. Sed si sit caecus per peccatum proprium, tunc est culpabilis." (OTh VI, 366). The reference is to Aristotle, *Ethica Nichomachea*, III, 1109b 30-31; 1114a 26-27). Ockham, *In III Sent.*,7: "...in nullo actu consistit peccatum nisi exsistat in potestate voluntatis..." (OTh VI, 210). Also in this connection see A. Garvens, *op. cit.*, p. 376; E. Hochstetter, "Ockham-Forschung in Italien," *Zeitschrift für philosphische Forschung*, I (1947), p. 575; E. Iserloh, *op. cit.*, p. 47; G. De Lagarde, *La naissance de l'esprit laïque au déclin du moyen âge*. VI: *L'individualisme ockhamiste: La morale et le droit* (Paris: Universitaires de France, 1946), pp. 31, 70-74; S. Zuidema, *De Philosophie van Occam*, t. I (Hilversum: Schipper, 1936), p. 512.

[17] Ockham, *Quodl.*, III, 14: "Praeterea nullus actus est virtuosus nec vitiosus nisi sit voluntarius et in potestate voluntatis, quia peccatum adeo est voluntarium etc." (OTh IX, 254). *In III Sent.*, 11: "...solus actus voluntatis est bonus vel malus moraliter." (OTh VI, 375); *Ibid*: "...requiritur ad bonitatem actus quod sit in potestate voluntatis habentis illum actum." (OTh VI, 389). Cf. also *Quodl.*, I, 20 (OTh IX, 99-106); *Quodl.*, VII, I (OTh IX, 703-06); *In III Sent.*, 9 (OTh VI, 281-82).

[18] *Quodl.*, III, 14: "Solus actus voluntatis est intrinsece laudabilis et vituperabilis. Praeterea secundum Sanctos nullus actus est laudabilis vel vituperabilis nisi propter intentionem bonam vel malum; intentio autem est actus voluntatis; igitur etc. Praeterea secundum Anselmum sola voluntas punitur, quia sola peccat; igitur etc." (OTh IX, 256). Cf. also *Quodl.*, I, 20 (OTh IX, 99-106).

CHAPTER III

to his will. Only the will can experience something as a punishment.[19]

Any act that is not immediately in the power of the human will is not moral of itself; but it receives its morality by extrinsic denomination only. Only an act of the will is first and principally good or evil morally.[20] And because of this primarily good act, the will itself can be called good or evil mediately, because of the act. And sometimes the resulting act commanded by the will is also called good or evil by extrinsic denomination; but it is not intrinsically good or evil of itself.[21] Any act, other than the act of the will which is immediately free, is moral only in virtue of an act of the will immediately in the power of the will. Any act which is not immediately free may be elicited by its proper faculty without any command by the will. In such a case the act is elicited "naturally," i.e. non-freely. Thus it is neither good nor bad of itself. Moreover, even if the act is commanded (as a true *actus imperatus*) it can be good or evil depending on whether it is performed with a good or an evil intention. Thus any such act can, while remaining the same act, be successively praiseworthy or vicious, since at one time it would be commanded with a right intention and later with an evil intention.[22] For example, a person may walk to church with the good intention

---

[19] St. Anselm, *De conceptu virginali et de originali peccato* in *S. Anselmi opera omnia*, tom. II, ed. F. Schmitt (Edinburgh: Nelson, 1946), p. 145: "Quidquid igitur faciunt, totum imputandum est voluntati. Quod cum ita sit, miratur forsitan aliquis, cur pro culpa voluntatis membra puniuntur et sensus. Verum non ita est. Non enim punitur nisi voluntas. Nam nihil est alicui poena nisi quod est contra voluntatem, et nulla res poenam sentit nisi quae habet voluntatem." The text continues: "Membra autem et sensus per se nihil volunt. Sicut igitur voluntas in membris et sensibus operatur, ita in illis ipsa torquetur aut delectatur. Quod si quis non accipit: sciat in sensibus et membris non nisi animam in qua est voluntas sentire et operari, et ideo in illis torqueri aut delectari." Cf. *Ibid.*, p. 143-144.

[20] Ockham, *In III Sent.*, 11: "...solum actus voluntatis qui primo est imputabilis est primo bonus vel malus moraliter." (OTh VI, 390). Cf. also *Quodl.*, III, 15 (OTh IX, 257-62).

[21] *In III Sent.*, II: "...voluntas denominatur bona vel mala mediante actu, et aliquando actus etiam denominantur denominatione extrinseca." (OTh IX 253-57); *In III Sent.*, II (OTh VI, 359).

[22] *Quodl.*, III, 14: "...nullus actus alius ab actu voluntatis est necessario virtuosus...quia omnis alius actus ab actu voluntatis, qui est in potestate voluntatis, sic est bonus quod potest esse malus, quia potest fieri cum malo fine et mala intentione. Similiter omnis alius actus potest elici naturaliter et non-libere, et nullus talis est necessario virtuosus. Praeterea quilibet alius actus idem manens potest indifferenter esse laudabilis et vituperabilis, et primo laudabilis et post vituperabilis, secundum quod potest successive conformari volitioni rectae et vitiosae..." (OTh IX, 253-54). Cf. *Quodl.*, I, 18 (OTh IX, 95); II, 16 (OTh IX, 182-86); III, 15 and 16 (OTh IX, 257-67); *In III Sent.*, 11 (OTh VI, 359-62, 383-88). See also L.

of honoring God. Later he may change this intention so that he is going to church out of pride. The external act of walking, the commanded act, remains the same, but its morality varies according to the intention of the will. Therefore, its morality is dependent on the fact of whether this intention is one of honoring God or, on the other hand, is an act resulting from pride. The mediately free acts, Ockham insists, are to be considered moral only in a secondary sense. In other words, they are moral only by extrinsic denomination.[23]

Another reason the commanded acts are not moral in the primary sense of the term is that these acts can be at first in the power of the will mediately and afterwards not. In other words, the will can command an act to be performed and later negate the command. But the second act of the will may be powerless to halt or to change the commanded act once it has actually begun. The example Ockham gives of this is of a man who throws himself voluntarily from a precipice, and afterwards, while falling, he repents of his act. To stop falling, however, is not in his will's power. So the descent, once evil because it was done voluntarily, is now not evil because it is no longer willed.[24] If the act would be evil, then the man would be evil and virtuous (because he repents of his act) at the same time. Consequently, he would have to be condemned because of his external act; and at the same time he would have to be rewarded because of his internal act of repentance.[25] Or we would have to say that he

---

Baudry (ed.), *Le Tractatus de principiis* ("Etudes de philosophie médiévale," 3XXIII: Paris: Vrin, 1936), pp. 77-81.

[23] Ockham, *In III Sent.*, 11: "Nullus actus nec habitus partis sensitivae dicitur virtuosus vel vitiosus nisi quadem denominatione extrinseca." (OTh VI, 360); *Quodl.* II, 15: "Dico quod propter passiones moderatas vel immoderatas laudamur et vituperamur, quando sunt in potestate nostra. Unde tales actus sive passiones non determinant sibi laudem vel vituperium, ita quod conveniant eis intrinsece; sed solum quadam denominatione extrinseca per conformitatem ad volitionem vel vitiosam..." (OTh IX, 181); cf. also *Quodl.*, I, 20 (OTh IX, 99-106).

[24] *Quodl.*, III, 14: "... actus alius ab actu voluntatis potest primo esse in potestate voluntatis, et post hoc non; puta quando aliquis dimittit se voluntarie in praecipitium, et post paenitet et habet actum nolendi illum descensum meritorie propter Deum; sed in descendendo non est in potestate voluntatis; igitur ille descensus non est necessario vitiosus." (OTh IX, 254).

[25] *Quodl.*, I, 20: "...sed si aliquis voluntarie dimittat se in praecipitium et in descendendo paeniteat et doleat et simpliciter nolit illum descensum, immo revocaret si posset, ille actus nolendi est virtuosus et meritorius; sed actus descendendi non est vitiosus quando paenitet, quia non est tunc in potestate voluntatis. Immo si esset vitiosus, ille homo simul foret vitiosus et virtuosus, damnandus propter actum exteriorem et salvandus propter interiorem." (OTh IX, 103). Cf. A. Garvens, *op. cit.*, p. 389; O. Fuchs, *The Psychology of Habit according to William Ockham* ("Franciscan Institute Publications: Philosophy Series," No. 8; St. Bonaventure, N.Y.: Franciscan Institute, 1952), p. 81.

CHAPTER III

merits by repudiating his sin, yet at the same time he is sinning mortally--which is absurd.[26] Thus an impossible situation would arise.

A final argument is that every commanded act of a creature could, as a matter of fact, be produced by God alone as the total cause. To explain: the act can be produced by God, not, of course, as a true commanded act in the sense in which this act depends on a free act of the will of the creature; but the act itself--seeing, walking, knowing--can be produced by God as the total cause. Now if the act is produced by God as the total cause, it would not be moral as far as the creature is concerned, for it lacks the first condition for a moral act, namely, that the act be under the power of the will.[27] In this case, however, the act would not be a true commanded act as far as the creature is concerned. It is not in the power of the creature's will even mediately. Therefore, such an act cannot be moral, much less intrinsically or necessarily moral in the sense that, given this act, it is always good or always evil. The situation, however, is not the same with an immediately free act of a creature. The term "free act" implies that it is in the power of the creature, hence cannot be produced by God as the total cause, for such an act could not be called a free act. Thus if God would cause the hatred of himself in the will of a creature--if he would cause the act of hatred as the total cause just as he now always causes it as a partial cause--then the creature could not sin in this case. For the act would not be in his power.[28] Similarly, all other acts caused by God as total cause would have to be regarded in the above way and considered according to the same governing principles.[29]

---

[26] Ockham, *Quaest. Variae*, 6, 9: "...aliquis voluntarie descendit in praecipitum, et in descendendo poenitet et dolet simpliciter nolendo illum actum propter Deum. Ille actus tunc descendi non est voluntarius nec in potestate voluntatis. Igitur tunc in illo non consistit peccatum quia tunc meretur per volitionem illius peccati et peccaret mortaliter quod falsum est." (OTh VIII, 263-64).

[27] *Quodl.*, III, 14: "Praeterea omnis actus alius a voluntate potest fieri a solo Deo, et per consequens non est necessario virtuosus creaturae rationali." (OTh IX, 254).

[28] *In IV Sent.*, 10-11: "Unde si Deus causaret odium in voluntate alicuius sicut causa totalis, sicut semper causat sicut causa partialis, neuter peccaret: nec Deus, quia ad nihil obligatur; nec alius, quia actus ille non esset in potestate sua." (OTh VII, 198).

[29] See for example *In IV Sent.*, 10-11: "Omne positivum quod est in peccato potest poni per Deum sicut per causam totalem in voluntate hominis, et tamen non diceretur peccatum, quia nec ex parte Dei nec ex parte hominis, quia numquam dicitur homo peccator propter aliquem actum nisi habeat respectu illius activitatem. Sed si Deus sit causa totalis actus, tunc homo non habeat activitatem aliquam respectu illius; igitur etc." (OTh VII, 225); see also *In III Sent.*, 11 (OTH VI, 389).

THE HUMAN WILL AND RIGHT REASON

We will now conclude this particular section of the chapter with a consideration of the relation of morality to the following types of acts: external acts, intellectual acts, commanded acts of the will, and acts of the sensitive appetites.

What then of the external act? If only an act of the will can be virtuous or evil in the primary sense, can the external act be said to have in any sense its own moral goodness or evil? According to the opinion of Duns Scotus exterior acts have a distinct morality.[30] Scotus' argument is based on the existence of distinct precepts for interior and exterior acts. Since there are distinct precepts, there are distinct sins; and since there are distinct sins, there is a distinct morality for interior and exterior acts. Exterior acts, therefore, have their own proper moral goodness or evil, distinct from that of the interior act of the will.[31] In addition to Duns Scotus, St. Augustine also seems to hold the existence of a distinct morality for external acts. We have his words, "A bad will in itself is enough to make a man a sinner; but the fulfillment of his evil desire makes him even more a sinner."[32]

The question of the morality of exterior acts discussed here is to be understood in the following terms: when an interior good act is elicited and an exterior act is performed in conformity with this interior act, does the exterior acts by its conformity with the interior act receive or acquire any morality beyond that of the interior act? Thus the question is not concerned with whether the physical nature of the exterior act is distinct from that of the interior act; for it is manifest that they are distinct. Nor is this question concerned with whether the exterior act has any essential morality, i.e. whether it is intrinsically good or evil; for it is manifest that such acts are not intrinsically good. Any exterior act can be elicited by an insane person, who, while he is insane,

---

[30]Duns Scotus, *Quaestiones quodlibetales*, q. 18, n. 1 in *Joannis Duns Scoti opera omnia*, tom. XXVII, ed. Vivès (Paris: 1895), p. 228: "Utrum actus exterior addat aliquid bonitatis vel malitiae ad actum interiorem...quae praeceptis negativis distinctis prohibentur, habent propriam et distinctam rationem illiciti; nunc autem alio praecepto prohibetur actus exterior, et alio interior, ut patet de istis praeceptis: *Non maechaberis, et non concupisces uxorem*, etc. Et similiter de istis praeceptis:
Non furtum facies, et non concupisces rem proximi, etc."

[31]Ockham, *Quodl.*, "Utrum actus exterior habeat propriam bonitatem moralem et malitiam.... In ista quaestione dicit Scotus quod sic, *Quodlibet*, q. 18. Quod probatur primo sic: distincta peccata prohibentur distinctis praeceptis negativis; sed distincto et distincto praecepto prohibetur actus exterior et interior; igitur sunt distincta peccata, et per consequens habent distinctam bonitatem et malitiam." (OTh IX, 99--100). See E. Iserloh, *op. cit.*, p. 63.

[32]St. Augustine, *De Trinitate*, XIII, 5: "Etiam mala enim voluntate vel sola quisque miser efficitur: sed miserior potestate, qua desiderium male voluntatis impletur."

CHAPTER III

cannot elicit any virtuous act whatsoever. Furthermore, the question is not concerned with a comparison of acts of different persons, nor with the acts of the same person at different times; but it is in reference to the same person at the same time.[33] For instance, a person intends to pray. Does the resultant external act of prayer in this case have a morality which is distinct from the morality embodied in his intention to pray?

Ockham is of the opinion that the exterior act does not have any morality distinct from that of the interior act. The external act is called "moral" only by extrinsic denomination. This conclusion follows directly and necessarily from Ockham's position explained above: only an act of the will is virtuous or evil; any act not immediately in the power of the will is not moral of itself, but receives its morality by extrinsic denomination. Thus the exterior act cannot have its own proper morality--a subjective or internal morality--distinct from that of the interior act.[34]

In answer to Scotus' argument from the distinct precepts, Ockham concedes that there are distinct precepts corresponding to interior and exterior acts. But at the same time he maintains that these distinct precepts are not given in the sense that one precept forbids a certain interior act and another percept forbids only the corresponding external act. This second precept is to be understood as forbidding both the internal and the external act. For there are distinct precepts on account of distinct acts, one interior and the other exterior. But the fact that these acts are distinct physically does not necessarily argue to their

---

[33] Ockham, *Quodl.*, I, 20: "...dico quod non intelligitur quaestio de substantia actus interioris et exterioris, utrum scilicet sit alia et alia substantia actus, quia manifestum est quod est alius et alius actus. Nec intelligitur de essentiali bonitate, utrum scilicet actus exterior sit essentialiter bonus vel malus circumscripto omni alio actu, sicut actus voluntatis est bonus et malus; quia manifestum est quod non, quia omnis actus exterior potest elici a phrenetico et furioso, qui tamen pro tunc nullum actus virtuosum possunt habere. Nec intelligitur de actu interiore et exteriore in diversis, sed in eodem. Nec etiam intelligitur de eodem subiecto in diversis temporibus, sed in eodem tempore." (OTh IX, 101).

[34] *Ibid.*: "Est igitur iste intellectus quaestionis: quando actus interior bonus elicitur et actus exterior conformiter elicitur, utrum actus exterior per talem conformitatem ad interiorem aliquid recipit vel adquirit praeter actum. Et sic intelligendo quaestionem, probo quod non. Quia si sic, aut illa bonitas moralis est ipse actus aut aliquid praeter actum. Et sic intelligendo quaestionem, probo quod non. Quia si sic, aut illa bonitas moralis est ipse actus aut aliquid praeter actum. Non actus, quia ille actus exterior qui nunc est bonus, idem potest esse malus; patet de actu ambulandi ad ecclesiam propter honorem Dei vel vanam gloriam; igitur illa bonitas est aliquid praeter actum. Non actus, quia ille actus exterior qui nunc est bonus, idem potest esse malus; patet de actu ambulandi ad ecclesiam propter honorem Dei vel vanam gloriam; igitur illa bonitas est aliquid praeter actum. Aut igitur est subiective in actu aut non. Si non, tunc illa bonitas non potest poni nisi actus interior. Si sic, contra: non potest esse qualitas inhaerens sibi nec respectus..." (OTh IX, 101-102).

distinct morality. The morality of the exterior act depends on the interior act and the exterior act could not be evil unless caused by an evil interior act which imparts its morality to the exterior act elicited in accord with the aforementioned interior act. For example, the tenth commandment of the Decalogue forbids the interior act of coveting another's possessions. The seventh commandment forbids the exterior act of stealing; but implicitly it also includes the interior act of willing to steal. And another argument Ockham mentions is that there are distinct precepts so that the naive and simple-minded will not make the mistake of thinking that only external acts are sins.[35]

Another argument sometimes advanced in favor of the distinct morality of interior and exterior acts is that exterior acts are punished more than internal acts, therefore they must be morally distinct. This state of affairs, Ockham answers, may take place repeatedly under civil codes of law which frequently punish rather minor external violations of the law with great severity on the grounds that these violations constitute greater occasions of detriment to the state. According to civil law it may even happen that the theft of a sheep is punished more severely than defamations of a citizen's character although in God's sight the latter would be a graver injustice.[36]

In Ockham's opinion, then, the external act is good by its own proper goodness in the physical order; it is ontologically good. But morally and causally the external act is good only by reason of the moral goodness of the interior act of the will. The external act is called good only by extrinsic denomination.[37]

In Ockham's mind Scotus' theory that the exterior act has its own proper morality distinct from the moral goodness of the interior act en-

---

[35] *Ibid.*: "...sunt distincta praecepta propter distinctionem actuum, quamvis unus actus non sit malus nisi quia causatur ab alio malo actu. Unde per unum praeceptum prohibetur actus interior, per aliud prohibetur tam actus interior quam exterior....Aliter potest dici quod sunt distincta praecepta ne detur simplicibus occasio errandi, qui credunt quod non est peccatum nisi in actu exteriore." (OTh IX, 104-105). Cf. *In III Sent.*, 11 (OTh VI, 375-76).

[36] *Quodl.*, I, 20: "...non plus punitur a Deo actus interior et exterior simul quam interior per se, nisi intendatur actus interior quando elicitur actus exterior. Sed a lege humana actus exteriores plus puniuntur, quia frequenter plus punit peccata minora quia sunt maiores occasiones destructionis rei publicae. Exemplum est de furari ovem et diffamare hominem; quorum primum est minus peccatum secundo, et tamen plus punitur apud homines quam secundum, licet non coram Deo." (OTh IX, 105). This argument is developed further in *In III Sent.*, 11 (OTh VI, 376-79). See also *Quodl.*, II, 12 (OTh IX, 165-67). See also L. Baudry, *op. cit.*, pp. 81-82; E. Hochstetter, "Viator mundi" *Franziskanische Studien*, XXXII (1950), p. 13.

[37] Ockham, *Quodl.*, I, 20: "...actus exterior est bonus bonitate sua propria, quae est ipse actus naturalis; sed moraliter et causaliter est bonus bonitate actus interioris, quia solum est bonus quadam denominatione extrinseca." (OTh IX, 106).

CHAPTER III

tails, consequently, that exterior acts would be virtuous or evil even when performed by a person who does not have the use of reason.[38] Accordingly, it seems that someone without the use of reason, who fights valiantly against an aggressor, would act virtuously; and if such a person would commit an act of fornication he would act evilly. But this cannot be, because only an act of the will which is elicited feely can be virtuous or evil, meritorious or demeritorious. No other act is called evil or virtuous except by extrinsic denomination. Therefore, if a man is incapable of a free act of the will, none of his acts can be virtuous or vicious, neither essentially nor denominatively. However, it could be said that the act by which a person places himself in a condition in which he would lose his use of reason may be called vicious or virtuous accordingly; for that act is, or at least it could be, willful. And so a sin does not consist in anything but that act which is voluntary and is in the power of the will immediately, or at least mediately. Now it is possible that someone would have an exterior act which is first elicited according to an evil intention and while this exterior act continues he could interiorly deny or repudiate the exterior act. His interior negation would be meritorious; therefore, the external act could no longer be a sin, because there is no interior act to which it conforms. The example of this is, as we have mentioned before, the man who jumps from a precipice.[39]

As an act performed by man externally is said to be moral only by a certain extrinsic denomination, so the same may be said for an act of the intellect when it is a commanded act of the will. The act of the intellect can remain the same while its morality changes, depending on the corresponding act of the will to which the act of the intellect is related. The will may command the intellect to be occupied in study, first out of pride and later, while the studying continues on the part of the intel-

---

[38] Ockham, *Quaest. Variae*, 6, 9: "Est dubium...utrum aggressio terribilium sit virtuosus in forti pro tunc quando suspenditur usus rationis et fornicatio viciosa in alio...Johannis, qui ponit quod actus exterior habet propriam bonitatem distinctam ab actu interiori, habet ponere quod praedicti actus essent virtuosi vel viciosi, quantumcumque non haberent usum rationis. Sed haec opinio videtur falsa." (OTh VIII, q. 6, 9: 262-3).

[39] *Ibid.*: "Solus actus voluntatis libere elicitus est virtuosus vel viciosus, meritorius vel demeritorius, et nullus alius actus dicitur viciosus vel virtuosus nisi quadam denominatione extrinseca, puta quantum potest conformari illi volitioni. Et ideo quando non est aliqua volitio in homine, nullus est actus virtuosus in eo, nec viciousus essentialiter nec denominative. Sed actus ille per quem voluntarie posuit se in tali statu in quo amitteret usum rationis dicitur viciosus vel virtuosus. Et ille fuit actus volendi...Nunquam in aliquo consistat peccatum nisi actus ille sit voluntarius et in potestate voluntatis mediate vel immediate. Sed nunc possibile est quod aliquis habeat actus exteriorem, primo elicitum iuxta volitionem viciosam et quod, stante illo actu exteriori, simpliciter nollet illum actum et meritorie, et per consequens in tali actu non consistet peccatum." (OTh VIII, 263).

lect, the intention of the will changes so that studying on the part of the intellect is now commanded out of love of God. The act of the intellect is at first evil; later it is virtuous. But the point is that there is no change in the act of the intellect all during this time. In so far as its activity is concerned the intellect remains engaged in study. Its activity has changed in its morality, however. And this change in morality, from evil to good, is dependent solely on the change which has taken place in the act of the will.[40]

The same holds true for any commanded act of the will. For instance, the will simply commands "go to church", at first without adverting to any purpose for the act of going to church, either good or bad. Later the will would command that the good intention of honoring God should be the purpose of going to church. The first act is indifferent, but the second is virtuous. In so far as the act of the will commanding the going to church is concerned, there has really been no change at all. But the point is that a new act of the will is elicited in commanding that the good intention should prevail. That these two acts of the will (one commanding simply "go to church", the other commanding "go to church out of love of God") are distinct can be seen from the fact of their separability. The act of walking to church is at first indifferent, but later it becomes virtuous when the good intention is elicited by the will. The external act of walking, however, has not changed in so far as its physical nature is concerned. But it has changed morally.[41]

By way of explanation, Ockham would insist that the phrase "an act of the will which is in the power of the will" is preferable and more accurate than the simpler phrase "an act of the will". Not every act of the will is in the power of the will immediately. For although the will, considered absolutely, is free regarding any act which it elicits, the will's liberty may be restricted in virtue of a prior act of the will itself. An example of this would be: the object of charity is God and all that God wills. Now I love God by such an elicited act of charity, so that I love God and all that God wills. And it is possible that I do this by one act of the will. Now if I know by my intellect, through revelation or in some

---

[40] *Quodl.*, I, 18: "Eodem modo est de actu intellectus, quando voluntas imperat sibi studere primo propter vanam gloriam, et secundo imperat continuationem illius actus propter honorem Dei. Iste actus intellectus primo est vitiosus, et secundo virtuosus; et tamen nulla mutatio est in ipso intellectu sed solum in voluntate." (OTh IX, 95).

[41] *Ibid.*: "Eodem modo est de aliquo actu voluntatis, puta quando voluntas absolute imperat homini quod vadat ad ecclesiam, et non propter aliquem finem bonum vel malum; post stante ista volitione, imperat quod vadat ad honorem Dei et laudem. In isto casu primus actus imperatus est primo actus indifferens, et secundo est virtuosus; et tamen nulla mutatio est in illo actu, licet voluntas eliciat novum actum." (OTh IX, 96).

CHAPTER III

other way, that God wills me to love a certain creature, then while the love of God remains in my will I must love this particular creature also. There is a distinction between the act of loving God and the act of loving this particular creature. The will is not free regarding the second act while the first remains in force and the required knowledge is present as stated. That this second act is distinct from the first is evident from the fact of their separability; the one precedes the other; and the second is in reference to an individual while the first is general, "to love all that God wills". And it is possible that I do this by one act of the will. Now if I know by my intellect, through revelation or in some other way, that God wills me to love a certain creature, then while the love of God remains in my will I must love this particular creature also. There is a distinction between the act of loving God and the act of loving this particular creature. The will is not free regarding the second act while the first remains in force and the required knowledge is present as stated. That this second act is distinct from the first is evident from the fact of their separability; the one precedes the other; and the second is in reference to an individual while the first is general, "to love all that God wills".[42] The point is, the second act, the act of loving this particular creature, is not immediately free even though it is an act of the will. A prior act of the will has already determined the second act. The second act is not immediately, but only mediately free. For it is impossible that I love God and everything that God wills me to love in general while at the same time I do not love this particular creature whom God wills me to love. Consequently, there would be merit primarily in the first act of the will, because it is immediately in the power of the will; but merit would only be mediately in the second act of the will, because it is only mediately in the power of the will. Thus it

---

[42] *In III Sent.*, 7: "Potest dici quod licet voluntas sit libera respectu cuiuscumque actus ab ea eliciti absolute considerando, tamen considerando aliquem actum voluntatis in quantum alius actus antecedit in voluntate, non est voluntas libera respectu illius actus. Exemplum: ponamus quod obiectum caritatis sit totum istud: 'Deus et omne quod Deus vult diligi,' et quod diligam Deum caritative actu elicito, ita quod aliquo uno actu diligam Deum et omne quod Deus vult diligi a me, quod est possibile. Si tunc cognoscam per intellectum quod Deus vult Ioannem diligi a me per revelationem vel quamcumque aliam viam, stante prima dilectione in voluntate cum cognitione praedicta, necessario habeo diligere Ioannem actu caritativo. Et ille actus est alius a primo, quia possunt separari. Et unus praecedit alium. Et unus, scilicet secundus, est praecise respectu unius incomplexi, puta Ioannis; alius, puta primus, non." (OTh VI, 210-11). See also L. Baudry (ed.), *op. cit.*, p. 147: "Non omnis actus voluntatis est liber quia, licet actus amoris quo actu amo sanitatem ante quam amem alia propter eam, qui est amicitie solum, sit liber, secundus tamen ejus actus qui est actus amicitie et concupiscentie simul non est liber, sed necessario sequitur alium supposito dictamine rationis quod tale amatum sit necessarium ad consecutionem talis finis; si actu volo sanitatem et ratio dictet quod comedam quia sic potest haberi sanitas et aliter non, stante actuali voluntate sanitatis et illo dictamine, statim necessario volo comedere."

can be said that the will is not immediately free regarding every act that it elicits. It is immediately free regarding some acts and not regarding others.[43]

Similarly, we are praised or blamed for moderate or immoderate passions when they are in our power mediately. These passions are not themselves praiseworthy or blameworthy, as if this were something due them intrinsically. But it is only by extrinsic denomination that they are worthy of praise or blame, that is, in so far as they are in conformity with a virtuous or an evil act of the will. Both praiseworthy and blameworthy passions are commanded by a virtuous or a vicious will respectively.[44] Thus the passions themselves are called praiseworthy or blameworthy on account of an act of the will to which they are related. However, they are praiseworthy or blameworthy only by extrinsic denomination.[45]

What has been said concerning the morality of acts holds also concerning the morality of habits. As only acts of the will are virtuous, so only habits of the will are virtuous. There are habits in the strict sense in the will.[46] And only these are moral in the sense that only acts of the will are moral.[47] No habit other than a habit of the will is intrinsically and perfectly virtuous, for every other habit inclines in-

---

[43] Ockham, *In III Sent.* 7: "...voluntas non est libera respectu secundi actus, stante primo actu cum apprehensione praedicta. Quia impossibile est quod uno actu diligam Deum et omne quod Deus vult diligi a me in generali, et quod sciam quod Deus vult Ioannem diligi a me, nisi diligam Ioannem in speciali, quia contradictio est dicere oppositum. Et tunc, licet in primo actu voluntatis consistat meritum, quia est in potestate voluntatis, non tamen in secondo actu qui non est in potestate voluntatis." (OTh VI, 211).

[44] *Quodl.*, II, 15: "...dico quod propter passiones moderatas vei immoderatas laudamur et vituperamur, quando sunt in potestate nostra. Unde tales actus sive passiones non determinant sibi laudem vel vituperium, ita quod conveniant eis intrinsece; sed solum quadam denominatione extrinseca per conformitatem ad volitionem virtuosam vel vitiosam....dico quod tam passiones laudabiles quam vituperabiles imperantur a voluntate virtuosa vel vitiosa." (OTh IX, 181). Cf. *In III Sent.* 11 (OTh VI, 359-62).

[45] *III Sent.*, 11: "...passio...solum dicitur laudabilis vel vituperabilis propter electionem voluntatis propter finem bonum vel malum. Et ita dicitur talis denominatione extrinseca." (OTh VI, 367). See O. Fuchs, *op. cit.*, pp. 91-92.

[46] Ockham, *Quodl.*, II, 18: "dico quod 'habitus' dupliciter accipitur, scilicet large et stricte....Habitus accepti primo modo sunt in corpore et in parte apprehensiva; secundo modo, sunt in voluntate." (OTh IX, 189-90). *In I Sent.*, prolog., 10: "...proprie loquendo omnis habitus moralis est in voluntate..." (OTh I, 299). Cf. also *Quodl.*, III, 20 (OTh IX, 281-84); *In III Sent.*, 7 (OTh VI, 201-03); 11 (OTh VI, 358, 363-5); 12 (OTh VI, 416). See also O. Fuchs, *op. cit.*, pp. 64-69; A. Garvens, *op. cit.*, p. 368.

[47] Ockham, *In III Sent.*, 11: "...solus habitus voluntatis est proprie virtus." (OTh VI, 358). Cf. *In I Sent.* prolog., 10 (OTh I, 299); *In III Sent.*, 11 (OTh VI, 356-62, 366-72).

differently to praise worthy and blameworthy acts.[48] And no habit is more virtuous than the act elicited by the habit. Habits are also virtuous in so far as they incline to virtuous acts.[49]

II. Right Reason

In the foregoing we saw that only an immediately free act of the will can be called moral in the strict sense. It is, of course, immediately obvious that not every free act of the will is a morally good act. Freedom is but the first condition of a morally good act. While all morally good acts are free acts, not every free act is a morally good act. Free acts may also be morally evil. What, then, in man determines the morality of the free act so that it is morally good or morally evil? This question is answered by the second condition required for a moral act: the act must be elicited in conformity with the dictates of right reason if it is to be a morally good act. Right reason embodies a type of practical knowledge which is directed toward a true praxis. In its actual operation it is directive, but more than that it is also dictative. Hence the frequently used term the "dictates" of right reason. This knowledge is usually, and also in Ockham, termed simply "right reason", or in a more precise designation of its activity, "the dictates of right reeason." In fact, Ockham continually emphasizes the dynamic aspect of right reason, considering it not so much as an habitual body of practical knowledge but rather in its operation of regulating, directing, dictating, commanding acts of the will. At times Ockham also uses the more accurate expression "the dictates of right reason" or "right reason dictating"; at other times he uses simply the term "right reason". In view of a problem to be considered later, it should also be mentioned that Ockham refers to right reason as a form of actual prudence, which is right reason as applied to things to be done.[50]

---

[48] *Quodl.*, III, 14: "...solus habitus voluntatis est intrinsece et necessario virtuosus, quia quilibet alius habitus inclinat indifferenter ad actus laudabiles et vituperabiles." (OTh IX, 257). Same wording in *Quodl.* III, 13.

[49] *In III Sent.*, 11: "...habitus non est magis virtuosus quam actus elicitus ab habitu. Hoc patet, quia habitus non dicitur virtuosus nisi...inclinat ad actum virtuosum qui proprie est virtuosus." (OTh VI, 359). Cf. also *Ibid.*, (OTh VI, 366).

[50] *Quaest. Variae*, 7, 2: "Prudentia...accipitur pro omni notitia directiva respectu cuiuscumque agibilis mediate vel immediate." (OTh VIII, 330); *ibid.*, 8: "Cum igitur de ratione prudentiae sit regulare actum voluntatis, quia est recta ratio agibilium." *Ibid.*, 413); cf. also *ibid.* 416ff., 423-7. *In III Sent.*, 12: "Recta autem ratio est prudentia in actu vel habitu." (OTh VI, 422). This is prudence used in the improper sense, i.e. the fourth meaning of prudence as explained in Ch. II. A. Garvens comments, *op. cit.* p. 375: "Mit Aristoteles und der Scholastik stimmt Ockham darin überein, dass der Mensch zum sittlichen Handeln des Regulativs durch die Vernunft bedarf. Sie tritt ihm in der recta ratio--vielfach von ihm prudentia genannt

THE HUMAN WILL AND RIGHT REASON

We have spoken of a free act of the will, a morally good act in the primary sense. But such an act cannot be elicited by the will unless it is in conformity with the dictates of right reason. That right reason is required for such an act to be morally good is mentioned over and over again in Ockham's writings.[51] The nature of the created will as a faculty which can freely choose good or evil makes it necessary that there be some norm for its actions. The created will is not necessarily a right will in and by itself, nor is it necessarily an evil will. Any will which can act either rightly or evilly requires some directive norm other than itself in order to act rightly.[52] This clearly does not apply to the divine will. The nature of the will excludes any necessity of having any external rule of action. The divine will, because it is a right will in and by itself, cannot act evilly. It is its own directive norm. But the created will, since it can act rightly or not, needs such a norm of action.[53]

Thus Aristotle defined virtue as an elective habit regarding the mean determined by reason.[54] And he held that there is never any moral virtue without prudence.[55] There cannot be a right or virtuous act without right reason. A right and virtuous act of the will is necessarily

---

und mit dem scholastischen Begriff der conscientia im wesentlichen gleichbedeutend--entgegen." And E. Iserloh remarks in *op. cit.*, p. 54: "So gebraucht Ockham recta ratio gleichbedeutend mit conscientia und besonders mit prudentia wobei diese eine auf das Handeln gerichtete Erkenntnis, eine 'notitia directiva respectu cuiuscumque agibilis est.'"

[51] Ockham, *Quaest. Variae*, 8: "Primo sciendum est quod ad hoc quod actus recte eliciatur a voluntate necessario requiritur aliqua recta ratio in intellectu." (OTh VIII, 409); cf. *ibid.*, 7, 3-4 (*ibid.*, 347-50, 360f).

[52] *Ibid.*, 8: "Illa voluntas quae potest, quantum est de se, indifferenter bene agere et male, quia de se non est recta, necessario ad hoc quod recte agat, indiget aliqua regula dirigente alia a se." (OTh VIII, 410). For the contrast on this point between Ockham and Luther see note 9, *supra*.

[53] Ockham, *Ibid.*: "Voluntas divina non indiget aliquo dirigente, quia illa est primo regula directiva et non potest male agere. Sed voluntas nostra est huiusmodi, quod potest recte et non recte agere. Igitur, indiget aliqua ratione dirigente." (OTh VIII, 410). See A. Garvens, *op. cit.*, p. 376; E. Hochstetter, "Viator mundi," p. 12.

[54] Aristotle, *Ethica Nicomachea*, II, 6, 1106b-1107a: "Virtue, then, is a state of character concerned with choice, lying in a mean, i.e. the mean relative to us, this being determined by a rational principle, and by that principle by which the man of practical wisdom would determine it."

[55] Ockham, *In I Sent.*, 35, 6: "Similiter virtus moralis, secundum Aristotelem, VI *Ethicorum*, numquam est sine prudentia." (OTh IV, 510). Cf. Aristotle, *Ethica Nicomachea* VI, 10 (1144b 14-17).

CHAPTER III

in conformity with an act of prudence.[56] Perfect moral virtue, then, cannot exist without prudence, although prudence may exist without moral virtue. The essence of a perfect virtue and its act is that it is elicited in conformity with right reason.[57]

But it must be emphasized that right reason or prudence does not consist in the mere judgment of the intellect expressed, for example, in the categorical proposition, "this act is good." It involves a further assent to this proposition, resulting in the normative statement, "this act should be done." Without this further assent, the act would not be virtuous when it is performed. Ockham refers to an act performed only in conformity with the proposition "this act is good" as good from its nature since it involves a naturally good act, directed towards a worthy object. But because such an act is not an object of right reason dictating "this act should be done," it cannot be virtuous, since the essence of a virtuous act is that it is elicited in conformity with right reason over and above the fact that the act is in reference to a worthy object.[58] It is in this sense, says Ockham, that Aristotle's dictum: First he knows; then he chooses" is to be understood.[59] Thus the act of dictating by right reason is not formally embodied in the proposition "this act is good"; but it is an act of assenting or dissenting to this propo-

---

[56] Ockham, *Quaest. Variae*, 8: "Et multae aliae auctoritates sunt ad hoc quod non potest esse rectus et virtuosus nisi habeat rationem rectam." (OTh VIII, 410). Cf. *Quodl.* III, 19 (OTh IX, 275-81); *In I Sent.*, prol., 11: "Non potest prudentia separi in adquisitione ipsius a virtute morali." (OTh I, 320); cf. *Quodl.*, III, 19 (OTh IX, 275-81). See L. Baudry, *op. cit.*, p. 80: "...nullus virtuose agit nisi regulatus recta ratione dictante sic esse agendum." Also E. Bonke, *op. cit.*, p. 65; F. Copleston, *A History of Philosophy*, Vol. III: *Ockham to Suarez* (Westminster: Newman, 1953), pp. 105-105).

[57] Ockham, *In III Sent.*, 12: "...prudentia potest esse sine virtutibus moralibus....virtus moralis perfecta non potest esse sine prudentia...quia de ratione virtutis perfectae et actus eius est quod eliciatur conformiter rectae rationi..." (OTh VI, 421-22). Cf. *In III Sent.*, 11 (OTh VI, 385-86). See also L. Baudry, *op. cit.*, p. 81.

[58] Ockham, *In III Sent.*, 12: "Si dicas quod ostenso aliquo obiecto diligibili sine omni dictamine rationis, potest voluntas illud diligere, et iste est bonus moraliter quia diligit quod diligendum est, et eodem modo etc. Puta si formatur hoc complexum 'hoc bonum est diligibile' et intellectus non assentiat, est tunc dubium utrum illa dilectio sit bona moraliter: Respondeo: licet actus ille sit bonus ex genere et non sit malus moraliter, tamen non est virtuosus, quia de ratione actus virtuosi est quod eliciatur conformiter rationi rectae et respectu obiecti convenientis....Unde si omnes circumstantiae requisitae ad actum virtuosum ponantur praeter rectam rationem, non erit ille actus perfecte virtuosus." (OTh VI, 422).

[59] The reference is to Aristotle, *Ethica Nicomachea*, II, 4, 1105a; "The agent also must be in a certain condition when he does them (i.e. acts in accordance with the virtues); in the first place he must have knowledge; secondly, he must choose the acts, and choose them for their own sakes."

sition already formed. It is from this act of assent that prudence results, not from the formation of the proposition itself.[60]

But suppose that a person has acquired a virtuous habit. Can he then elicit an act corresponding to this habit so that the act will be virtuous without prudence? Ockham answers that no one acts virtuously unless he acts knowingly and freely. Any act of the will performed without an act of prudence cannot be called virtuous. This holds true also for an act following from a virtuous habit. It may happen, for example, that an insane person performs acts in virtue of some habit remaining in the will. He may have willed these acts virtuously before he lost his sanity. And now the habit he acquired inclines him to continue these same acts which were once done virtuously while he was in his right mind. But the acts are no longer virtuous acts, because such a person is not acting freely and is not, consequently, responsible for his acts. He is not worthy of either praise or blame, because he does not know what he is doing and does not have prudence or right reason.[61] The conclusion is that no moral virtue or virtuous act can exist without prudence. No act is virtuous unless it is in conformity with right reason, because right reason is included in the very definition of virtue. Therefore, every virtuous act and habit necessarily requires some kind of prudence.[62]

But what kind of prudence is required? Prudence may be aptitudinal, habitual, or actual. Aptitudinal prudence is only a certain potency or aptitude, existing before the act, to have prudence. Aptitudinal prudence is parallel to the case of interpretative intention, an intention which never existed and does not exist, but which would exist if the

---

[60] Ockham, *In III Sent.*, 12: "Et sciendum quod actus dictandi intellectus non est formaliter complexum, sed est actus assentiendi vel dissentiendi complex iam formato. Et ex illo actu assentiendi generatur prudentia, non autem ex formatione complexi." (OTh VI, 422-23); *Quaest. Variae*, 7, 4: "...recta ratio, sive actus assentiendi qui vocatur recta ratio..." (OTh VIII, 393).

[61] *Quaest. Variae*, 7, 3: "Et si quaeras utrum post generationis virtutis possit elici actus virtuosus sine actu prudentiae: respondeo quod non, quia nullus virtuosus agit nisi scienter agat et ex libertate. Et ideo si aliquando talis actus voluntatis elicitur a tali habitu sine actu prudentiae, non dicetur virtuosus nec est, sed magis elicitur sicut actus appetitus sensitivi habituati, sicut in fatuis patet quod aliquid volunt, quod prius virtuose voluerunt, propter habitum derelictum in voluntate, qui inclinabat ad actus virtuosos quando fuit in bono statu, sed nunc non est actus virtuosus, quia nec est laudabilis nec virtuperabilis propter actus suos. Et tota ratio est, quia nescit quid facit, eo quod non habet prudentiam sive rectam rationem." (OTh VIII, 362-3).

[62] *Ibid.*: "Nulla virtus moralis nec actus virtuosus potest esse sine omni prudentia, quia nullus actus est virtuosus nisi sit conformis rectae rationi, quia recta ratio ponitur in definitione virtutis...igitur quilibet actus et habitus virtuosus necessario requirit aliquam prudentiam." (*Ibid.*, 362). See Copleston, *op. cit.*, p. 105f.

CHAPTER III

person made an intention. So aptitudinal prudence does not really exist; but an act is performed which would conform to a dictate of right reason if such a dictate actually existed. It is clear that aptitudinal prudence is not sufficient to fulfill the requirements necessary for a virtuous act.[63]

Nor does the conformity of the act to habitual prudence suffice for a virtuous act. Ockham holds that as a general principle one habit never inclines immediately to a different habit's act. It can neither cause or regulate nor otherwise influence this other virtue's act except through its own proper act to which it inclines primarily. In other words, there is a mediate influence at work here; but the mediate influence takes place through the habit's own act, which, therefore, is necessarily required before any influence can take place. Applying this general principle to the question of prudence, we may then say that the virtue of prudence inclines primarily to an act of prudence, but not to an act of the will. The act of the will is neither caused by nor regulated by the habit of prudence. Only an act of prudence can regulate the acts of the will. Since it is the very essence of prudence that it regulate the acts of the will--for it is the right reason in regard to things to be done--it is impossible that it regulate as a habit in the intellect except through its own proper act. Therefore, if prudence is to regulate, functioning in such a manner that it directs and dictates what acts are to be done and what acts are to be avoided, habitual prudence would not suffice.[64]

The phrase "according to the dictates of right reason" demands that the dictates be in some way actualized. Consequently, the prudence that is required here is actual prudence. For the rectitude of an act of the

---

[63] Ockham, *Ibid.*, 8, 1: "Dico quod prudentia aptitudinalis non sufficit ad actum virtuosum. Quia supposito quod conformitas ad prudentiam aptitudinalem non est aliud nisi quod ille actus dicatur rectus qui elicitur sicut ratio recta dictaret illum actum esse eliciendum si inesset,--licet modo non insit de facto--, ita quod prudentia aptitudinalis non est nisi potentia sive aptitudo ante actum ad habendum prudentiam." (*Ibid.*, 410-11).

[64] *Ibid.*: "Dico quod conformitas actus voluntatis ad prudentiam habitualem non sufficit ad actum virtuosum. Quod patet quia, sicut saepe dictum est, habitus unus numquam inclinat ad actum alterius habitus, causando vel regulando vel quomodocumque, nisi mediante actu proprio ad quem primo inclinat. Patet de habitu principii qui numquam inclinat ad actum conclusionis nisi mediante actu respectu illius principii ad quem primi inclinat....Cum igitur de ratione prudentiae sit egulare actum voluntatis, quia est recta ratio agibilium etc., impossibile est quod regulet habitus quicumque in intellectu nisi mediante actu suo, non plus quam si talis habitus non inesset intellectui. Igitur prudentia habitualis non sufficit ad actum rectum, sed necessario requiritur prudentia actualis." (*Ibid.*, 416). Cf. also *In IV Sent.*, 3-4 (OTh VII, 49-50). See L. Baudry, *op. cit.*, p. 82: "...quod ad actum virtuosum intrinsece requiritur ut objectum prudentia actualis et non sufficit habitualis solum." Cf. a. Garvens, *op. cit.*, pp. 382 ff; E. Iserloh, *op. cit.*, p. 60.

will actual prudence, actually inhering in the person who performs the right act, is required. All admit that some kind of prudence is necessarily required for a virtuous act. However, neither aptitudinal nor habitual prudence suffice. Therefore, actual prudence is necessarily required.[65]

Thus far Ockham's position on the role that right reason plays as a condition and determinant of morality is still vague. How are we to understand the statement that actual prudence is required for a virtuous act? Ockham's answer to this question is of major importance in understanding his position on moral goodness and evil. In analyzing Ockham's answer to this question let us first consider the matter from a negative point of view. He first criticizes what he considers a false, or at least a misleading, interpretation of the necessity of actual prudence for a virtuous act. This interpretation he attributes to Duns Scotus.[66] According to this view if a person would elicit an act of the will while all the required circumstances are present for a virtuous act, with, however, the exception of prudence or right reason, then the act of the will in this case would become virtuous as soon as the deficiency (the lack of prudence) would be supplied. In other words, an act of the will which at first was not virtuous because prudence was lacking, now becomes virtuous through the mere presence of prudence without any change taking

---

[65] Ockham, *Quaest. Variae*, 8, 1: "dico quod ad rectitudinem actus voluntatis requiritur prudentia actualis actualiter inhaerens illi cuius est talis actus rectus. Hoc patet, quia secundum omnes ad actum virtuosum aliqua prudentia requiritur necessario; sed nec aptitudinalis nec habitualis sufficiunt; igitur necessario requiritur prudentia actualis." (OTh VIII, 414); see also *ibid.* 7, 4 (393 ff.).

[66] *Ibid.*, 8, 1 (414ff.); *ibid.*, 7, 4 (379-84). See for example Duns Scotus, *Ordinatio* I, d. 17, p. 1, qq. 1-2 n. 65: "Idem enim habitus in natura, qui generaretur ex actibus abstinentiae elicitis cum ratione erronea in eliciente, manens post cum recta ratione, esset post virtus abstinentiae et prius non habitus virtutis, quamdiu non fuit ratio recta abstinendi; nec tamen aliquid mutatum est circa illum habitum in se, sed tantummodo nunc coniungitur prudentiae et prius non." (ed. Vaticana, V., 187f.); *ibid.*, n. 97: Est autem avertendum quod ista bonitas, ut attribuitur prudentiae sic inclinanti...non necessario competit habitui prudentiae, nec soli, sed actui illi qui natus esset esse actus prudentiae, qui est dictamen rectum....Itaque, prudentia quando non inest, sufficit ad actum rectum dictandum actus ille qui est rectum dictamen; quando autem prudentia inest, non sufficit sine actu mediante actu proprio prudentiae." (V, 187f.)

For additional detail on this dispute see E. Iserloh, *op. cit.*, pp. 57ff. Iserloh summarizes the dispute (p. 57): "Gegen Scotus betont Ockham immer wieder, dass ein indifferenter Akt nicht moralisch wird durch einen blossen Akt der Klugheit, dass der Mensch sich nämlich der Übereinstimmung seines Handelns mit der recta ratio bewusst wird bzw. Gebotensein des Aktes erkennt. Es bedarf vielmehr eines neuen Willensaktes, der nun auch die recta ratio zum Gegenstand hat. Scotus vertritt nämlich die ansicht, dass die Moralität des freien Aktes in seiner Relation zur recta ratio besteht und sie mit dem Akt und der recta ratio notwendig gegeben ist, dass also ein akt oder Habitus, der mangels der recta ratio schlecht oder indifferent ist, durch Hinzukommen der letzteren ipso facto gut wird."

CHAPTER III

place in the act of the will itself. Now this interpretation, if taken strictly, Ockham insists, cannot be correct. For if the interpretation were correct, then there would no longer be any possibility of having any act intrinsically and necessarily virtuous. All acts could be only contingently and extrinsically virtuous, because the same act of the will would be virtuous (if it is in accord with the dictates or right reason) and non-virtuous (if the dictates of right reason are not present). Hence such an act cannot be intrinsically or necessarily virtuous, since there is the possibility of its being non-virtuous.[67]

Scotus' opinion seems to follow as a consequence of his position on the indifferent act. The indifferent act is one which is not yet morally good in a formal sense; it is, in Scotus' words, "natus esse conformis rectae rationis." Scotus holds that not only a habit but also a deliberate act of the will can be morally indifferent in this sense. For example, an act which follows naturally from a habit of abstinence is a natural act and, consequently, indifferent. But later this same act of abstinence can become intrinsically good if the dictate of right reason would arise directing that abstinence should take place. The act of abstinence is then in conformity with right reason and becomes virtuous on that account. But Ockham argues against this view, basing his argument on this principle: it is impossible for an act which is non-virtuous to become virtuous by means of something which is purely natural, that is, through something which is in no way in the power of our will.[68] An act of prudence or right reason is only a natural act and is no more in our power than is an act of seeing. No one is praised or blamed for a purely natural act, therefore it is impossible that an indifferent act of the will

---

[67] Ockham, *Quaest. Variae*, 8, 1: "Sed quod prudentia actualis requiratur, potest duplicitur intelligi. Uno modo quod primo eliciatur aliquis actus voluntatis secundum omnes circumstantias requisitas ad actum virtuosum, excepta prudentia sive recta ratione, et quod post, manente isto eodem actu in voluntate praecise et nullo alio elicito, per generationem prudentiae fita iste actus [virtuosus], quia prius non fuit virtuosus propter defectum prudentiae....Et iste intellectus est impossibilis....Quia hoc dato nullus actus esset intrinsece et necessario virtuosus sed solum contingenter et extrinsece. Quia per generationem prudentiae fieret ille actus virtuosus et per eius corruptionem fieret vitiosus semper manente eodem actu in voluntate." (OTh VIII, 414-415).

[68] The word "natural" may have a variety of meanings. See Ockham's *In III Sent.*, 6 (OTh VI, 173-76) where he distinguishes five meanings of the word "natural." In the present context he seems to use "natural" in its most general sense as distinct from voluntary or free. Thus, *In III Sent.*, 6: "...principium activum dividitur in agens a natura et a voluntate. Et sic omne agens non liberum dicitur naturale." (OTh VI, 173). See also *In I Sent.*, 1, 6: "Et sic libertas est quaedam indifferentia et contingentia, et distinguitur contra principium activum naturale." (OTh I, 501). Cf. L. Baudry, *Lexique philosophique de Guillaume d'Ockham* (Paris: Lethielleux, 1958), pp. 136, 169-70.

should become virtuous solely on the basis of a co-existing act of prudence.[69]

Furthermore, if a non-virtuous act would become virtuous by means of an act of prudence, which is only naturally produced and not in our power in any way, the same would hold true for a non-meritorious act. A non-meritorious act would become meritorious in the same way that a non-virtuous act becomes virtuous, that is, through an act of prudence, an act which is only naturally produced and not in our power. The consequences of a meritorious act resulting from a non-meritorious act in this way are absurd. For example, it would follow that a person who is not worthy of eternal life would become worthy of it through something not in his power. And on the contrary, by the destruction of the act of prudence alone, a virtuous and meritorious act could become non-virtuous and unworthy on account of something which is in no way in his power. It would seem that this second case is even more absurd than the first.[70]

Moreover, according to the interpretation presented by Duns Scotus, it would seem that the virtuous act is not really one simple act at all; it would seem that what Scotus really means by the virtuous act formally includes two acts, namely, the indifferent act and the act of prudence.[71] We could reach for an escape from this difficulty by saying that there is only one act, the indifferent act, and alone with it a relation of conformity to prudence. But even this attempted solution would not answer Ockham's fundamental argument that an indifferent act cannot possibly become virtuous by means of something which is purely natural. For in

---

[69] *Quaest. Variae*, 7, 4: "Respondet Ioannes...quod tam habitus quam actus voluntatis potest esse indifferens, sic quod idem habitus abstinentiae generatus solum in esse naturae, cuius actus solum est actus naturalis, potest postea per coexistentiam actus prudentiae esse intrinsece bonus....Contra [Scotum]: impossibile est quod de actu non virtuoso fiat virtuosus per aliquem actum pure naturalem qui nullo modo est in potestate voluntatis, quia propter talem nullus laudatur nec vituperatur, ex quo solum est actus naturalis; sed actus prudentiae secundum eum et secundum veritatem est solum actus naturalis et nullo modo in potestate nostra plus quam actus videndi; igitur impossibile est quod actus voluntatis indifferens et non virtuosus fiat virtuosus per solum coexistentiam prudentiae." (OTh VIII, 380-81). Duns Scotus, *Ordinatio* I, d. 17, p. 1, qq. 1-2, nn. 64-65 (ed. Vaticana, V, 164-8).

[70] Ockham, *Quodl.*, III, 16: "...si per solam positionem actus prudentiae fieret actus voluntatis virtuosus, qui prius non erat virtuosus propter carentiam talis actus, cum actus ille prudentiae sit mere naturalis et nullo modo in potestate nostra, sequitur quod de actu non-virtuoso fieret virtuosus, et econverso, per positionem et destructionem alicuius mere naturalis quod nullo modo est in potestate nostra; et de non-digno vita aeterna fieret dignus vita aeterna per aliquid mere naturale quod nullo modo est in potestate nostra." (OTh IX, 264-65).

[71] *Quaest. Variae*, 7, 4: "Praeterea secundum istam viam videtur quod actus virtuosus non est unus et simplex actus, sed quod includit formaliter duos actus, puta actum illum indifferentem et actus prudentiae...quod videtur absurdum." (OTh VIII, 381).

CHAPTER III

the solution just previously mentioned an act would still become formally virtuous by means of a relation which arises naturally when the extreme term (that is, the act of prudence) is given. Here we find that Scotus readily admits that the extreme term is posited naturally, because prudence is caused naturally. Hence it follows that if prudence is given, the relation to prudence naturally arises.[72]

An act which is non-virtuous can never become virtuous merely through something which is only produced naturally. How then can an indifferent act become virtuous? An act which is itself only contingently and extrinsically virtuous cannot determine the morality of an indifferent act. This would seem to involve an infinite regress. From this standpoint Ockham's answer is that an indifferent act can become virtuous in only one way: through an act which itself is intrinsically virtuous.[73] But only an act of the will, as we have seen, can be intrinsically virtuous or evil. No other act is virtuous or evil except by extrinsic denomination, because every other act, whether it be an interior or an exterior act, can be elicited by the will successively with either a good or a bad intention and, consequently, can be only contingently good or evil. Such an act would, of course, not be necessarily and intrinsically good or evil. And as a result it would be impossible for a non-virtuous act of the will to become good solely by means of an act of prudence.[74] The reason is that prudence is only a naturally produced act. But even if prudence were produced deliberately and freely in some way or other, an act resulting naturally from such an act of prudence would still be good or evil only contingently and extrinsically. It seems, in other words, that even if the will would command that an act of prudence be posited, the resultant act of prudence would be called good since it is in conformity with the commanding act of the will. But here again we are

---

[72] *Ibid.*: "Si dicis quod solum includit respectum conformitatis ad prudentiam ultra substantiam actus: hoc videtur magis absurdum quod aliquis actus fiat formaliter virtuosus per unum respectum qui naturaliter oritur posito extrmo, quod etiam naturaliter ponitur secundum eum [Scotum], quia prudentia naturaliter causatur, et ipsa posita naturaliter oritur ille respectus, igitur etc." (*Ibid.*).

[73] *Ibid.*: "Igitur impossibile est quod actus voluntatis indifferens et non virtuosus fiat virtuosus per solam coexistentiam prudentiae.--Praeterea numquam de actu non virtuoso intrinsece potest fieri virtuosus nisi per actum intrinsece virtuosum, et non solum extrinsece et contingenter, quia aliter esset processus in infinitum." (*Ibid.*, 380-81).

[74] *Ibid.*: "Solus actus voluntatis est intrinsece virtuosus vel vitiosus, et nullus alius nisi extrinseca denominatione, quia quilibet alius,--tam actus intellectus quam exterior--potest idem manens fieri successive bona intentione et mala, et per consequens est contingenter bonus vel malus, et non necessario et intrinsece; igitur impossibile est quod aliquis actus voluntatis non bonus fiat bonus per solum actum prudentiae." (*Ibid.*, 381).

involved with extrinsic denomination, since the act of prudence is a commanded act of the human will.

Perhaps it would be good at this point to insert an observation regarding the meaning of "intrinsically" good and evil. In Ockham's use of the term "intrinsic" an act is called intrinsically good only in the sense of necessity. An act is intrinsically good only if it is necessarily so; no other act can be called intrinsically or necessarily good. In other words, it is impossible that an act be at first intrinsically good and later evil or indifferent, just as it is impossible that an act be at first intrinsically evil or indifferent and later good.[75] Thus Ockham argues against the opinion attributed to Duns Scotus because the latter's opinion makes it possible for an act to be at first only natural and morally indifferent, while the same act afterwards can become intrinsically good and even intrinsically meritorious.[76] Such a situation Ockham considers absurd.

We can now summarize and elaborate briefly on the points mentioned in the preceding paragraphs. An act can be called virtuous intrinsically or extrinsically. Speaking of the intrinsically virtuous act, it is impossible that an indifferent act can become morally good merely through the co-existence of an act of prudence. For it is impossible that some act which is non-virtuous becomes virtuous through something merely naturally produced. Let us give an example of this. Suppose that a person wills to study. If all the circumstances required for the moral goodness of this act are present, except the circumstance of right reason, then the act of the will to spend some time in studying is of itself something good (*bonus ex genere*). But now, after this original situation in which the will elicits the act of studying, there is also an act of the will to study including the circumstance of right reason. What is the moral situation in this case? The will certainly follows and, in fact, fulfills this dictate of right reason by willing that its first act should continue. The difference lies in this: that the studying is now willed according to the dictates of right reason. This second act of the will is perfectly

---

[75] *Ibid.*: "Et quando arguitur de actu primo intrinsece bono et post malo, dico quod casus iste impossibilis est. Et ideo actus primo intrinsece bonus non potest fieri post intrinsece malus nec indifferens nec extrinsece malus nec e contra." (*Ibid.*, 385).

[76] *Ibid.*: "Quantum ad secundum quod dicit Ioannes, dico quod impossibile est quod actus quicumque sit primo indifferens et naturalis solum, et postea intrinsece bonus moraliter vel meritorie..." (*Ibid.*, 385-6). Cf. Duns Scotus, *Quaestiones Quodlibetales*, q. 17 (ed. F. Alluntis, Matritii 1968) 612-7).

CHAPTER III

virtuous because it is in complete conformity with the dictates of right reason. It is an intrinsically virtuous act.[77]

But in this case has not the act of willing to study become virtuous merely through the presence of the dictate of right reason? Or to use our previous terminology, is not Scotus correct when he says that an act of the will, which at first was not virtuous because prudence was lacking, now becomes virtuous through the generation of prudence, without any change taking place in the act of the will itself? It seems that nothing new has been added in the above case except the dictate of right reason or, in other words, the act of prudence now coexists with the act of the will to study. Such would actually be Scotus' position. But Ockham answers that the first act of the will has not become virtuous; instead, an entirely new act of the will is elicited. And it is this second act, an act of the will elicited in complete conformity with right reason, that is intrinsically virtuous. What is important is that this second act is a new act, distinct from the first act, of willing to study. This is evident from the fact that they can be separated; the first act can exist without the second. Furthermore, these two acts of the will are distinct because they have distinct objects. The second act has right reason for its object, but the first act did not. It is this second act which is intrinsically virtuous. The first act does not "become" virtuous; but this second act must be understood as a new act of the will. It should go without saying that it is not the act of prudence or right reason which is intrinsically virtuous. The dictate of right reason in this case would only be extrinsically good on the basis of its conformity to an act of the will which itself is intrinsically virtuous. The act of prudence cannot be intrinsically good because only an act of the will is capable of being intrinsically good.[78]

---

[77] *Quaest. Variae*, 7, 4: "Actus potest dici virtuosus vel intrinsece vel extrinsece. Primo modo, impossibile est quod actus indifferens fiat bonum moraliter per coexistentiam actus prudentiae, quia impossibile est quod aliquis actus non virtuosus, per mere naturale fiat virtuosus....Exemplum: aliquis vult studere circumscribendo omnem circumstantiam. Iste actus est bonus ex genere. Et post intellectus dictat quod iste actus volendi sit continuandus secundum omnes circumstantias requisitas, et voluntas vult primum actum continuare secundum dictamen rectae rationis. Iste secundus est perfecte virtuosus, quia conformis rectae rationi complete dictanti, et est intrinsece virtuosus." (OTh VIII, 384).

[78] *Ibid.*: "Et primus est solum virtuosus denominatione extrinseca, quia scilicet conformatur secundo actui. Et est secundus actus distinctus a primo; patet per separabilitatem eorum et per distinctionem obiectorum, quia secundus habet rectam rationem pro obiecto, primus non. Unde si solum esset primus actus,--et ideo iste primus actus non est aliter bonus quam actus exterior potentiae apprehensivae vel exsecutivae --, cum actu prudentiae, non diceretur virtuosus intrinsece nec extrinsece...bonus nisi quia conformatur alicui actui intrinsece bono, cuiusmodi non est actus prudentiae sed solum actus voluntatis." (*Ibid.*, 384-5).

THE HUMAN WILL AND RIGHT REASON

Prudence or right reason is necessary for a virtuous act. An act is virtuous only if it is elicited in conformity with the dictates of right reason. But again, lest any misunderstanding arise on this account, it must be added that it is not precisely because an act is elicited in conformity with right reason that it is virtuous. Suppose that God would place in my will an act that conforms in a most perfect and complete manner with an actually existing command of my reason, and yet in this act my own will remains completely passive. Such an act would not be virtuous even though it is in complete accord with a dictate of right reason. The explanation, of course, of why this act would not be virtuous is that the first condition for a virtuous act is absent: the act must be under the control of my will. But in the supposed case we do not have a freely willed act. It is always required for the goodness of an act that it be in the power of the will of the person acting.[79] So even though the act of the will is in conformity with a dictate of right reason, it is not precisely on that account that the act is virtuous. This is not meant to minimize in any way the importance of the second condition for a virtuous act: the act is willed according to the dictates of right reason. This second condition is certainly necessary for a virtuous act; but it is not in itself a sufficient condition for the producing of such an act.

Ockham criticized Scotus' opinion on the role that right reason or prudence plays in the production of virtuous acts. This criticism we treated in considering Ockham's theory on the role of right reason as a condition for moral acts from a negative viewpoint. He also offers a more positive theory of his own, some features of which have already been mentioned. According to Ockham's viewpoint two propositions must be maintained: first, prudence is required as a partial efficient cause of the virtuous act; secondly, prudence is also required as a partial object of the virtuous act.

As an efficient cause prudence precedes the virtuous act, or at least it is simultaneous with the act. "Simultaneous" is taken here in a temporal sense--for by nature prudence must be prior to the virtuous act because it can exist apart from the virtuous act, but the virtuous

---

[79] *In III Sent.*, 11: "Ad aliud dico quod ex hoc quod praecise est conformis rationi rectae non est virtuosus, quia si Deus faceret in voluntate mea actum conformem rationi rectae, voluntate nihil agente, non esset ille actus meritorius nec virtuosus. Et ideo requiritur ad bonitatem actus quod sit in potestate voluntatis habentis illum actum." (OTh VI, 389). See E. Bonke, *op. cit.*, p. 65; "Formaliter bonitas actus concreti et in individuo non dependet a bonitate obiecti et circumstantiarum, ed ab electione voluntatis. Nam si Deus produceret in voluntate actum conformem rationi rectae, voluntas necessario recte ageret, ita ut actus non esset meritorius vel virtuosus." See also E. Iserloh, *op. cit.*, p. 47.

CHAPTER III

act cannot exist apart from prudence.[80] Here again we can see how in Ockham's view there is no question of an act "becoming" virtuous through the generation or coexistence of prudence. It would not be a question of the same act becoming virtuous, but of an entirely new act being elicited. For the point is that prudence does not follow but precedes the act, and, therefore, any question of non-virtuous acts becoming virtuous through the generation of prudence is an impossible situation. The question is meaningless, since it presupposes that the act exists before prudence.

First, prudence is a partial efficient cause of the virtuous act. Since actual prudence is necessarily required for a virtuous act and is in some way prior to the act, it follows that the act of prudence is a true efficient cause which is essentially and necessarily required for a virtuous act. It is as much an essentially required condition for a virtuous act as the will, acting freely, is necessarily required as an efficient cause. So if the activity of right reason or the act of prudence were suspended, the act which follows could not be called virtuous in any way. And the reason for this is that "virtuous"--or "vicious"--are connotative terms. They signify the act, not absolutely, but also connote the activity of both the free will and of right reason. So in case either of these connoted elements is lacking, the act which follows cannot be called virtuous. This is just another way of stating what we have previously emphasized regarding the two required conditions for a virtuous act, namely: the act must be in the power of the will; the act must be elicited according to the dictates of right reason.[81]

---

[80] Ockham, *Quaest. Variae*, 8, 1: "Potest intelligi quod requiratur prudentia tamquam obiectum partiale et causa efficiens partialis ipsius actus virtuosi. Et per consequens, vel oportet quod prudentia praecedit illum actum virtuosum...vel saltem quod simul producatur cum illo actu--simul dico tempore--licet necessario prudentia sit prior natura actu virtuoso quia potest separari ab eo et non e converso. Et iste intellectus est bonus, sanus et verus." (OTh VIII, 415). Cf. G. Biel, *Repertorium generale...Gabrielis Biel super quatuor libros Sententiarum* (Tuebingen, 1527), III Sent., d. 23, q. 1, I; and A. Garvens, *op. cit.*, p. 385.

[81] Ockham, *Ibid.*: "Cum prudentia actualis necessario requiratur ad actum virtuosum et est aliquo modo prior, sequitur quod actus prudentia sit vere causa efficiens essentialiter et necessario requista ad actum virtuosum, ita essentialiter sicut voluntas necessario requiritur tamquam causa efficiens ad hoc quod actus sit virtuosus vel meritorius. Et per consequens sequitur ultra quod suspensa activitate voluntatis vel actus prudentiae, nullo modo dicetur talis actus virtuosus. Et ratio est quia virtuosus et meritorium sunt nomina connotative et significant ipsum actum non absolute, sed connotando cum hoc activitatem voluntatis et prudentiae, et quando deficit aliquod connotatum non dicitur talis actus virtuosus." *Ibid.*, 417-8); *ibid.*: "Actum elici conformiter rationi rectae est ipsum elici secundum rectam rationem regulantem et dictantem talem actum esse efficiendum, quod quidem 'dictare' sive 'regulare' non est aliud quam speciali modo illum actum causare." (*Ibid.*, 418). See G. Biel, *op. cit.*, III Sent., d. 23, q. 1, I; A. Garvens, *op. cit.*, p. 386; E. Iserloh, *op. cit.*, p. 55.

THE HUMAN WILL AND RIGHT REASON

It may be well to interject here a few remarks regarding a recent treatment of the above problem which comes to a conclusion which contradicts the above interpretation of Ockham's view. In a doctoral dissertation undertaken in 1952 Fuchs treats of the notion of right reason as a partial object of the virtuous act, while denying, however, its activity as a partial cause of the virtuous act.[82] Now it is perfectly true that Ockham emphasizes right reason or the act of prudence as an object of the virtuous act. This emphasis does not mean, however, that he did not consider the right reason as a partial cause of the virtuous act. The texts of Ockham seem too clear on this point to admit of any interpretation to the contrary. I think that possibly Fuchs was misled on this point by overlooking the fact that Ockham, in most of the texts on this topic, was engaged in controversy with Duns Scotus regarding the interpretation of the principle that actual prudence is required for a virtuous act.[83] Hence I understand this to mean that Scotus admitted the causal influence of actual prudence on the virtuous act, but denied that prudence was also a partial object of the virtuous act. Ockham then opposed this view of Scotus that actual prudence was only a cause of the virtuous act. Ockham, therefore, rather naturally, stresses very heavily the aspect of actual prudence as a partial object of the virtuous act. His statements regarding right reason and prudence as an object of the virtuous act should be viewed in the light of his disagreement with Scotus.[84]

Prudence, therefore, is a necessarily required efficient cause, though partial, of a virtuous act. Without the activity of prudence it would be impossible for an act to be virtuous, at least as long as the present divinely constituted order remains in force. Prudence is only a partial efficient cause, because besides the activity of prudence there is also the activity of the will involved in a virtuous act. The free will

---

[82] O. Fuchs, *op. cit.*, pp. 89-90.

[83] This controversy was discussed earlier in this chapter; see note 66ff.

[84] See L. Baudry (ed.), *Le Tractatus de principiis theologiae*, p. 80: "...quod recta ratio sive prudentia est objectum et causa partialis actus virtuosi..." See also G. Biel, *op. cit.*, III Sent., d. 23, q. 1, I: "...dicit (Ockham) prudentiam actualem necessario requiri ad actum virtuosum; immo ita essentialiter sicut voluntatem; cum tam voluntas quam prudentia actualis sit causa efficiens actus virtuosi...ostendit actum prudentiae esse vere causam efficientem actus virtuosi sic quod impossibile est actum esse virtuosum...sine actu prudentiae." And G. De Lagarde remarks, *op. cit.*, pp. 74-75: "Accomplir un acte moral, c'est poser *librement* un acte conforme *à un jugement de la raison pratique*. La *raison pratique* concourt ainsi avec la volunté et devient une cause partielle de l'acte."

CHAPTER III

and right reason cooperate, with the added concurrence of Almighty God, in producing the virtuous act.[85]

Secondly, prudence is also a partial secondary object of the virtuous act. Unless this is true no act of the will would be necessarily and intrinsically virtuous, but only extrinsically and contingently so. This can be shown, for instance, in the case of temperance. If right reason were not the object of the act of temperance, and food were the object, then it would follow that by apprehending food without right reason (and even with erroneous reason), the will could elicit a perfectly virtuous act. For to cause an act of the will nothing more is required than God, the will, and the apprehension of the object. These suffice as partial causes in the production of an act of willing. And so if the will could produce a virtuous act in this case without right reason as the partial object, so it could also conserve without right reason an act once elicited with right reason. But then the act would at first be virtuous and later non-virtuous; thus it could not necessarily be virtuous, but only contingently so. It is for this reason that prudence, or the act of assenting which is called right reason, must be the partial object of the virtuous act.[86]

It is not enough to say that right reason is required as a partial efficient cause without adding that it is also required as a partial object of the virtuous act. This point, as indicated above, was at stake in the controversy between Ockham and Scotus regarding the role of right reason in the production of a virtuous act. For if right reason is required only as a partial and essential cause, then if God would supply

---

[85] Ockham, *Quaest. Variae*, 7, 3: "[Actus prudentiae] est causa efficiens necessario requista ad actum virtuosum, sine qua impossibile est actum esse virtuosum, stante ordinatione divina quae nunc est, quia ad actum virtuosum necessario requiritur activitas actus prudentiae et activitas voluntatis, ita quod illae duae causae sunt causae partiales cum Deo respectu actus virtuosi." (OTh VIII, 363). Cf. also *In III Sent.*, 12 (OTh VI, 425-8). See A. Garvens, *op. cit.*, p. 386: "Der Vorgang des "regulare" und "dictare," worin die Aufgabe der Vernunft gegenüber dem Willen besteht, stellt sich demnach bei Ockham als ein Verursachen dar. Wenn vom sittlichen Akt gesagt wird, dass er "conformiter rationi rectae" hervorgebracht wird, so bedeutet das in Ockhams Denkweise nichts anderes, als dass die recta ratio den Willensakt verursacht. Denn "dictare sive regulare non est aliud quam speciali modo actum causare." See also G. Biel, *op. cit.*, III Sent., d. 23, q. 1, I; E. Iserloh, *op. cit.*, p. 55; G. De Lagarde, *op. cit.*, pp. 74-77.

[86] Ockham, *Quaest. Variae*, 7, 4: "Dico quod tam finis quam recta ratio et omnes aliae circumstantiae sunt obiecta partialia secundaria actus virtuosi. Cuius ratio est, quia aliquis est actus voluntatis qui est intrinsece et necessario virtuosus, stante ordinatione divina quae nunc est, et nullo modo contingenter virtuosus. Nunc autem, si illa quae dicuntur circumstantiae non essent obiecta actus virtuosi, nullus actus voluntatis esset necessario et intrinsece virtuosus sed solum contingenter et extrinsece." (OTh VIII, 393). The text continues, illustrating the above by the use of examples. See E. Iserloh, *op. cit.*, pp. 59-60.

the causality exercised by right reason--and it appears that he can, since he can supply the causality exercised by any secondary--then the act of the will in cooperation with God would be perfectly virtuous without an act of prudence. But that is manifestly false. For no act is perfectly virtuous unless it is elicited in conformity with right reason actually inhering in the subject who elicits the act. Therefore, says Ockham, right reason is required as a partial object of the virtuous act as well as its partial cause.[87]

We can explain a step further. Perhaps it would be clearer if we said that no act is perfectly virtuous unless the will by this act wills what is dictated by right reason because it is dictated by right reason. That is what the phrase "a partial object of the act" really means. It would not be sufficient, therefore, that an act be elicited in conformity with right reason. What is really necessary is that it is elicited according to, and because of, the dictates of right reason. The will can elicit an act, and this act may be what is dictated by right reason; but it may happen that in eliciting this act the will does so not because it is dictated by right reason but for some other motive, for instance, because of the pleasure involved in the act or the satisfaction it affords the person acting. Ockham would not consider such an act to be perfectly virtuous, because it is not elicited in conformity with right reason, understanding this phrase as qualified by and including the condition "because it is dictated by right reason."[88] To elicit an act in conformity with right reason means eliciting the act according to right reason regulating and dictating that such an act is to be elicited.[89] The act is elicited, therefore, because right reason dictates that it is to be elicited.

---

[87] Ockham, *Quaest. Variae*, 7, 4: "Si recta ratio solum requireretur sicut causa partiales et essentialis...cum Deus omnem causalitatem causae secundae possit supplere--si Deus suppleret causalitatem rectae rationis, stante causalitate voluntatis et apprehensionis, posset ille actus esse perfecte virtuosus sine actu prudentiae; quod est manifeste falsum, quia...nullus actus est perfecte virtuosus nisi eliciatur conformiter rectae rationi actualiter inhaerenti. Ideo dico quod recta ratio est obiectum actus virtuosi." (OTh VIII, 394).

[88] *Ibid.*: "Nullus actus est perfecte virtuosus, nisi voluntas per illum actum velit dictatum a recta ratione propter hoc quod est dictatum a recta ratione, quia si vellet dictatum a ratione, non quia dictatum, sed quia delectabile vel propter aliam causam, iam vellet illud dictatum si solum esset ostensum per apprehensionem sine recta ratione; et per consequens ille actus non esset virtuosus, quia non eliceretur conformiter rationi rectae." (*Ibid.*, 395). See also *Quodl.* III, 16 (OTh IX, 262-7). Cf. F. Copleston, *op. cit.*, p. 106.

[89] Ockham, *Quaest. Variae*, 8: "Actum elici conformiter rationi rectae est ipsum elici secundum rectam rationem regulantem et dictantem talem actum esse eliciendum." (OTh VIII, 418). Cf. G. Biel, *III Sent.*, d. 23, q. 1, I.

CHAPTER III

In other words, to elicit an act in conformity with right reason really means this: to will what is dictated and because it is dictated by right reason. Right reason itself is, consequently, an object of the virtuous act. It is an object of the will because it is impossible for someone to will what is dictated by right reason itself. All this is in accordance with the general principle that one who wills something because of another thing necessarily wills this other thing also. Therefore, since I will virtuously what is dictated by right reason, it follows that I will right reason itself. And this willing of what right reason dictates because it is dictated is not to be considered as two acts of the will but only one. For if two acts were involved then the first act, the act of willing what is dictated by right reason, would not be virtuous. An act is not virtuous unless I will what is dictated by right reason because right reason dictates it. There is only one act involved in this, just as by one act alone I can love some particular creature and still at the same time love God for whose sake I ought to love the creature.[90]

If we would suppose for the moment that right reason or the act of prudence is not an object of the virtuous act, then we would be faced with two difficulties. The first is that no act would be necessarily and intrinsically virtuous, but only contingently so. And the second difficulty is that a non-virtuous act could become virtuous by something that is merely naturally produced, that is, by something which is not in our power or control.[91] We have already spoken of these two difficulties

---

[90] Ockham, *Quaest. Variae*, 7, 4: "Hoc est elicere conformiter rectae rationi: velle dictatum a ratione propter hoc quod est dictatum. Nunc autem est impossibile quod aliquid velit aliquid propter aliud nisi velit illud, quia si nolit vel non velit illus aliud, iam vult primum magis propter se quam propter illud aliud. Igitur ad hoc quod virtuose velim dictatum a ratione recta, oportet necessario quod velim rectam rationem per eundem actum, non per alium, quia si per alium, ille actus quo volo dictatum a ratione non esset virtuosus, quia non est virtuosus nisi propter hoc quod per illum volum dictatum a ratione propter hoc quod ratio sic dictat. Erit igitur per eundem actum, sicut per eundem actum utor creatura et diligo Deum, propter quem diligo creaturam." (OTh VIII, 395). Cf. Aristotle, *Ethica Nicomachea*, II, 4, 1105b: "Actions, then, are called just and temperate when they are such as the just or the temperate man would do; but it is not the man who does these that is just and temperate, but the man who also does them *as* just and temperate men do them. It is well said, then, that it is by doing just acts that the just man is produced, and by doing temperate acts the temperate man; without doing these no one would have even a prospect of becoming good." See F. Copleston, *op. cit.*, p. 106; A. Garvens, *op. cit.*, pp. 384 ff.

[91] Ockham, *Quaest. Variae*, 7, 4: "Melior et fortior ratio ad probandum rationem rectam sive prudentiam esse obiectum actus virtuosi est haec: quia aliter sequerentur duo inconventientia. Primum est quod nullus actus esset intrinsece et necessario virtuosus sed solum contingenter...Secundum, quod de actu non virtuoso fieret virtuosus per aliquid mere naturale quod non est in potestate nostra." (OTh VIII, 398). See A. Garvens, *op. cit.*, p. 387.

previously, and especially the second one.[92] But a further explanation of the first difficulty seems necessary, or would appear profitable at least, at this time.

The first difficulty was stated: there would be no intrinsically virtuous act if prudence were not the partial object of the virtuous act. This can be shown by the following: first, as a general principle we can say that whatever act the will can elicit with right reason, that act the will could also elicit without right reason. Thus, for example, a person can will to abstain from meat out of the love of God, at the proper time and place, and with all the other required circumstances according to the dictates of right reason. But he can also will to abstain out of the love of God, at the proper time and place and with all the other required circumstances, but without a prior act of prudence dictating that this act should be done. The proposition "abstinence should be willed out of love for God" may be merely apprehended by the intellect without any consent being given to this proposition and without, therefore, right reason directing or dictating that abstinence should be carried out. In other words, there would be no directive-dictative influence exercised by the right reason in this case. But even in this case the will is still able to elicit an act of willing abstinence without the prior act of prudence. Now, Ockham asks, is that act of the will intrinsically virtuous or not? It cannot be said to be intrinsically virtuous because the second condition he has proposed for a virtuous act—that the act must be willed in conformity with the dictates of right reason—is lacking. The act is not elicited in conformity with right reason, which includes the notion "because it is dictated by the right reason" and which, as we have explained previously, is necessarily required for a virtuous act.[93]

However, even if we grant that an act of willing abstinence without the dictates of right reason is not virtuous, can we not explain its lack of virtue solely on the basis of the fact that right reason is lacking only as a partial efficient cause of the act? Or is it actually necessary to maintain that right reason, besides acting as a partial cause, is also the partial object of the act? Here Ockham supposes that the act of

---

[92] See note 70 *supra*.

[93] Ockham, *Quodl.*, III, 16: "...quemcumque actum respectu quorumcumque obiectorum aliorum a recta ratione potest voluntas elicere mediante recta ratione, potest elicere sine ea cum sola apprehansione illorum obiectorum. Hoc patet, quia sicut voluntas potest velle abstinere propter Deum loco et tempore mediante actu dictativo intellectus, ita potest velle abstinere propter Deum loco et tempore cum sola apprehensione istius propositionis 'volendum est abstinere propter Deum loco et tempore' sine omni assensu respectu eiusdem. Hoc supposito tunc quaero: aut ista volitio est virtuosa intrinsece, aut non; si sic, contra; non elicitur conformiter rectae rationi, quod necessario requiritur ad actum intrinsece virtuosum; igitur non est virtuosa intrinsece." (OTh IX, 263).

CHAPTER III

prudence coexists with the act of the will, with prudence functioning only as a cause and not as the object of the act. He then asks whether the act of the will is virtuous or not, even if it does not have prudence as an object of the act. If the act is not virtuous, then no reason for its lack of virtue can be given except that right reason is not its object, because nothing else is lacking in the case given. If, however, the act of the will is actually virtuous, then it would follow that an act changes from non-virtuous to virtuous merely through the coexistence of prudence. And since the will can either conserve or destroy this act of prudence, then it would also follow that the same act can be either virtuous or non-virtuous. Consequently, such an act would only be contingently virtuous and not intrinsically so. There could be no intrinsically virtuous act. The conclusion is: if an act is to be intrinsically virtuous it must have right reason not only as a partial cause, but also as a partial object of the act. And only such an act, one which has prudence as a partial object and partial cause of the act, can be intrinsically virtuous. On the other hand, any other act must be called only contingently and extrinsically virtuous.[94]

We can conclude, therefore, regarding the two acts of abstinence spoken above (the one without right reason; the other with right reason) that they are not the same numerically nor specifically. For these two acts of the will have different objects. One has right reason for a partial object and the other does not. Since acts are specified by their objects, these acts are specifically distinct.[95]

Right reason is an object of the virtuous act; but it is only a partial object. Along with right reason as a partial object, those things which are usually called only circumstances of the virtuous act are also its partial objects. Acts are distinct if they have different objects;

---

[94] *Quodl.*, III, 16: "Si autem dicis quod talis actus non est virtuosus propter defectum prudentiae, contra: pono quod coexistat tunc actus prudentiae, et tunc quaero utrum ille actus voluntatis sit virtuosus vel non. Si non, nulla causa huius potest dari nisi quia recta ratio non est eius obiectum, quia nullum aliud obiectum requisitum deficit per cassssum, et recta ratio coexistit. Si sit virtuosus, sequitur quod actus non prius virtuosus modo sit virtuosus per solam coexistsentiam prudentiae; et tunc cum voluntas potest conservare eumdem actum stante prima apprehensione complexi, destructo illo actu prudentiae propter aliquod medium sibi apparens, sequitur quod idem actus numero fieret iterum non-virtuosus, quia non coexistit prudentia, et per consequens erit contingenter virtuosus; et ita si sit intrinsece virtuosus et necessario, oportet quod habeat rectam rationem pro obiecto; et ille solus erit necessario virtuosus." (OTh IX, 264).

[95] *Quodl.*, III, 16: "...recta ratio deberet dictare quod volendum est abstinere propter Deum quia sic est dictatum a recta ratione, aliter non esset recta sed erronea; sed volitio habens Deum et alias circumstantias a recta ratione pro obiecto non est eadem numero cum volitione quae haberet rectam rationem pro obiecto, propter variatione obiecti..." (OTh IX, 263-64). See E. Iserloh, *op. cit.*, p. 56.

they are not distinct, however, merely by a variation in the circumstances as such. Another way of expressing this is that an act can and will remain the same act only if its object remains the same; but on the other hand the act can and will remain the same act even if its circumstances, but not its object, change. If this generally accepted principle is true, says Ockham, then it is necessary that those things usually called only circumstances are really nothing else than partial objects of the virtuous act. They are not only "circumstances" as such. Why is this so? It is because otherwise the act would be the same whether it is accompanied by its "circumstances" or not. [96] It is evident that at least this is true of the intrinsically virtuous act. The intrinsically virtuous act must have the circumstances as partial objects of the act. For otherwise the same two difficulties would follow that were involved in the question of whether right reason is a partial object of the act or not: no act would be intrinsically and necessarily virtuous but only contingently virtuous; secondly, a non-virtuous act would become virtuous by reason of something purely natural.[97] We have treated these two difficulties at some length in the preceding paragraphs when Ockham used the same arguments for proving that right reason is a partial object of the virtuous act. We can omit their explanation and proof here and dwell instead on the other argument that Ockham uses in this connection: a variation of the "circumstances" involves a variation in the acts themselves and, therefore, the "circumstances" are not merely circumstances but are actually partial objects of the act. Let us turn now to the circumstances in general as objects of the virtuous act.

Against the opinion of the philosophers who hold that the circumstances are merely circumstances and are not true objects of the act, Ockham argues that in speaking of the necessarily and intrinsically virtuous act we must look upon these "circumstances" as partial objects of the act. However, if we are speaking of any act which is only virtuous by extrinsic denomination, then the circumstances are merely circumstances and not objects of the act. For such an act can and will remain the same while these circumstances vary. For instance, the act of walking to church remains the same whether it is performed at the proper time or not, whether it is performed with a good or an evil intention, in conformity with right reason or contrary to it. Walking to church still remains walking to church under any and all of these different circum-

---

[96] Ockham, *Quodl.*, III, 16 (OTh IX, 263-64). *In III Sent.*, 12 (OTh VI, 424), 11 (OTh VI, 362).

[97] *Quodl.*, III, 16: "Secundum actus [intrinsece virtuosus] habet pro obiecto circumstantias. Quod probo, quia aliter sequerentur duo inconvenientia: primum quod nullus actus sit intrinsece et necessario virtuosus, sed solum contingenter...secundum, quod de actu non-meritorio fieret actus meritorius per positionem alicuius mere naturalis." (OTh IX, 263).

CHAPTER III

stances. Therefore, in reference to an act which is only contingently virtuous the circumstances are properly called "circumstances". But the same cannot be said regarding those acts which are intrinsically good. For the intrinsically good acts vary with any variation in the so-called "circumstances". If this is true, then the "circumstances" are not really circumstances at all; they are, rather, true objects of the act. And when the object of the act varies, the act itself must also vary in its nature. This is a general rule which Ockham applies consistently in his treatment of ethical questions.[98] For instance, the act of the will to walk to church with an evil intention, to walk to church out of pride, is an act which is specifically distinct from the act of the will to go to church with a good intention, to will to go to church to honor God. Here the purpose of the act, a so-called "circumstance" of the act, but really a true object of the act, varies, and with its variation there is a variation in the nature of the act itself. The same principle would hold true for any of the other "circumstances" of the act. Hence we can conclude that in reference to the intrinsically virtuous acts the so-called "circumstances" of the act are not really circumstances but are actually objects of the act.[99]

While all of the circumstances of the act of the will are really partial objects of the act, the purpose of the act, however, is the principal object, as will appear later. The other circumstances are partial secondary objects of the act. If someone wills to pray to God, these circumstances are required for the act to be perfectly virtuous: he wills to pray, for the honor of God, according to the dictates of right reason, at the proper time (for example, on Sunday), in the proper place (for example, in church). In this case the virtuous act has the honor of God as its principal object, for the honor of God is the purpose of the act of praying. The act of praying itself is the common object; the secondary partial objects are right reason, Sunday and the church. But all of these "circumstances" are really objects of the act and as such are also

---

[98] *Ibid.* : "...dico quod non sunt circumstantiae respectu actus necessario et intrinsece virtuosi, sed sunt obiecta respectu illius actus; sunt autem circumstantiae respectu cuiuscumque actus qui solum dicitur virtuosus per denominationem extrinsecam, per conformitatem ad actum necessario virtuosum, quia quilibet talis actus potest semper idem remanere, et circumstantiae possunt variari; sicut idem potest esse actus ambulandi ad ecclesiam propter bonum finem et malum, cum recta ratione et contra rectam rationem. Ideo respectu talis actus dicuntur circumstantiae. Actus autem intrinsece virtuosus variatur propter variationem cuiuscumque circumstantiae, quia variato obiecto non potest esse idem actus..." (OTh IX, 266-67). Cf. E. Iserloh, *op. cit.*, p. 59.

[99] Ockham, *Quaest. Variae*, 7, 4: "Et ideo respectu talis actus [intrinsece virtuosi] non sunt proprie circumstantiae." (OTh VIII, 400). Ockham speaks of only three of the seven circumstances usually discussed in moral texts: cur, quando, ubi.

effective partial causes of the act of the will which is intrinsically virtuous. But what of the external act, the act of praying, an act which is only contingently virtuous? In reference to the external act or the common object of the act the circumstances remain really circumstances and merely circumstances. For this act remains the same whether the circumstances are present or absent. The act of praying has only "prayer" for its object; and merely as an external act, it does not necessarily involve praying at a certain time or place, with a good or an evil intention, in conformity with the dictates of right reason or contrary to them. This same rule holds true for any other external act. The circumstances, in so far as they pertain to the external act, do nothing else but "stand around," that is, they accompany the act but do not exercise any causal influence and do not form the partial objects of the act.[100]

Since the circumstances as partial objects of the act have meaning only in reference to the intrinsically virtuous act, we may conclude that they are partial objects of the act of willing itself. For only an act of the will is capable of being intrinsically virtuous, and all other acts, either external or internal, are only contingently virtuous or virtuous by extrinsic denomination.[101] The exterior act is sometimes referred to as the "common object," because it can remain the same in regard to, or it is common to, a variety of acts of the will. Suppose that I will to go to church for the honor of God. Walking to church is the common object of the act of the will. The honor of God is one of the circumstances, the purpose, of the act of walking. It is also a partial object of the act of the will, however. Now I will afterwards to go to church for the honor of God, and with the added condition that I go at the proper time. The act of willing has changed, in fact a new act of the will is elicited because

---

[100] Ockham, *In III Sent.*, 11: "...omnes circumstantiae actus voluntatis sunt obiecta partialia illius actus, ita quod finis in omni actu est obiectum principale....Aliae circumstantiae sunt obiecta secundaria partialia respectu illius actus. Exemplum: si enim ad hoc quod actus voluntatis quo aliquis vult orare Deum sit perfecte virtuosus requirantur necessario istae circumstantiae: quod velit orare propter honorem Dei, secundum rectum dictamen rationis, in tempore statuto, puta die dominico, in loco debito, puta in ecclesia, tunc iste actus sic virtuosus habet honorem Dei pro obiecto principali, actum orandi pro obiecto communi, rectam rationem, diem dominicum et ecclesiam pro obiectis secundariis et partialibus, ita quod respectu actus voluntatis istae circumstantiae sunt obiecta et causae effectivae partiales respectu illius actus. Sed respectu actus exterioris non sunt obiecta partialia, qui actus dicitur obiectum commune, quia actus orandi vel ambulandi vel aliquis talis exterior actus non habet tempus pro obiecto nec locum nec rectam rationem nec finem, sicut alius, puta actus comendendi habet cibum pro obiecto, actus ambulandi, viam. Et aliae circumstantiae quantum ad istum actum nihil faciunt nisi stant iuxta, id est, circumstant illum actum sine aliqua causalitate." (OTh VI, 381-82). Cf. also *Ibid.*, 11 (OTh VI, 388). See G. Biel, *op. cit., III Sent.*, d. 23, q. 1, M; E. Bonke, *op. cit.*, p. 65; A. Garvens, *op. cit.*, pp. 392-396.

[101] See notes 15-23, *supra*.

CHAPTER III

a new object of the act has been specified. But the external act of walking remains unchanged because "time" is not an object of the act of walking. It is, on the contrary, merely a circumstance. The exterior act of walking remains the same, but the act of willing now embraces a new and different object and is, accordingly, a new and different act of the will. Thus the exterior act is called the "common object" because it can be the object of many acts of the will and because it remains the same whether it is accompanied by certain circumstances or not. In addition, it is evident that whenever the "circumstances" change in regard to an act of willing, then the act of the will must also change. But this rule does not apply to the exterior act.[102]

The "circumstances," therefore, are nothing else but partial objects of the intrinsically virtuous act, the act of the will. And through a variation is these "circumstances" there necessarily follows a change in the act of the will. To put the matter more clearly, we would say that a new act of the will is elicited. Therefore, it becomes clearer again why there is no such thing as an act of the will which is at first intrinsically virtuous and afterwards evil. We mean here, of course, numerically the same act. An act of the will, it is true, can be elicited first with a good intention and later with an evil one. But the intention or purpose is one of the "circumstances" of the act; and by a change in the purpose (or any of the other "circumstances") from good to evil, there would necessarily be a change in the act of the will itself. And this is true because the so-called "circumstances" are really objects of the act, and a change in the objects means a corresponding change in the act itself. Nor can it ever happen that the numerically same act is at first only imperfectly virtuous because it lacks one or more of the circumstances required for a perfectly virtuous act, and later it becomes perfectly virtuous. Such a case would be impossible, because by the addition or subtraction of anything which is an object of the act, the act itself is changed.[103]

---

[102] Ockham, *In III Sent.*, 11: "...actus exterior est obiectum commune, quia potest idem manere respectu multorum actuum voluntatis. Puta, si primo velim ire ad ecclesiam pro honore Dei, hoc 'ambulare ad ecclesiam' est obiectum commune, et 'honor' circumstantia. Sed si post velim ire tempore statuto, tunc variatur actus voluntatis, et potest manere idem actus ambulandi. Si adhuc velim ire propter honorem Dei tempore statuto et secundum rectam rationem, et hoc semper in ambulando, semper iste actus exterior manet idem, tamen actus volendi variatur. Et ideo dicitur obiectum commune, quia potest esse obiectum multorum actuum volendi, et potest manere idem cum circumstantiis et sine circumstantia aliqua respectu actus volendi, variatur ipse actus voluntatis licet non exterior." (OTh VI, 383).

[103] *In III Sent.*, 11: "Respondeo primo quod [actus] idem numero non potest primo esse indifferens et post intrinsece bonus vel malus....quia...circumstantiae non sunt nisi obiecta partialia actus voluntatis virtuosi ad quorum variationem variatur necessario actus. Et

THE HUMAN WILL AND RIGHT REASON

At this point a question could be raised whether the purpose is really the primary and principal object of the act. For it seems at first glance that the external act is what is principally intended by the will and, therefore, the external act should be called the primary and principal object of the will. Thus, for example, it seems that if a person wills to go to church in order to honor God, his walking to the church is what is principally intended. But walking to church is the external act. Is then the external act itself or the purpose of the act of the will to be considered the principal object of the act of the will?

In presenting an answer to this question of the principal object of an intrinsically virtuous act, Ockham maintains that the purpose of the act must occupy the primary position. And this is true, he says, because the love of the end is what is principally intended by the will in acting. The exterior act is only the common object of the act of the will. It is called the "common object" for the reasons previously given.[104]

The purpose is the principal object of the act of the will because the love of the end is what is principally intended by the will in acting. Expressing this in another way, we may say that when the will wills something on account of an end, it loves the end more, because unless it loved the end it could not love anything else for the sake of the end.[105] The end, which is one of the "circumstances"--the purpose--is an object of the virtuous act. Whenever I will something dictated by right reason, I will it for an end. Hence by that same act I also will the end itself. And when I will something for the sake of attaining some end, I will the

---

propter eanden causam non potest aliquis actus voluntatis primo esse virtuosus intrinsece et post vitiosus--idem dico actus numero--quia non potest esse mutatio nisi per mutationem circumstantiarum, puta quia nunc actus bene circumstantionatur et post male, et hoc non potest esse sine mutatione actus. Et hoc semper tenet, quia circumstantiae sunt obiecta actus ad quorum variationem sequitur variatio in actibus. Nec--propter eanden rationem--potest esse unus actus primo imperfecte virtuosus, puta quia habet aliquas circumstantias requisitas ad actum perfecte virtuosum, et secundo perfecte virtuosus, puta quando habet omnes circumstantias requisitas. Quia semper per additionem vel subtractionem alicuius circumstantiae quae est obiectum et cuasa partialis respectu actus, variatur actus." (OTH VI, 383-85).

[104] *Quodl.*, III, 16: "Secundum dubium est, quia videtur quod finis non sit obiectum principale actus virtuosi, quia actus principaliter intentus a voluntate est obiectum primarium et principale illius actus; sed ille est actus exterior; puta quando quis vult ire ad ecclesiam propter Deum, hic ambulare ad ecclesiam principaliter intentitur; igitur etc....Ad secundum dubium dico quod finis est obiectum principale actus virtuosi intrinsece, et hoc quia dilectio finis principaliter intenditur; sed actus exterior est obiectum commune isti actui voluntatis et multis aliis;...et finis est obiectum principale." (OTh IX, 266-67). See the same wording *In III Sent.*, 11 (OTh VI, 382-83).

[105] *In III Sent.*, 11: "...quia quando voluntas non diligit aliquid nisi propter finem, magis diligit finem, quyia sine illo non diligeret aliud." (OTh VI, 380). See *Quodl.*, III, 16 (OTh IX, 267).

CHAPTER III

end more than the means used to attain it.[106] Now that object is the principal object of the act of the will, the love of which is principally intended by the will. Since the purpose as an object of the act of the will is principally intended by the will, it is, therefore, the principal object of the will.[107]

But at this time it would be worth while mentioning again that just as conformity to the right reason is not precisely the reason why an act is virtuous, so also the primary goodness of an act does not reside in its purpose and intention--or in any of the other partial objects of the act--but only an act of the will itself can be primarily morally good or evil.[108]

The other "circumstances," for instance those of place and time, are also objects of the intrinsically virtuous act, though these are only secondary objects, while the purpose is the primary and principal object of the act of the will. Place and time are really objects of the will's act, because otherwise the act of the will could be just as perfectly virtuous without these conditions as it is with them. And that, of course, would be a false viewpoint. For the will to eat, for example, is a virtuous act if it is willed at the right time and the right place. But without these circumstances the will to eat could be an evil act. Briefly, then, all of the "circumstances" are really partial objects of a necessarily virtuous act.[109]

For a virtuous act the circumstances of place and time would have to be apprehended by the right reason and dictated in the same way that the right reason apprehends and dictates the purpose or intention of the act. Can we not say, then, that place and time--and all the other cir-

---

[106] *Quaest. Variae*, q. 7, a. 4: "Et eodem modo potest probari quod finis, qui est una circumstantia, sit obiectum actus virtuosi; quia volo tale dictatum propter talem finem, igitur per illum actum volo finem, quia propter quod unumquodque, et illud magis." (OTh VIII, 396).

[107] *In III Sent.*, 11: "...illud est obiectum principale actus voluntatis cuius dilectio principaliter intenditur; huiusmodi est finis." (OTh VI, 382).

[108] *Ibid.*: "Similiter, non plus est actus virtuosus propter rectam rationem quam propter finem vel aliam circumstantiam, quia sicut recta ratio est obiectum partiale actus virtuosi vel vitiosi, ita finis et tempur aliquando. Et tamen nullus ponit quod prima bonitas actus est a fine vel a tempore, sed solum actus voluntatis qui primo est imputabilis est primo bonus vel malus moraliter." (OTh VI, 389-90).

[109] *Quodl.*, III, 16: "Idem patet de loco et tempore, quod sunt obiecta, quia aliter esset actus voluntatis ita perfecte virtuosus sine illis sicut cum illis; quod falsum est, quia velle comedere est actus virtuosus, si velit loco et tempore, et aliter est magis vitiosus quam virtuosus. Dico igitur breviter quod omnes circumstantiae sunt obiecta partialia actus necessario virtuosi, et finis est obiectum principale." (OTh IX, 265). See the same wording in *Quaest. Variae*, q. 7, a. 4 (OTh VIII, 396).

cumstances--are objects of the act of dictating but are not objects of the act of the will? It seems that the object of the will would be merely what is dictated by right reason and that anything beyond this is unnecessary. But here we must remember that an act of the will is perfectly virtuous only if it is elicited in complete conformity with the dictates of right reason. If an act of the will would conform only partially to the dictates of right reason, the act would not be virtuous. Right reason, for example, may dictate that an act take place with a good intention and at a certain determined place and time. In this case if the will follows the dictates of right reason regarding the good intention but does not take into account the "circumstances" of time and place, the act of the will would not be perfectly virtuous. It would be an evil, or at least indifferent, act of the will. It is necessary for an act of the will to be perfectly virtuous that it is in complete conformity with the dictats of right reason. This means, of course, that the will must include everything that the right reason dictates should be willed. And, therefore, if the right reason would dictate that an act is to be performed at a certain place and time, the perfectly virtuous will must conform to the right reason regarding the proper place and time. Consequently, whatever is an object of the act of dictating by right reason must also be an object of the perfectly virtuous act of willing. It is not sufficient to say, therefore, that place and time are merely objects of the act of dictating by the right reason, that it is unnecessary for them to be objects of the act of the will. And the reason behind this is: the will must be in complete and perfect conformity with the dictates of the right reason in eliciting an act which is to be perfectly virtuous.[110]

Ockham's insistence that the will must conform completely with the dictates of right reason may be interpreted as nothing else but an application of the generally accepted dictum, "Bonum ex integra causa, malum ex quovis defectu." Ockham's discussion of the circumstances of a

---

[110] *Quaest. Variae*, q. 7, a. 4: "Si dicas, quod requiritur ad actum virtuosum, quod locus et tempus apprehendantur et dictentur a ratione, sicut finis, et aliter non potest ratio causare actum virtuosum; et per consequens tam locus quam tempus sunt obiecta partialia apprehensionis et actus dictandi, non tamen sunt obiecta volitionis virtuosae, contra: volitio dicitur perfecte virtuosa quia in omnibus conformiter elicitur rationi rectae, quia si in aliquo conformiter eliceretur et in aliquo non, iam non esset perfecte virtuosa. Exemplum: si aliquis vellet actum carnalem propter talem finem dictatum a ratione recta, et nullum actum volendi haberet respectu loci et temporis, quamquam ista dictentur a ratione, ista volitio non est perfecte virtuosa sed potius vitiosa vel indifferens; igitur ad hoc quod sit perfecte virtuosa, oportet quod conformetur rationi rectae et omnibus dictatis a ratione recta sibi debitae competere; igitur si recta ratio dictet quod talis actus sit volendus loco et tempore, voluntas perfecte virtuosa debet velle talem actum in loco et tempore; et per consequens quidquid est obiectum actus dictandi recte, erit obiectum actus perfecte virtuosi." (OTh VIII, 396 f.). See A. Garvens, *op. cit.*, p. 394.

CHAPTER III

good act and the integrity of circumstances show that he would accept the above formula as true.[111] But he makes one restriction or, rather, an observation, regarding the interpretation of the formula. He remarks that not every defect in a circumstance required for a morally good act would render that act evil. For if every defect of a required circumstance would be sinful, then ignorance would never excuse a person from responsibility. However, according to the authorities ignorance sometimes excuses completely. Therefore, it would be more correct to say that when some circumstance is lacking to which the one performing the act is obligated at the time, then the act is evil. If, on the other hand, the person is not obliged at that time to some particular circumstance--for instance, he is inculpably ignorant that a certain circumstance is required--then, as should be evident, the resulting act would not be evil.[112] This observation would apply in the case in which someone would seek something as an end which ought to be sought only as a means to an end. But the person may be inculpably ignorant of the fact that the thing he seeks is only a means to an end. He may even be ignorant of the end itself. In this case the act of the will which this person elicits would not be evil even though a required circumstance is lacking, because the person is not obliged in this case to will that circumstance as a partial object of the act. Or, to put the entire matter more simply, the circumstance is not a required circumstance for a virtuous act in this case.[113]

In all of the foregoing, what has been said concerning the necessity of right reason and of the "circumstances" as objects of the virtuous act also holds, *mutatis mutandis*, in reference to the moral habits or virtues. As it is impossible for a virtuous habit to exist without its

---

[111] See Ockham, *In III Sent.*, 11 (OTh VI, 379-80).

[112] *In I Sent.*, 1, 1: "...non omnis defectus circumstantiae requisitae ad actum moraliter bonum facit actum esse malum vel peccatum. Tunc enim ignorantia nunquam excusaret, cum tamen secundum doctores et Sanctos ignorantia aliquando excuset a toto. Sed quando deficit aliqua circumstantia ad quam eliciens actum pro tunc obligatur tunc est actus malus, si autem non obligetur tunc ad illam circumstantiam non est actus malus." (OTh I, 378). F. Copleston, *op. cit.*, pp. 106-107, gives Ockham credit for clarifying the position of the erroneous conscience in morality: "Conscience is always to be followed, even if it is an erroneous conscience...A man is morally obliged to do what he in good faith believes to be right. This doctrine, that one is morally obliged to follow one's conscience, and that to follow an invincibly erroneous conscience, so far from being a sin, is a duty, was not a new doctrine in the Middle Ages; but Ockham expressed it in a clear and unequivocal manner."

[113] Ockham, *Ibid.*: "Et si dicatur quod ille actus est malus quando diligitur aliquid quod est ad finem et non propter finem, respondeo quod actus respectu alicuius ad finem potest non esse malus quamvis non diligatur vel non referatur positive ad finem, et hoc maxime si non apprehendatur finis." (OTh I, 378).

proper objects, so also it would be impossible for a virtuous habit to exist without its proper objects. The partial objects of moral virtue are the circumstances of place and time, and especially right reason, to which an act of the virtue must conform completely if it is to be a perfectly virtuous act.[114] And to an even greater degree the purpose or intention as a partial object of the moral virtues would play an important role.

From a consideration of the objects of the virtuous act, especially the purpose, we can see that the virtues of the Christian are basically different from those of the pagan. For the moral virtues, even though identical as far as the common object or the exterior act is concerned, are distinct if any of their partial objects are distinct. Now the purpose or inteniton is a true partial object of a virtue as we have seen. With little doubt it can be said that the intention of the Christian in acquiring, practising, and developing the moral virtues is different from the intention of the pagan. The Christian observes continence, for example, out of love for God and because of God's command in this matter. So the love of God or of God's command is the reason why continence is observed by the Christian. This same intention is found in the practice of the other virtues also. God is always the principal end intended by the Christian. The non-Christian philosopher, however, although he would observe continence and the other virtues, would do so for a completely different motive, for instance, to conserve his health or devote himself to study. In this way the partial object of the virtues differs for the Christian and the non-Christian. And consequently, since the "same" virtue for the Christian and for the non-Christian has a different basis in the intention of each of these, they are really specifically distinct.[115]

---

[114] *In IV Sent.*, qq. 3-4: "Impossibile est, virtutem moralem esse sine suo obiecto...Nunc autem obiecta partialia virtutis moralis sunt circumstantiae, puta locus et tempus, inter quas est praecipua recta ratio, cuius actus debet conformari quod sit virtuosus perfecte." (OTh VIII, 49 f.).

[115] *Ibid.*, 3, S: "Et quando dicitur, quod virtutes philosophorum fuerunt eiusdem rationis cum virtutibus nostris, nego quia virtutes morales distinguuntur secundum distinctionem obiectorum partialium. Nunc autem finis est obiectum partiale virtutis, sicut alius dictum est. Philosophi autem in adquirendo virtutes morales habuerunt alium finem quam christiani gratia: abstinere ab actu fornicandi propter Deum, et quia Deus praecepit sic abstinere, ita quod Deus est hic causa finalis, vel preceptum Dei, istius abstinentiae. Et sic est de omnibus aliis virtutibus adquisitis a bono christiano, quia semper Deus est principalis finis intentus. Philosophus autem, licet abstineat a talibus, tamen totaliter propter aliam finem vel propter conservationem naturae vel ad perficiendum in scientia vel propter aliquid tale. Igitur aliud fuit obiectum partiale abstinentiae philosophi et boni christiani, et per consequens, alia virtus et alterius rationis." (OTh VII, 58).

CHAPTER III

In fact, for a perfect moral virtue a supernatural object is required. First of all, there can be moral virtues in reference to a supernatural object. Not only is such a virtue possible, it is also virtue which is fully perfect. And from this it follows also that the moral virtues of a pagan philosopher and those of a Christian differ specifically. Since the object, either total or partial, is different specifically in each case, then the act and habit also differ specifically. Since God is the object of whatever perfectly virtuous act which the pagan performs, and since God is specifically distinct from any object that the pagan would have in mind, it follows that the acts and virtues of the Christian differ specifically from those of the pagan.[116]

Thus the pagan philosophers, as Ockham mentions, did not hold that moral virtues have any reference to a supernatural object in the way that we believe they do. Likewise, they did not believe that abstinence, continence, or any of the other moral virtues should be willed out of love for God or out of obedience to the commandments of God. But such supernatural motives form the basis for the Christian's abstinence, continence, or the practice and development of any of the moral virtues. But for the pagan these virtues are sought because they are in some way naturally good, that is, in so far as they conserve and perfect human nature.[117] Thus we cannot say that the virtues of the pagan, although they have reference to the same common object that the virtues of the Christian have, are the same as the virtues of the Christian. The difference between the virtues of the pagan and those of the Christian lies in the difference between the partial objects, the intentions, of each.

In the last few paragraphs, when we began to speak of the distinction between the virtues of the Christian and the virtues of the pagan,

---

[116] *Quaest. Variae*, q. 7, a. 4: "Dico quod respectu obiecti supernaturalis potest esse virtus moralis, immo nulla est perfecta virtus nisi inclinet ad actum respectu obiecti supernaturalis....Et es hoc etiam sequitur quod virtus moralis quam poneret philosophus et bonus christianus differunt specie...quia universaliter quorum obiecta totalia vel partialia differunt specie, illorum actus et habitus differunt specie; sed Deus non est eiusdem speciei cum quacumque creatura, cum igitur Deus sit obiectum alicuius actus virtuosi quem eliceret philosophus vel paganus, sequitur quod ibi actus et habitus differunt specie." (OTh VIII, 402f.)

[117] *Quaest. Variae*, q. 7, a. 4: "Philosophus tamen non ponit virtutem moralem esse respectu obiecti supernaturalis sicut nos ponimus, quia non ponit quod abstinentia vel continentia sit volenda propter honorem divinum tamquam propter finem,--nec talia et simila sunt praecepta a Deo--quo modo bonus christianus vult talis, sed tantum ponit talia esse volenda quia sunt honesta vel conservativa naturae vel aliquid mere naturale." (OTh VIII, 402f.) Cf. *In III Sent.*, 11 (OTh VI, 385-86). E. Hochstetter, "Viator mundi," p. 12, refers to Ockham's quote of St. Jerome in this connection "Er verweist in diesem Zusammenhang auf das Wort des hl. Hieronymus, 'quod relinquere omnia est philosophorum, sed relinquere propter Christum omnia et sequi Christum est perfectorum.'"

we entered into a new phase of Ockham's ethical thought. We introduced a new notion which, it turns out, is of vital importance in any examination of the virtuous act and the conditions required for such an act. The Christian, says Ockham, elicits virtuous acts out of love for God and in obedience to His divine commands. This can be expressed rightly, I think, as a third condition for a virtuous act. This third condition is in addition to the two conditions already expressed and explained in this chapter--namely, that the act be freely willed and that it be willed in complete conformity with the dictates of right reason. The additional third condition, that the act be performed out of love of God and in obedience to His divine commands, would hold at least for the Christian, who is not excusable out of ignorance. It would not render the pagan entirely incapable of performing virtuous acts, but the virtues of the pagan would not be on the same level as those of the Christian. In this sense, then, the pagan could be said to be "lacking" in virtue, because he cannot fulfill the third condition required for a perfectly virtuous act. Here, it seems, we get the first real glimpse of Ockham's theory of a peculiar, a proper "Christian" morality. And it is this notion he is most interested in developing in his theory of ethics.

Writing some years ago, E. Hochstetter seems to have claimed that what we have called the third condition for a virtuous act really applies to the notion of a meritorious act, while the first two conditions apply and suffice for the virtuous act.[118] There is undoubtedly some basis for this distinction in the third *Quodlibet* of Ockham.[119] However, in spite of this basis I would prefer to keep the term "virtuous" for several reasons. First of all, Ockham himself sometimes uses the terms "meritorious" and "virtuous" interchangeably without making any effort to distinguish between them. And it is at these times that he may use the term "meritorious" and at the same time be speaking of conditions which apply equally well to the virtuous act. Secondly, the third condition as expressed above, that the act is to be performed out of love for God and in obedience to His divine commands, is really required, according to Ockham, for the perfectly virtuous act on the part of the Christian who knows what the will of God is. Thirdly, there is no real need to use the term "meritorious" to distinguish the virtuous act of the Christian from that of the pagan, if it is remembered that their virtuous acts are

---

[118] E. Hochstetter, "Viator mundi," pp. 11-12: "So verwendet er (Ockham) den Virtus-Begriff der aristotelischen Ethik, für die caritas notwendig ist, wahrend das christliche meritum ohne sie nicht sein kann, kontrastiert demgemäss das virtuose agere gegen das meritorie agere und betont, dass die Philosophen tagendhaft waren ohne jegliche Liebe, aber eine verdienstliche Tat ohne sie nicht vollbringen konnten."

[119] Ockham, *Quodl.*, III, 15 (OTh IX, 257-62).

CHAPTER III

specifically distinct on the basis of their different partial objects, the intentions underlying each. And finally, the meritorious act in the complete sense would demand a fourth condition over and above the three conditions required for a virtuous act, namely, that it be accepted by God as worthy of merit. In other words, the merely virtuous act would become meritorious only if it were accepted by God as meritorious. This fourth condition distinguishes the meritorious act from the perfectly virtuous yet, absolutely speaking, possibly non-meritorius act.[120]

Hochstetter is perfectly correct, however, in pointing out that when we introduce the third condition, love and obedience to God, we are entering into the realm of the theological-ethical problem of virtuous acts.[121] The first two conditions, which were discussed in this chapter, refer directly and exclusively to the philosophical-ethical problem of moral acts. Ockham certainly recognized the distinction between the philosophical and theological realms and the corresponding distinction between the problems of the virtuous act in each realm. This recognition is clearly expressed in his distinction between the virtues of the Christian and those of the pagan. But Ockham is also faced with the knowledge that for the Christian actually existing in this world the realms of the philosophical and the theological in relation to ethical acts are indeed inseparable. "For God is always the object of the good Christian's perfectly virtuous acts."[122]

The position of the Christian can be more accurately and clearly delineated if we take another look at the first two conditions for a virtuous act. First, the act must be freely willed. Only an act of the

---

[120] *In I Sent.*, 17, 2: "...Deus libere acceptat bonum motum voluntatis tamquam meritorium, quando elicitur ab habente caritatem." (OTh III, 472). See also *ibid.*, qq. 1 et 2 (OTh III, 464f., 440ff., 472f., 475).

[121] E. Hochstetter, "Viator mundi," p. 11: "Der actus meritorius aber erweist sich hier, wie auch an vielen anderen Stellen, als ein theologisch-ethisches und nicht als ein philosophisch-ethisches Problem. Der Liebesakt greift jedoch auf beide Problemgebiete über, ist aber auf letzterem nicht unbedingt erforderlich. Ockham behandelt die Unterscheidung beider Fragenkreise nicht in extenso, aber gelegentliche Bemerkungen zeigen, dass er sie macht, wie ihm auch sonst die traditionelle Gegenüberstellung der philosophi oder sapientes und der theologi natürlich geläufig ist." See also F. Copleston, *op. cit.*, p. 197: "It would seem, then, at least at first sight, that we are faced with what amounts to two moral theories in Ockham's philosophy...The authoritarian conception of morality expresses Ockham's conviction of the freedom and omnipotence of God and they are revealed in Christianity, while the insistence on right reason would seem to represent the influence on his thought of Aristotle's ethical teaching and of the moral theories of his mediaeval predecessors. It would seem, then, that Ockham presents one type of ethical theory in his capacity as theologian and another type in his capacity as philosopher."

[122] Ockham, *Quaest. Variae*, q. 7, a. 4: "Deus est obiectum cuiuscumque actus perfecte virtuosi quem eliceret bonus Christianus." (OTh VIII, 403).

will is primarily and immediately free. From this Ockham goes on to conclude that only an act of the will is of itself virtuous or evil. Any other act, interior or exterior, is only mediately free and consequently receives its morality from an act which is immediately free. These mediately free acts are virtuous only by extrinsic denomination. They have no morality distinct from the act of the will by which they were brought into being.

Secondly, the freely willed act must be elicited in conformity with the dictates of right reason. Not every free act is a morally good act of itself. The will, since it has the capability of acting rightly or not, needs a directive norm for its actions. This norm is the right reason directing and dictating which acts are to be performed and which acts are to be avoided. When the will elicits its acts in complete conformity with the dictates of right reason, the act of the will is virtuous. Right reason, consequently, is really a partial cause of the virtuous act. Right reason is also a partial object of the virtuous act, however, and, therefore, the will not only must elicit its acts according to, but also because of, the dictates of right reason. Furthermore, the will must also will everything that the right reason dictates should be willed. Thus the "circumstances" of the act, and principally the purpose or intention are also really objects of the virtuous act. Since they are objects of the virtuous act, these, too, must be willed if the act of the will is to be considered as perfectly virtuous.

The foregoing could be considered a summary of the conditions necessary for a virtuous act. But can we stop here? Is not the Christian, at least, faced with a further problem--a problem, it is true, which carries him over into the theological-ethical realm? Probably the question which arises most immediately is in connection with the principal object of the virtuous act, the end or purpose of the act. Clearly, the purpose as principal object of the virtuous act occupies a special position, a position of major importance and concern in any questions of an ethical science which is supposed to deal with moral acts. It should, therefore, receive attention proportionate to its importance in the realm of ethics.

But what is the end required? Surely it cannot be left up to right reason itself to determine arbitrarily the end to be sought. In its activity of dictating, right reason itself must have a norm according to which it acts so that it will be right, and not erroneous, reason. It would seem to be impossible for right reason to be its own norm of morality, as the Kantian School would have us believe. Much less, right reason could not be the ultimate norm of morality, as the Stoics held that it was. To maintain the complete autonomy of human reason would lead us into the errors of moral rationalism of either the Stoic or the

CHAPTER III

Kantian variety.[123] Nor, in Ockham's view, as P. Boehner has pointed out, can the norm of morality be any impersonal law of natures or essences.[124]

Here we see how and why Ockham turns to the love of God, and the love of God as expressed through obedience to God's will, as the norm for right reason. Right reason is not autonomous; it is to be governed in its activity of directing, regulating and dictating what acts are to be performed and what acts are to be avoided. Right reason is regulated by the will of God as manifested in his divine commands. When the divine will commands, the right reason must dictate to the human will that the command of God be fulfilled. The will of God or obedience to the will of God out of love thus becomes the motive and object, the end and purpose, of the virtuous act. Thus, regarding the purpose, Ockham says, "Right reason must dictate that we should will to abstain out of love for God or obedience to Him, because this is what right reason demands. Otherwise it would not be right, but erroneous, reason."[125] Reason cannot be right reason unless it conforms to its norm. In all things dictated by right reason, the will of God is the norm. As Ockham expresses it, "By the very fact that God wills anything, human right reason must dictate that the will of God be followed."[126] The will of God, then, can be called, according to Ockham, the highest norm of morality. How this doctrine is to be understood will form the content of the following chapter.

---

[123] See J. Donat, *op. cit.*, pp. 195 ff; C. Bittle, *Man and Morals: Ethics* (Milwaukee: Bruce, 1950), pp. 156 ff.

[124] P. Boehner, "A Recent Presentation of Ockham's Philosophy," *Franciscan Studies*, IX (1949), p. 454: "Thus Ockham does not base his ethics on some anonymous and impersonal law pervading nature, or on something to which God Himself is subject, for instance on 'ethical values,'...Ockham bases his ethics on one Personal principle, on God who is most powerful, most good and most wise and most just." See also E. Gilson and P. Boehner, *Christliche Philosophie* (3. ed.; Paderborn: Schoeningh, 1954), p. 622: "Demnach ist Wilhelms Ethik nicht einfachhin die Statuierung eines blinden Wollens, nach welchem der Willie des Menschen sich richten muss, *wohl aber* eine stärkere Verankerung des Sittlichen in der persönlichen Sphäre und nicht in der anonymen Sphäre der recta ratio oder der Natur und dem naturgemässen handeln."

[125] Ockham, *Quodl.*, III, 16: "...recta ratio deberet dictare quod volendum est abstinere propter Deum quia sic est dictatum a recta ratione, aliter non esset recta sed erronea..." (OTh IX, 263).

[126] *In I Sent.*, 41, un.: "Sed eo ipso quod voluntas divina hoc vult, ratio recta dictat quod est volendum." (OTh IV, 610).

CHAPTER IV

GOD:
THE OBJECTIVE NORM
OF
MORALITY

Most, if not all, of our modern authors concur in interpreting Ockham's ethics as a system which holds that the will of God is the highest norm of morality.[1] As a typical example of this interpretation we offer the words of P. Boehner, certainly one of the foremost students of Ockham's writings:

> God's will is the ethical norm and must be obeyed by every creature. As soon as a human person knows that a certain command is the will of God, he is bound to obey. To do the will of God or, equivalently, to love God, is the supreme ethical rule.[2]

---

[1] All of the following speak of the will of God as the highest norm of morality in these or equivalent terms. P. Boehner, *Ockham. Philosophical Writings* ("The Nelson Philosophical Texts"; London: Nelson, 1957), p. xlix; P. Boehner, "A Recent Presentation of Ockham's Philosophy," *Franciscan Studies*, IX (1949), p. 453; F. Copleston, *A History of Philosophy*, Vol. III: *Ockham to Suarez* (Westminster: Newman, 1953), pp. 14, 384; A. D'Entrèves, *Natural Law: An Introduction to Legal Philosophy* ("Hutchinson's University Library"; London: Hutchinson, 1955), p. 68; M. De Wulf, *Histoire de la philosophie médiévale*, t. II (5. ed. rev.; Louvain: Institut supérieur de philosophie; Paris: Alcan, 1924-1925), p. 172; A. Garvens, "Die Grundlagen der Ethik Wilhelms von Ockham," *Franziskanische Studien*, XXI (1934, pp. 262-273; E. Gilson, *La philosophie au moyen âge* (3. ed.; Paris: Payot, 1947), p. 652; E. Gilson and P. Boehner, *Christliche Philosophie* (Paderborn: Schoeningh, 1954), p. 622; O. Fuchs, *The Psychology of Habit according to William Ockham* ("Franciscan Institute Publications; Philosophy Series," No.8; St. Bonaventure, N.Y.: Franciscan Institute, 1952), pp. 84-88; J. Hirschberger, *Geshchichte der Philosophie*, I. *Altertum und Mittelalter* (Freiburg: Herder, 1949), pp. 459-460; F. Ueberweg and B. Geyer, *Grundriss der Geschichte der Philosophie*, II. *Die patristische und scholastische Philosophie* (Basel, 1951), p. 582. E. Gilson and P. Boehner, *Christliche Philosophie*, p. 632, write: "Das Omnipotenzprinzip bleibt für Wilhelm oberste Norm seiner Lehre. Das zeigt sich auch in der Ethik. Die letzte Norm für die sittlichkeit eines Aktes kann nicht ausserhalb Gottes, und vor allem nicht ausserhalb des Willens Gottes gesucht werden. Was Gott will, ist darum gut, weil Gott es will. Um diese Behauptung Wilhelms sondertes in Gott bedeutet, sondern mit Gottes Wesen identisch ist...Nun ist aber Gott ein vernünftig wirkendes und darum auch vernünftig wollendes Wesen."

[2] P. Boehner, *Ockham. Philosophical Writings*, p. xlix.

CHAPTER IV

One must admit that to interpret Ockham's ethics as holding that the will of God is the supreme ethical rule is undoubtedly correct, although there is present the danger on the part of some of misunderstanding Ockham's position. To understand the notion that God's will is the highest ethical norm correctly it is important, first of all, to keep in mind certain leading ideas in Ockham's theologico-philosophical speculations regarding the Supreme Being. For these ideas are fundamental in Ockham's writings and, as such, also exert considerable influence on his ethical theories. The purpose of this chapter is to attempt to examine these fundamental ideas and apply them to the realm of ethics. We will try to avoid as much as possible any unnecessary detail by sidestepping much of the controversy that has arisen around some of the questions to be discussed. It is not our purpose to attempt any settlement of the controversial aspects of the following topics but to sketch the main points of Ockham's views and apply them to ethical problems.

We can begin by stating that according to Ockham, while we cannot prove from natural reason alone the existence or necessity of an infinite good, we can know this proposition from natural reason: God is the greatest good.[3] And it is because God is the greatest good that He is to be loved above all.[4] The act of the will whereby we love God above all and for Himself is of such a nature that, given this act, it is necessarily virtuous. It cannot be either indifferent or evil. And it is this act which is the first, the principle or source, of all good acts.[5]

Now it is this love of God, the greatest good, which I will term the highest or ultimate norm of morality according to Ockham's teaching. If we cast this in formula form it would be expressed: Love God and will what he wills. But this formula calls for some detailed examination. The formula's explanation will serve a twofold objective: in a positive way, to include any related ideas involved in an understanding of the formula; and negatively, to exclude any wrong or misleading interpretation of the

---

[3] Ockham, *In I Sent.*, 1, 5: "...concedo quod ex puris naturalibus possumus cognoscere istam propositionem 'Deus est summum bonum.'.. (OTh I, 464).

[4] *In I Sent.*, 1, 4: "...dico quod solus Deus est summe diligendus, quia est summum bonum." (OTh I, 447).

[5] *Quodl.*, III, 14: "...nam iste actus [quo Deus diligitur super omnia et propter se] sic est virtuosus quod non potest esse vitiosus, nec potest iste actus causari a voluntate creata nisi sit virtuosus; tum quia quilibet pro loco et tempore obligatur ad diligendum Deum super omnia, et pro consequens iste actus non potest esse vitiosus; tum quia iste actus est primus omnium actuum bonorum." (OTh IX 255-56). This point is emphasized by P. Boehner in "A Recent Presentation of Ockham's Philosophy," pp. 453-454. See also O. Fuchs, *op. cit.*, p. 83; A. Garvens, *op. cit.*, p. 390; E. Iserloh, *Gnade und Eucharistie in der philosophischen Theologie des Wilhelm von Ockham* (Wiesbaden: Steiner, 1956), pp. 48-51.

GOD: THE OBJECTIVE NORM OF MORALITY

formula. Accordingly, there are three parts of the formula that seem in need of explanation. These three parts are as follows:

1. What is meant by "love God"?
2. What does "God wills" mean?
3. What does it mean for us to "will what he wills"?

1. LOVE GOD

To love God means here to love God above all and to love whatever God wills to be loved.[6] First, let us explain that the love of God above all includes the notion that he is loved for Himself and not for any other reason. The reason why God is loved, the end of the act of loving, is a primary object of the will. But whenever the primary objects of any acts differ, the acts themselves are also specifically distinct. The act is specified by its object. As a consequence it is impossible for one and the same act to terminate at one primary object at one time and at another primary object at another time.[7]

Let us put this same idea in another way. When God is loved not for Himself but for some other reason, then we cannot say that he is loved above all. For if the will loves anything on account of something else (A is loved on account of B), then this something else (B) is loved more than the other (A). Because if it were not for this something else (B), the other (A) would not be loved at all. Or to put this in other words, (B) is something that cn be considered as an end in itself, and (A) is only the means to this end. The end is therefore the primary object of the will, for except for the end the means to the end would not be sought. No one seeks the means alone; the means are always sought in relation to some end. This is equivalent to saying that the love of the end is the cause of the love of the means to the end. I would not love the means unless I also loved the end. Therefore, given the fact that I

---

[6] Ockham, *Quodl.*, III, 14: "Hoc est diligere Deum super omnia: diligere Deum et diligere quidquid Deus vult diligi." (OTh IX 257).

[7] *In III Sent.*, 11: "...actus diligendi Deum propter se tamquam propter finem, et post propter aliud, sunt actus distincti etiam specie. Quod autem sunt distincti actus patet, quia quandocumque obiecta primaria aliquorum actuum variantur, necessario variantur illi actus, quia impossibile est quod unus actus nunc terminetur ad unum primarium obiectum et non ad aliud, et post terminetur ad aliud obiectum primarium." (OTh VI, 380). See A. Garvens, *op. cit.*, p. 391.

love the end, I can also love the means; but if I do not love the end, there is no reason for loving the means.[8]

In consideration of the ideas expressed in the above paragraphs there are two points I would emphasize as being involved in the notion of loving God above all. First, the notion of loving God above all includes the fact that he is loved for Himself, as an end and not as a means, and this motive or end is the primary object of the will. And secondly, loving God for any other reason except for Himself is an act which is specifically distinct from the act of loving God for Himself. Any act of loving God in which he is not loved for Himself cannot be the love of God above all. A further development of these ideas can be made, employing the familiar notions of the love of friendship (*amor amicitiae*) and the love of desire (*amor concupiscentiae*). From a consideration of these notions it will be seen that God, the highest good, is to be loved by the love of friendship; and this love is specifically distinct from any kind of love of desire.

The act of the love of friendship terminates in God Himself.[9] Such a love which terminates in God, a love of God in and for Himself, is specifically distinct from a love of God by the love of desire. For in this case, too, we have a distinction of ends or primary objects, and from a variation or distinction of ends there follows a variation or distinction of acts.[10] Now the love of God above all must be a love of friendship. For every love of desire in the strict sense presupposes the love of friendship. Whenever something is loved by the love of desire, there must be something else which is loved more by the love of friendship. Therefore, if God would be loved precisely by the love of desire, there

---

[8] Ockham, *Ibid.*: "...quia quando voluntas non diligit aliquid nisi propter fine, magis diligit finem, quia sine illo non diligeret aliud. Et patet aliter, quia si essent duo respectu duorum obiectorum quorum unus actus esset causa alterius, si illa duo obiecta post diligerentur unico actu, illud obiectum esset primum cuius actus est causa alterius quando diliguntur distinctis actibus. Sed si diligeret finem unico actu et aliud propter finem alio actu, actus quo diligo finem esset causa respectu alterius actus, quia non diligo aliud nisi quia diligo finem. Et ita, posito actu respectu finis, potest alius ponit; et non posito, non potest poni, per casum. Igitur est causa..." (OTh VI, 380-81). See A. Garvens, *op. cit.*, p. 392.

[9] Ockham, *In I Sent.*, 1, 4: "...amor amicitiae respectu cuiuscumque obiecti est perfectissimus...amor amicitiae terminatur ad ipsum Deum in se..." (OTh I, 441). Cf. also *In I Sent.*, 1,4 (OTh I, 444-45). See also L. Baudry (ed.), *Le Tractatus de principiis theologiae attribue a G. d'Occam* ("Études de philosophie médiévale," XXIII; Paris: Vrin, 1936), p. 146: "...omnis finis amatur et amore amicitiae et concupiscentiae; amatur propter se et amatur amore quo alterum est propter ipsum amatum; et primus est amor amicitiae, secundus est amor concupiscentiae."

[10] *In III Sent.*, 11: "Igitur ad variationem finium sequitur variatio actus, et per consequens sunt distincti actus....actus unus est actus amoris amicitiae et alius actus amoris concupiscentiae qui distinguuntur specie. (OTh VI, 381).

GOD: THE OBJECTIVE NORM OF MORALITY

would be something else which is loved more than God, that is, by the love of friendship. Thus God would not be loved above all in such a case.[11] God as the highest good must be loved by the love of friendship. For if there are two ends and one of them is loved by the love of desire, and the other by the love of friendship, then the one which is loved by the love of friendship is the more perfect of the two.[12] So if God is loved only by the love of desire, this would imply that there must be some other end more perfect than God, the highest good. But to repeat, because God is the highest good, he is to be loved above all.[13]

When Ockham speaks, therefore, of the act of loving God as a necessarily virtuous act, one which is perfectly virtuous, the first or source of all good acts, he means that act by which God is loved for Himself, loved above all, loved by an act of the love of friendship. He does not mean, certainly, that God can be loved in a true sense by the love of desire, even though he speaks of loving God for an unworthy end. For it is false to assume, says Ockham, that the love of God is always for a worthy end. Sometimes it can be for an unworthy end and thus not a good act but an evil act, that is, when God is loved by the love of desire. But this type of love certainly would not be a true love of God.[14] As far as our formula "Love God and will what he wills" is concerned, the love of God must be understood as meaning the love of friendship, a true love of God, and that God himself is the end of this act of love.

It may be well to digress briefly at this point to examine Ockham's discussion of the use of the term "end." The term "end," he tells us, is sometimes understood as being synonymous with "final cause," one of the four causes; or it can mean something final in a reality or an operation, for instance, a period is the "end" of a line.[15] Improperly speaking, the

---

[11] *In I Sent.*, 1, 4: "...omnis amor concupiscentiae, qui est praecise concupiscentiae, praesupponit amorem amicitiae, ita quod quando aliquid diligitur amore concupiscentiae est aliquid magis dilectum amore amicitiae. Igitur si Deus praecise diligeretur amore concupiscentiae esset aliquid magis dilectum quam Deus, quod est inconveniens." (OTh I, 444).

[12] *Quaest. Variae*, q. 4: "Duplex ist finis: quidam amatus amore concupiscentiae, et quidam amatus amore amicitiae. Finis autem amatus amore amicitiae perfectior est." (OTh VIII, 150).

[13] *In I Sent.*, 1, 4, (OTh I, 447). See footnote 4 of this chapter.

[14] *In II Sent.*, 15: "...est falsum quod dilectio Dei sit semper bona [et] propter debitum finem, quia aliquando potest esse mala et propter indebitum finem, ut quando amo Deum amore concupiscentiae." (OTh V, 354).

[15] *Quaest. Variae*, q. 4: "...finis quandoque accipitur pro causa finali, quae est una de quattuor causis...Alio modo accipitur finnis pro quolibet ultimo in re vel operatione, sicut dictum est, quod punctus est finis lineae." (OTh VIII, 99). See A. Garvens, *op. cit.*, p. 250.

CHAPTER IV

ultimate operation can be called an end, as for instance, in the case of the ultimate perfection a being attains.[16] Or it can be called an end by reason of the fact that it is the ultimate--and in some way the best--in a series of effects. But properly speaking, the end is not the ultimate operation, nor even the best, but precisely that something which belongs to a loved thing, on account of which something, the loved thing is loved by an agent. It may happen, of course, that the ultimate operation is that loved thing itself and the final cause; but it is not the final cause precisely, because it is the term of this operation, but because it is that which is loved in this particular case by the agent as well as the reason why the agent loves it.[17]

When we speak of God as the final cause, we certainly do not mean that he is an end in the sense of "first in intention, ultimate in execution." Such an end is always some produced term or operation. But if God were said to be an end in this sense, then he would be posterior to something else as an effect is posterior to the producer.[18] From faith we know that every effect has a final cause in the proper sense. But it does not always have a final cause distinct from the efficient cause, since God is both the efficient and final cause of many effects. From reason alone we cannot prove, either from principles which are self-evident or known from experience, that every effect has a final cause, distinct or not from the efficient cause, because we cannot prove sufficiently that every effect has a final cause. It does not follow that if something is the efficient cause of some particular effect, it is also that effect's final cause; not, vice versa.[19]

---

[16] Ockham,.*Quaest. Variae*, q. 4: "Patet, ultima operatio agentis non est causa finalis proprie loquendo, quamvis potest dici finis aliquo modo, sicut dicitur ultima perfectio acquisita rei." (OTh VIII, 103f.).

[17] *Ibid*.: "Dico quod licet ultima operatio alicuius posset aliquo modo dici finis quia est ultimum et aliquo modo optimum inter effectus causatos et ita aliquam rationem habet, quae est causa finalis--tamen proprie loquendo de causa finali nec est operatio ultima, nec etiam obiectum quod per illam attingitur inquantum tale, sed est praecise illud propter quod amatum ab agente, agens dat aliquibus esse tanquam aliquid ordinatum ad amatum. Et illud sic amatum est causa finalis facti. Quandoque autem contingit quod obiectum ultimae operationis ist illud amatum et causa finalis, non quia terminua operationis, sed amatum ab agente propte quod amans agit." (OTh VIII, 104). See A. Garvens, *op. cit.*, pp. 250 ff.

[18] Ockham, *Quodl.*, IV, 2: "...alius est finis intentus ab agente, qui quamvis sit primum in intentione, est tamen ultimum in executione; et talis finis est semper terminus productus vel operatio profucta. De isto...fine non est quaestio, quia non est dubium quin Deus non sit causa finalis cuiuscumque isto modo, quia tunc Deus esset posterior aliquo quod est ad finem, sicut effectus productus est posterior producente." (OTh IX, 301-02).

[19] *Quodl.*, IV, 1: "...dico quod aliter dicendum est ad quaestionem secundum veritatem fidei, et aliter dicerem si nullam auctoritatem reciperem. Nam primo modo loquendo, dico

GOD: THE OBJECTIVE NORM OF MORALITY

However, we can know from experience, and only from experience, that a free agent, such as man, acts for an end. And in these free acts the effect sometimes has a final cause which is distinct from the efficient cause; and sometimes these acts have a final cause which is not distinct from the efficient cause.[20] Furthermore, we can know from experience that God can be the final cause of the effects produced by man. Everyone ought to know from experience that he can perform some actions, at least, for the honor and glory of God as the final cause of irrational creation. Moreover, that the whole universe is ordered to one principle as its final cause cannot be demonstrated.[21]

As far as the attainment of God as the ultimate end in a state of beatitude is concerned, again we find Ockham using extremely cautious language. So we cannot demonstrate, he says, that the human will is capable of desiring any good beyond finite goods. The reason for this is that we cannot prove that there is any good which is infinite, though we can, as mentioned previously, know that God is the highest good to be loved above all. Likewise, we cannot prove that the human will is drawn to desire a good which is infinite--not any more than we can prove that it is inclined to desire the impossible.[22] Our will does not have a desire for an infinite good. It does not follow that since our will can de-

---

quod secundum veritatem fidei quilibet effectus habet causam finalem, proprie loquendo de causa finali; sed non semper habet causam finalem distinctam ab efficiente, quia quandoque idem est causa finalis et efficiens; sicut Deus quandoque est efficiens et finis multorum effectuum....Sed secundo modo loquendo dicerem, si nullam auctoritatem reciperem, quod non potest probari ex per se notis nec per experientiam quod quilibet effectus habet causam finalem nec distinctam nec indistinctam ab efficiente, quia non potest probari sufficienter quod quilibet effectus habet aliquam causam finalem ....ex hoc ipso quod aliquid est causa efficiens, non sequitur quod est finis, nec econverso." (OTh IX, 295-96). See A. Garvens, *op. cit.*, p. 253.

[20] *Ibid.*: ""Et probari potest evidenter per experientiam et non aliter, quod agens liberum agit propter finem; et in talibus actionibus aliquando effectus habet causam finalem distinctam ab efficiente, aliquando habet finem non distinctum ab efficiente." (OTh IX, 299).

[21] *Quodl.*, IV, 2: "...dico quod potest evidenter sciri per experientam quod Deus potest esse causa finalis effectuum productorum ab agentibus liberis hic inferius, quia quilibet experitur quod potest facere opera sua propter honorem Dei sive propter Deum tamquam propter causam finalem....dico quod non potest probari quod Deus sit causa finalis agentis naturalis sine cognitione....dico quod non potest demonstrari quod universum ordinatur ad unum principem in dependendo." (OTh IX, 303, 308).

[22] *Quodl.*, III, 1: "...dico quod non potest demonstrari quod voluntas potest velle maius bonum quolibet bono finito, quia non potest probari aliquod bonum infinitum esse. Similiter non potest probari quod voluntas inclinatur ad volendum bonum infinitum, non plus quam quod inclinatur ad volendum impossibile." (OTh IX, 207-08).

CHAPTER IV

sire a good that is greater or more perfect than any particular finite good, therefore it naturally desires an infinite good.[23]

Furthermore, since the human will is absolutely free it is capable of loving or not loving beatitude; it can seek or not seek beatitude. A persuasion for this statement is the following argument: if the intellect can judge that something is to be refused, then the will can refuse it. But it is possible for the intellect to make a false judgment that no beatitude is possible, believing that the present state is the only one possible. Consequently, the will could refuse anything that is opposed to the present state, thus refusing beatitude.[24] And even in a situation in which the intellect would judge rightly concerning the final end of man, the will could still refuse this end. For the will is an absolutely free faculty having the power to desire or refuse any object presented to it by the intellect. If the will can desire God freely, then by the same token--its freedom--it can also refuse God. If the end proposed by the intellect is not particularized but is only some good in general, it is still not necessary that the will desire it.[25] Therefore, the will can desire or not desire or refuse the ultimate end. And this would hold whether such an end is proposed in general or in particular.[26]

---

[23] *Quodl.*, VII, 15: "Aliter potest dici quod non est in voluntate inclinatio naturalis in bonum infinitum intensive. Nec sequitur omni bono finito voluntas potest maius bonum appetere, igitur naturaliter appetit bonum infinitum." (OTh IX, 754).

[24] *In I Sent.*, 1, 6: "...voluntas contingenter et libere--modo exposito--fruitur fine ultimo ostenso in universali, quia scilicet diligere beatitudinem potest et non diligere, et potest appetere sibi beatitudinem et non appetere. Ista conclusio persuadetur primo sic: illud potest esse nolitum a voluntate quod potest intellectus dictare esse nolendum; sed intellectus potest credere nullam beatitudenem esse possibilem, quia potest credere tantum statum quem de facto videmus esse sibi possibilem; ergo potest nolle omne illud quod isti statui quem videmus repugnat, et per consequens potest nolle beatitudinem." (OTh I, 503). See A. Garvens, *op. cit.*, pp. 257-58.

[25] *In IV Sent.*, q. 16: "Dico quod intellectu iudicante hoc esse finem ultimum, potest voluntas nolle illum finem. Quod probatur, quia potentia libera quae est receptiva duorum actuum contrariorum, qua ratione potest in unum et in reliquum. Sed voluntas tamquam potentia libera est receptiva nolle et velle respectu cuiuscumque obiecti, igitur si potest in velle respectu Dei, eadem ratione potest in nolle respectu Dei...osteno bono in universali, puta in aliquo conceptu communi, non est necessarium voluntatem velle illud bonum,sed potest illud nolle, quia non necessario appetit illud in quo credit se non posse quietari." (OTh VIII, 350f.).

[26] *In I Sent.*, 1, 6: "...dico quod finem ultimum, sive ostendatur in generali sive in particulari...potest absolute voluntas eum velle vel non velle vel nolle." (OTh I, 506); *In IV Sent.*, q. 16: "Sed [voluntas] non necessario vult bonum in particulari, sed potest illud nolle. Igitur non necessario tendit in bonum in universali, sed potest illud bonum nolle...dico primo quod voluntas pro statu isto potest nolle finem ultimum sive ostendatur in generali sive in speciali." (OTh VII. 351, 350). See F. Copleston, *op. cit.*, p. 102: "According to Ockham, the

GOD: THE OBJECTIVE NORM OF MORALITY

Complete beatitude, a fruition in which the will rests completely satisfied, is, as we know, unattainable in this life. Nor can we prove from reason alone that such a complete fruition will ever actually be attained in some future state or even that it is attainable by a mere creature. Ockham says that the philosophers who diligently investigated the question of the ultimate end of man could not provide a satisfactory answer to the question, hence it is not likely that we can find the answer by reason alone concerning man's last end. Moreover, all the reasons adduced to prove complete beatitude or fruition is possible can be refuted. Finally, all the Saints held that Faith is required to prove that such an end is possible for us.[27] As a matter of fact, of course, the complete fruition of the divine essence is to be posited; but this is an object of Faith, not an object of natural reason.[28]

Beatitude is to be attained through the performance of meritorious acts. These meritorious acts include, above all, the act of the love of God through the supernatural virtue of charity, an act which must not be natural, but supernatural. But how does this supernatural act of loving God differ from the natural act of loving God, if we understand the natural act to include those characteristics previously mentioned as belonging to the notion of loving God above all? In discussing this question we do not have in mind what Ockham refers to as a simple natural love of God--simple, that is without the notes of "above all" and "for Himself".[29] What we do have in mind is the love of God above all and for Himself. And this means a complete or perfect act of love, although confined to the purely natural order. It is an act of perfect love, elicited not through the supernatural virtue of charity but solely by natural powers. It seems that Ockham holds that such an act is possible, or in other

---

will is free to will or not to will happiness, the last end; it does not will it necessarily." *In I Sent.*, 1, 6: "...dico quod finem ultimum, sive ostendatur in generali sive in particulari...potest absolute voluntas eum velle vel non velle vel nolle." (OTh I, 506).

[27] *In I Sent.*, 1, 4: "...quod talis fruitio [quietans voluntatem] est nobis possibilis non potest naturaliter probari, videtur, quia philosophi investigantes diligenter quis sit finis ultimus operum humanorum non potuerunt ad illum finem attingere, igitur non est verisimile quod hoc possit naturaliter probari....Praeterea, omnes rationes adductae ad probandum hoc sunt solubiles....Praeterea, secundum omnes Sanctos, ad tenendum talem finem nobis esse possibilem requiritur fides..." (OTh I, 433). Ibid.: "Ideo dico...quod non potest naturaliter demonstrari quod talis fruitio divinae essentiae est nobis possibilis, quia istud est mere creditum; et ita non potest naturaliter demonstrari." (OTh I, 433-34; cf. 431-33).

[28] *Ibid.*: ""...dico quod de facto talis fruitio est ponenda, sed hoc tantum est creditum et non per rationem naturalem notum." (OTh I, 439).

[29] *Quodl.*, III, 14: "Posset tamen Deum diligere simplici amore et naturali, qui non est dilectio Dei super omnia..." (OTh IX, 257).

CHAPTER IV

words, that man is capable by his natural faculties of eliciting this kind of act of the love of God.[30]

We can, however, distinguish between the act of natural love by which a person loves God above all and the supernatural act of love which is elicited by means of the virtue of charity. But both acts would be basically the same as far as the essence of the act is concerned.[31] But here it is necessary to remember that an act is specified by its object, that is, the specific difference between their objects. To explain further: a natural act, one elicited by the natural faculties, and a meritorious act, one elicited through the supernatural virtue of charity, can be of the same species essentially. Even if a higher grade of virtue in the meritorious act is attained through the virtue of charity, the meritorious act is still of the same species as that of the natural act, because a specific difference in causes does not argue necessarily to a specific difference in the effects. For instance, we could have the case in which many partial causes, specifically distinct, concur in producing one, identical effect. Although the causes are distinct in this case, there is no distinction in the effect. The effect remains simply one. According to this opinion, therefore, if the perfect natural act and the meritorious act have the same object, they could not be viewed as specifically distinct. However, if the purely natural act does not have the same object as the meritorious act, then the acts are specifically distinct.[32] Here

---

[30] *In I Sent.*, 17, 2: "...dico primo, quod nec actus meritorius, nec etiam actus caritatis, excedit totam facultatem naturae humanae. Quia omnis actus caritatis quem secundum communem cursum habemus in via, est eiusdem rationis cum actu et puris naturalibus possibili, et ita ille actus non excedit facultatem naturae humanae." (OTh III, 472). See E. Hochstetter, "Viator mundi," *Franziskanische Studien*, XXXII (1950), p. 10.

[31] *Quaest. Variae*, q. 1: "Sed actus naturalis dilectionis quo diligit viator [Deum] super omnia et actus elicitur mediante caritate sunt eiusdem rationis quoad substantiam actus." (OTh VIII, 20). See G. De Lagarde, *La naissance de l'esprit laïque au déclin du moyen âge*. VI: *L'individualisme ockhamiste: l'morale et le droit* (Paris: Universitaires de France, 1946), p. 83.

[32] *Quaest. Variae.* q. 6, a. 9: "Ex istis patet quod actus naturalis et meritorius possunt esse eiusdem speciei, quia ille gradus intensus causatus mediante caritate est eiusdem speciei, quia ille gradus intensus causatus mediante caritate est eiusdem speciei cum actu naturali praecedente, quia distinctio specifica in causa non arguit distinctionem specificam in effectu. Patet de multis causis partialibus distinctis specie concurrentibus ad eundem effectum...Immo, secundum istam viam, actus pure naturalis et actus meritorius faciunt unum actum numero...Unde quando actus naturales perfecte meritorii habent idem obiectum specie, tunc potest esse unus actus specie et numero modo praedicto. Quando autem non habent idem obiectum specie, tunc necessario actus naturalis et meritorius distinguuntur specie." (OTh VIII, 292). Cf. Introductio ad OTh VIII, 19*f. See P. Vignaux, "Nominalisme," *Dictionnaire de théologie catholique*, t. XIa (Paris: Letouzey et Ané, 1931), col. 771: "Il est essentiel de pouvoir accomplir l'action droite, éviter le péché et aimer Dieu par-dessus tout, *viatoris vol-*

GOD: THE OBJECTIVE NORM OF MORALITY

Ockham seems to indicate that the circumstances of the act, which form the distinct partial objects of the natural and of the supernatural act of loving God, would lead necessarily to specifically distinct acts. The act is specified by its object. Take first this case: a person would first love God above all, but would be deficient in some required circumstance, and then afterwards this same person would elicit the same act with the required circumstances. These two acts would be specifically distinct because of the specific difference in the matter of the circumstances, which are, according to Ockham, to be considered as partial objects of the act.[33] Hence, as mentioned previously, the virtues of the Christian are specifically different from those of the pagan or atheist since the virtues of the Christian have God as their primary object, the virtues of the pagan do not.[34] Now in the same way, the natural love of God and the supernatural love of God would be specifically distinct if there is a difference in the circumstances, partial objects of the acts, according to which the acts are elicited. Ockham seems to leave the question on this hypothetical plane. What seems important to him is to insist that the natural and supernatural acts of the love of God are not specifically distinct on the basis of the acts themselves or on the basis of their causes.

Ockham's view, by the way, differs from that of Duns Scotus, although the two views are quite similar. Scotus raises the question: Are a natural act of love and a meritorious act of love specifically identical?[35] Scotus holds that the natural act does not differ specifically from the supernatural act of the love of God in its essence as such (*in esse absoluto*). However, he does concede that over and above the act

---

untas humana ex suis naturqlibus potest diligere Deum super omnia. Biel, *Collect.*, II, dist. XXVIII, q. 1, J, K; dist. XXVII, q. 1, Q." See also E. Iserloh, *op. cit.*, pp. 93, 105.

[33] Ockham, *Quaest. Variae* q. 6, a. 9: "Sicut si aliquis diligeret Deum super omnia [sed] non secundum aliquam circumstantiam requisitam, et iste idem post diligeret Deum super omnia secundum omnes circumstantias, puta secundum rectam rationem, quia et finis ultimus, et sic de aliis, hic actus pure naturalis et meritorius necessario distinguuntur, non solum numero, sed etiam specie propter distinctionem specificam circumstantiarum quae sunt obiecta partialia actus meritorii." (OTh VIII, 292f.).

[34] *Quaest. Variae* q. 7, a. 3: "...iustitia in quinto gradu, prout est virtus heroica perfecta in uno christiano, qui talem actum imperaret propter honorem Dei, non compatitur secum aliquod vitium nec defectum culpabilem propter eandem causam. Tamen virtus heroica alicuius philosophi bene compatitur aliquod vitium...quia una habet Deum pro obiecto, alia non." (OTh VIII, 354f.). *In IV Sent.*, qq. 3-4: "Et ideo nullus actus est perfecte virtuosus vel meritorius sine actu caritatis." (OTh VII, 58). Cf. *Quaest. Variae*, q. 7, a. 3 (OTh VIII, 357).

[35] Cf. Ioannes Duns Scotus, *Quaestiones quodlibetales*, q. 17: "Utrum actus dilectionis naturalis et actus dilectionis meritoriae sint eiusdem speciei," ed. F. Alluntis (Matritii 1968, 611-628).

itself, the supernatural act involves a certain property (*ratio specifica*) which does not pertain to the natural act. What is involved here is a relation to merit which distinguishes the meritorious act of loving God from the natural act of the love of God.

To return to our main point, the act of loving God above all and for Himself, we repeat, is a necessarily virtuous act. It cannot be an evil act, nor can it ever be elicited by a created will without being virtuous. Everyone is obliged always, but not at all times, (*semper sed non pro semper*), to love God above all. Consequently, whenever this act is elicited it is virtuous, since the created will is obliged by divine precept to the love of God.[36] On the other hand, no one can hate God in a virtuous way.[37] Nor can anyone hate God in a meritorious way.[38] As long as God's command to love him remains in force, the hatred of God cannot be a morally good or meritorious act.[39] An act of hating God would always be morally evil because the divine command obliges us to the love of God.[40]

In the realm of the supernatural love of God, the act of charity is the loving of God above all; the opposite of this act is to love something else more than God. This opposite act is performed by loving something which God does not will to be loved, or to hate something which he does not will to be hated.[41] The object of charity, then, is God himself and

---

[36] Ockham, *Quaest. Variae*, q. 7, a. 4: "...quia non diligit Deum super omnia, quod tamen tenetur facere." (OTh VIII, 390). *In II Sent.*, 15: "...voluntas creata obligatur ex praecepto Dei ad diligendum Deum..." (OTh V, 353). See also footnote 5 of this chapter.

[37] In I Sent., 1,1: "...nullus potest ordinate odire Deum..." (OTh I, 375).

[38] *Quaest. Variae*, q. 4: "...quia nullus meritorie odit Deum." (OTh VIII, 132).

[39] *In II Sent.*, 15: "Sed stante praecepto divino ad eorum opposita non potest aliquis tales actus [sci]. odium Dei, furari, adulterari] meritorie nec bene exercere..." (OTh V, 352). See E Bonke, "Doctrina nominalistica de fundamento ordinis moralis apud Gulielmum de Ockham et Gabrielem Biel," *Collectanea franciscana*, XIV (1944), p. 60; E. Iserloh, *op. cit.*, pp. 68-69.

[40] Ockham, *In II Sent.*, 15: "...et ideo stante illo praecepto [diligendi Deum] non potest bene odire Deum nec causare actum odiendi, sed necessario male causat malitia moris. Et hoc quia obligatur ex praecepto Dei ad actum oppositum." (OTh V, 353).

[41] *Quaest. Variae*, q. 7, a. 3: "...actus caritatis adquisitae est diligere Deum super omnia, actus autem vitiosus est plus diligere aliud quam Deum, vel diligere aliquid quod Deus non vult diligi, vel odire aliquid quod Deus vult diligi." (OTh VIII, 360).

everything that God wills to be loved, so that in the act of charity I love God and everything that he wills me to love.[42]

The hatred of God and sin are not, however, necessarily equivalent. Not all hatred of God is a sin.[43] Not every sin involves the hatred of God.[44] Not every act of hating God is a sin, because such an act of hatred elicited, for example, by an insane person would not be culpable and, therefore, not sinful. Not every sin is an act of hating God. A pagan who does not believe in the existence of God could commit an unjust act against his better judgment, right reason, and yet this pagan could not be accused of hating what he does not even believe exists. Such an act could not be called an act of hating God. However, Ockham does refer to all mortal sin as a "turning away from God," because every sinner who commits a mortal sin either does something which God does not will him to do or he does not do what God commands to be done. And so the sinner loves something else more than God; he does not love God above all, something which he is bound by God's own law to do.[45]

The act of refusing and hating God, turning away from Him, must necessarily exclude any act of loving God as well as any good act. There is, in Ockham's terms, a formal repugnance between the acts of hating and loving God. In other words, the act of hating God is formally incompatible with the act of loving Him.[46] And in the same way a turning to God by an act of charity and the turning from him by an act of hatred of him are also mutually exclusive. To love God above all and to hate

---

[42] *In II Sent.*, 7: "...obiectum caritatis sit totum istud: 'Deus et omne quod Deus vult diligi', et quod diligam Deum caritative actu elicito, ita quod aliquo uno actu diligam Deum et omne quod Deus vult diligi a me, quod est possibile." (OTh VI, 211).

[43] *In II Sent.*, 15: "Item, odium [Dei] non est formaliter peccatum..." (OTh V, 343).

[44] *Quaest. Variae*, q. 7, a. 4: "...non omne peccatum etiam commissum est actus odiendi Deum." (OTh VIII, 390).

[45] *Quaest. Variae*, q. 7, a. 4: "Potest enim aliquis velle facere opera iniusta contra rectam rationem, et nec diligere Deum nec odire. Sed ideo dicitur omne peccatum avertere a Deo, quia omnis peccans mortaliter vel facit aliquid quod Deus non vult eum facere...vel non facit quod Deus vult fieri quia Deus praecipit illud fieri; et sic talis videtur diligere aliud a Deo plus quam Deum, et sic avertitur a Deo..." (OTh VIII, 390).

[46] *In II Sent.*, 15: "Et ille actus [odiendi Deum] non compatitur secum actum diligendi Deum nec aliquem actum bonum propter repugnantiam formalem inter illos actus. Et stante illo actu et conservato a Deo totaliter, non potest voluntas creata in oppositum de potentia sua absoluta. Et ideo quamdiu stat iste actus, est voluntas obstinata, sic quod non potest oppositum velle." (OTh V, 342).

CHAPTER IV

him are always contrary acts.[47] However, in the case of turning to God by an act of charity and the turning away from him by an act of loving a creature whom God does not wish to be loved (for instance, by an act of fornication), Ockham does not consider these as mutually exclusive acts, neither formally nor materially. But as far as the acts themselves are concerned, they can be reconciled. They are incompatible only by reason of some extrinsic cause, that is, by a commandment of God which would prescribe that this creature is not to be loved. And so if someone loves this person, then God is not loved above all, because the will of God is opposed. But the incompatibility between the love of the creature and the love of God arises only from the command of God or, in other words, from something extrinsic to the acts themselves. This is evident, because if the law of God would be revoked, then the love of this creature and the love of God would no longer be incompatible. And if the law would actually prescribe that this creature is to be loved, then not only are the love of God and the love of this creature compatible, but the love of the creature would even be a meritorious act in this case.[48]

In summary of the main points of this section, the following fundamental ideas bear repeating. In attempting to analyze the notion of "Love God," we find the first characteristic of such a love is that this must be a love of God above all. Nothing must be loved more than God who is the highest good. This love of God above all necessarily includes the notion that he is loved for Himself. For if he is loved only because of something else, then this other being is loved more than God, the highest good. Such an unworthy type of love would be specifically distinct from the true love of God, since the primary objects of each act are distinct. True love is a love of friendship, a love of God in and for Himself; the other type of love, the love of desire, is an unworthy love of God. Although we cannot know from reason alone that man can desire

---

[47] *Quaest. Variae*, q. 7, A. 4: "Si quaeras utrum conversio ad Deum actu caritativo et aversio ab eo actu odiendi Deum opponuntur formaliter, dico quod sic, quia diligere Deum super omnia et odire Deum sunt actus contrarii." (OTh VIII, 391).

[48] *Quaest. Variae*, q. 7, a. 4: "Si quaeras de conversione ad Deum actu caritativo et aversione actu quo diligitur creatura quam Deus non vult diligi, puta actum fornicandi, sic non repugnant illi formaliter et naturaliter inter se, sed compatiuntur se in eodem quantum est ex natura actuum; sed solum repugnant per causam extrinsecam, puta per Deum ordinantem talem creaturam nullo modo a voluntate creata diligi; et ita voluntas diligens talem creaturam non diligit Deum super omnia, quia si sic, non diligeret aliquam creaturam quam Deus odit vel vult non diligi; et ideo propter ordinationem talis causae extrinsecae videtur solum repugnantia. Quod patet, quia si lex statuta revocaretur, iam isti actus diligendi compaterentur se in eodem; et si lex illa praeciperet illam creaturam diligi, tunc posset non tantum simul stare cum alio actu, sed tunc meritorie diligeret illam creaturam." (OTh VIII, 391). See A. Garvens, *op. cit.*, p. 268; E. Iserloch, *op. cit.*, pp. 66-67.

GOD: THE OBJECTIVE NORM OF MORALITY

the attainment or the possession of God in and through the love of Him, we do know from experience that man can elicit acts of loving God. The love of God may be a purely natural act or it may be a supernatural act which is elicited through the supernatural virtue of charity. These two acts, as far as the acts themselves are concerned, are not distinct; but they would be specifically distinct if any of the circumstances which constitute the partial objects of these acts are distinct. Even the natural love of God, however, (and *a fortiori*, the supernatural act) is an act which is necessarily virtuous, so that, given this act, it cannot be evil or indifferent. The act of loving God is called by Ockham "the first the principle or the source, of all good acts."[49]

2. GOD WILLS

We are now in a position to turn to the second part of our formula: "Love God and will what he wills." In this second part we will take up the meaning of the phrase "God wills." The main topics to be treated here are: Ockham's teaching on the absolute simplicity of God; God's will toward creatures; and his freedom and omnipotence. This, indeed, covers a wide and deep field. The field will of necessity have to be limited to those elements which bear immediately on the present topic of Ockham's theory of ethics. Accordingly, the treatment will be selective rather than exhaustive.

First let us consider the absolute identity in God. As E. Bonke points out:

> Apart from the real distinction between the Three Persons in God and the formal distinction between the relations in the Holy Trinity, there is no distinction, either virtual or formal, between God's perfections and qualities, between his intellect and will, being and act. All of these notions refer to the one, identical, most simple divine essence.[50]

---

[49] Ockham, *Quodl.*, III, 14. See note five of this chapter.

[50] E. Bonke, *op. cit.*, p. 60: "Si excipiuntur distinctio realis inter Personas divinas et distinctio formalis inter diversas relationes in SS. Trinitate, in Deo nulla datur differentia neque virtualis necque formalis inter perfectiones et qualitates, inter intellectum et voluntatem, inter esse et agere. Omnes notiones unam eandemque simplicissimam divinam essentiam indicant."

CHAPTER IV

In Ockham's own words, "...the divine essence is really identical with anything that is really God."[51] And again he says, "It is impossible for anything in God to differ by reason from anything in God."[52]

The divine will is identical with the divine essence.[53] The divine will is in no way posterior to the divine essence, any more than the essence itself is posterior to the essence.[54] Nor is the essence any more the cause of creatures than is the divine will (nor vice versa), for there is no distinction of any kind between the divine essence and the divine will.[55] So that in every way that the essence is identical with the essence, the essence is also identical with the will. And therefore, if the divine will is the cause of creatures so is the divine essence.[56] And in addition, an act of the will is not any more distinct from the will than the will itself is distinct from the will.[57]

---

[51] *In I Sent.*, prolog., 2: "Sed essentia divina est eadem realiter cum quolibet quod est realiter Deus..." (OTh I, 111).

[52] *In I Sent.*, 19, 1: "...impossibile est aliquid quod est in Deo differre secundum rationem a quocumque quod est in Deo." (OTh IV 6).

[53] *In I Sent.*, 45, un.: "...essentia divina nullo modo distinguitur a voluntate divina..." (OTh IV 663). *Ibid.:* "...nulla penitus est distinctio inter essentiam et voluntatem nec inter voluntatem et intellectum..." (OTh IV, 664). *In I Sent.*, 46, 1: "...immo etiam divina voluntas nullo modo distinguitur ab essentia." (OTh IV 671). P. Boehner notes in *Ockham. Philosophical Writings*, p. xlix: "Once more, we have to remind the reader that God's will is identical with God's intellect, wisdom and love. The one living God, the omnipotent and merciful God, is the supreme rule of ethics." See also P. Vignaux, *op. cit.*, col. 763: "La volonté n'a aucun privilège sur l'entendement. Quand on pense au seul entendement divin, il faut penser qu'il est Dieu, en son acte indépendant de tout le reste; de même, quand on pense à la seule volonté divine, elle est Dieu et rien ne la précède; quand on pense a l'entendement et à la volonté à la fois, il faut concevoir qu'en Dieu ils sont un: la doctrine occamiste de l'entendement et de la volonté est dominée par cette pensee qu'en Dieu tout est également parfait et absolument simple." See also O. Suk, "The Connection of Virtues according to Ockham," *Franciscan Studies*, X (1950), p. 28.

[54] Ockham, *In I Sent.*, d. 10, q. 1: "...dico quod voluntas nullo modo est posterior quam essentia, non plus quam essentia sit posterior essentia." (OTh III, 328).

[55] *In I Sent.*, 45, un.: "...dico quod non magis est essentia causa creaturarum quam voluntas nec e converso..." (OTh IV, 664). See also E. Bonke, *op. cit.*, pp. 61-62.

[56] Ockham, *Ibid:* "...sed omni modo identitatis quo essentia est eadem essentiae etiam essentia est eadem voluntati; igitur si voluntas sit causa, essentia erit causa." (OTh IV, 663).

[57] *In I Sent.*, d. 10, q. 1: "...nec plus distinguitur actus voluntatis a voluntate quam distinguitur voluntas a voluntate. Verumtamen non est forte propria locutio 'actus voluntatis divinae,' sed magis proprie dicendum est 'actus volendi vel velle quod est voluntas divina.'" (OTh III, 329).

GOD: THE OBJECTIVE NORM OF MORALITY

It should be obvious also that such distinctions in the divine will, as, for example, the distinction between God's will of good pleasure and his signified will (*voluntas beneplaciti and voluntas signi*), do not refer to any distinct realities in God or in the will of God. God's will is absolute in its unity and simplicity.; Ockham points out that the term "will" (*voluntas*) is often used in an improper sense, just as the term "God wills" is often used in a wide sense in the Sacred Scriptures. When the Scriptures tell us that "God wills this," it may be equivalent to saying "God commands this"' or the phrase "this is against the will of God" may be equivalent to saying "this is against a commandment of God." And so the term "will" is often not taken in its strict sense but is equivalent to such words as "command," "prohibition," "counsel," "permission," "fulfillment." The same may be said of the phrase "God wills." It is not the will of God which is multiple and different; but there are different terms for speaking of the absolutely simple will of God and these terms are often to be understood in different ways. From this discussion it should be apparent that nothing multiple or distinct is involved here except the ways in which the term "will" or its corresponding words are used and understood.[58] We also spoke in a previous chapter of the different usages of the term "divine volition" in connection with the question of praxis on the part of God. There it was brought out that the term "divine volition" could signify not only the divine will itself but also connote its activity in relation to a creature.[59]

Although the will of God is absolutely one and simple, it is commonly distinguished according to a twofold division: the will of good pleasure (*voluntas beneplaciti*) and the will of expression (*voluntas signi*). The former refers to the divine will in so far as it remains an intrinsic act; the latter refers to the divine will in so far as it is manifested by some sign externally.[60] The will of expression is further subdivided into the will of prohibition, precept, counsel, fulfillment and

---

[58] *II Sent.*, 46, 1: "...ista distinctio non est alicuius quod est realiter in Deo et realiter Deus, quia in Deo non est aliquo modo multiplex voluntas, immo etiam divina voluntas nullo modo distinguitur ab essentia. Sed istae distinctiones sunt nominum et dictionum quae significant ipsam voluntatem quae Deus est....'Non est Dei voluntas diversa, sed locutio diversa est de voluntate, quia nomine voluntatis diversa accipit.'...Ex quibus patet quod nihil est ibi multiplex nisi hoc nomen 'voluntas' vel verbum sibi correspondens." (OTh IV, 671-72). Cf. *Ibid.*, 6 (OTh III, 89).

[59] *In I Sent.*, 35, 6 (OTh IV, 516). See chapter II.

[60] *In I Sent.*, 46, 1: "...dicitur communiter quod voluntas Dei est duplex: scilicet voluntas beneplaciti et voluntas signi, quae distinguitur in quinque: prohibitionem, praeceptum, consilium, impletionem et permissionem. (OTh IV, 671).

CHAPTER IV

permission.[61] When we speak, then, of willing what God wills, we are concerned with what we term the will of expression, especially the will of precept and prohibition. However, it must always be understood, of course, that these are merely different terms which all correspond to one and the same reality, the one absolutely simple will of God, or equivalently, his divine essence.

The divine will is not distinct in any way from the divine essence. Neither is the divine will in any way distinct from the divine intellect.[62] As a consequence, whatever would pertain to the divine intellect would also pertain to the divine will, and vice versa.[63] So when we say that God knows evil but does not will evil, we make this distinction not because of any distinction or lack of identity in God but because of a distinction which is made in reference to creatures. The phrase "God knows evil" merely means that God permits something to be done by a creature which the creature should not do. The phrase "to will evil" means to do something which must not be done. Consequently, it would imply that God is a creature, for only a creature can do something that must not be done.[64] God, on the other hand, is not obliged to anyone or to anything.[65] "God wills evil" must be a meaningless statement. In any case, the phrases "God knows evil" and "God does not will evil" connote in a different way, but not because of any distinction between the in-

---

[61] This seems to be a familiar Scholastic hexameter: "Praecipit et prohibet, permittit, consulit, implet." See J. Pohle, *Dogmatic Theology*, Vol. I: *God: His Knowability, Essence, and Attributes*, ed. A. Preuss (St. Louis: Herder, 1942), p. 438. For a further development of these divisions see, for example, A. Tanquerey, *Synopsis theologiae dogmaticae*, t. II: *De Fide, de Deo uno et trino, de Deo creante et elevante, de Verbo Incarnato* (12a ed.; Rome, Desclee, 1921), pp. 287-288.

[62] Ockham, *In I Sent.*, 45, un.: "...nulla penitus est distinctio inter essentiam et voluntatem nec inter voluntatem et intellectum..." (OTh IV 664). See E. Gilson and P. Boehner, *Christliche Philosophie*, p. 622; J. Hirschberger, *op. cit.*, p. 460.

[63] Ockham, *In I Sent.*, 2, 1: "...concedo quod quidquid convenit illi rei quae est intellectus divinus, convenit illi rei quae est voluntas divina, et e converso." (OTh II, 44).

[64] *Ibid.:* "...Deus intelligit mala et non vult, non propter aliquam distinctionem vel non-identitatem a parte Dei, sed propter non-identitatem a parte creaturae....Similiter, per istam 'Deus vult malum,' importatur totum istud 'Deus facit aliquid quod non debet,' et per consequens eo ipso importatur quod sit creatura, ita quod per faciens malum importatur res faciens aliquid quod non debet, quod potest soli creaturae convenire. Per istam autem 'Deus intelligit malum,' non imporatur nisi quod Deus facit vel permittit aliquid fieri ab aliquo creato quod non deberet illud facere." (OTh II, 47-48). See E. Bonke, *op. cit.*, p. 61.

[65] Ockham, *In II Sent.*, 15: "...Deus autem nulli tenetur nec obligatur tanquam debitor...." (OTh V, 343).

tellect and the will of God.[66] Nor does it make sense to say that the will of God depends on the divine intellect for guidance in right action or that the divine will needs some norm outside of itself so that it will not fall into error. To be sure, our own will, a will which can act virtuously or evilly, does need such a directive faculty so that it will always act rightly. But the divine will does not need such direction. It is its own directive norm and cannot act evilly.[67]

Furthermore, because of this complete identity of intellect and will in God, the phrase "nothing is produced by an act of the will unless it is foreknown," though it may be understood correctly in reference to any of God's creatures, is simply false regarding God Himself. For in God an act of the will, an act of the intellect, and the will itself, are all identical.[68]

The will of expression necessarily involves a reference to creatures. When the phrase "God wills" is used in this sense, it is termed God's will toward creatures (*ad extra*). But can we prove that God wills, or even knows, anything outside of Himself? Ockham answers that we cannot prove sufficiently, or strictly, from natural reason alone that God either knows or wills anything outside of Himself. There does not seem to be any necessity for holding that he knows anything outside of Himself. The reason for saying that God does know creatures is based on the argument that God acts rationally and therefore knows what he creates. But this argument presupposes that God is the sufficient cause of things, a proposition that cannot be proved sufficiently from natural

---

[66] *In I Sent.*, 2, 1: "Et ita aliud connotatur per unum et per aliud [i.e., Deus intelligit mala et non vult]; et propter hoc sine omni non-identitate a parte Dei possunt ista verificari." (OTh II, 48).

[67] Ockham, *Quaest. Variae*, q. 8: "...voluntas divina non indiget aliquo dirigente quia ipsa est prima regula directiva et non potest male agere. Sed voluntas nostra est huiusmodi quod potest recte et non recte agere. Igitur indiget aliqua ratione recta dirigente." (OTh VIII, 410).

[68] *In I Sent.*, 10, 1: "Ad tertium dico quod illa propositio 'nihil producitur actu voluntatis nisi praecognitum' potest intelligi dupliciter. Vel quod actus voluntatis elicitus sit quo voluntas producit, et sic potest concedi in creaturis, quia tale productum est volitum, et nihil est volitum a voluntate creata nisi praecognitum. Tamen in Deo est simpliciter falsa, quia in Deo actus volutatis et actus intellectus et voluntas sunt omnibus modis idem, nec plus distinguitur actus voluntatis a voluntate quam distinguitur voluntas a voluntate...Aliter potest intelligi quod quidquid producitur actu voluntatis est praecognitum, quia quidquid est a voluntate est praecognitum. Et sic est falsa etiam in creaturis, quia volitio quae producitur a voluntate non est praecognita." (OTh III, 329).

CHAPTER IV

reason. So the argument to prove that God knows things outside of himself is defective, at least as far as a strict proof is concerned.[69]

Similarly, we cannot prove from natural reason alone that God wills anything outside of Himself. Consequently, we cannot prove either that the will of God is always fulfilled. We cannot prove that everything willed by God is done by Him; nor can we prove that everything God wills someone else to do is done by this other being.[70] It comes out to this that basically the proofs for the propositions "God wills something outside of Himself" and, likewise, "The will of God is always fulfilled" depend on the proposition that "God is the immediate cause of all things"-- a proposition that cannot be proved, in the strict sense, from natural reason.[71]

A third fundamental idea that should be considered here because of its importance in connection with Ockham's ethical thought is the freedom and omnipotence of God. If we cannot prove that God wills anything outside Himself, then neither can we prove that he wills anything freely outside Himself. And if God is necessitated in regard to Himself, what then becomes of God's freedom, that is, as far as a proof from natural reason is concerned?

First, regarding the notion of necessity, it should be mentioned that there are really two kinds of necessity to be considered here: absolute and conditional. Something is absolutely necessary if it would be a contradiction for its opposite to be true. The statement "God exists" would be an example of a proposition that is absolutely necessary, because it is impossible that this proposition should be false and its contradictory true. Conditional necessity, on the other hand, occurs when a conditional proposition is necessary although both the antecedent

---

[69] *Quodl.*, II, 2: "...dico quod non potest sufficienter probari quod Deus intelligit aliquid extra se vel vult aliquid extra se, quia nulla videtur necessitas ponendi quod intelligat alia a se, cum non possit probari sufficienter quod Deus sit causa efficiens alicuius, cum tamen hoc videtur esse praecisa ratio, scilicet efficientia, ad ponendum Deum intelligere alia a se, ut cognoscat illud quod agit et sic rationabiliter agat." (OTh IX, 115).

[70] *In I Sent.*, 46, 2: "...dico quod si possit probari quod Deus vult alia a se, potest probari quod voluntas divina semper impletur. Ita scilicet quod si vult aliquid fieri a se, fit a se; si vult aliquid fieri ab alio, fit ab alio; si vult aliquid fieri tam a se quam ab alio, fit tam a se quam ab alio. Et eodem modo est de nolito a Deo. Sed non potest probari quod omne volitum a Deo fit a Deo, nec quod omne volitum a Deo fit ab alio. Et consimiliter est dicendum de nolito." (OTh IV, 677-78).

[71] *In I Sent.*, 46, 2: "...quia non potest probari naturali ratione quod Deus est causa omnium immediata, ideo non potest ratione naturali probari quod voluntas divina semper impletur a se. Cum hoc tamen stat quod possit ratione naturali probari quod voluntas divina semper impletur a se vel ab alio, et hoc si possit probari quod Deus vult alia a se." (OTh IV, 679).

and the consequent are contingent. For instance, this proposition is necessary: "If Peter is predestined, he will be saved." Both the antecedent and the consequent are contingent, but the proposition as a whole is necessary. When Ockham denies, then, that God acts toward creatures with any necessity, he understands this to mean "any absolute necessity." He admits a conditional necessity, as, for instance, in the matter of God's accepting an act as meritorious if it is in accord with the conditions that he has set down for a meritorious act.[72] In this connection the following statement of A. Pegis can certainly be viewed as an oversimplification of Ockham's position regarding liberty and necessity in God:

> If we say that there is necessity without liberty in the God of Aristotle and Avicenna, then we must add that there is necessity with liberty in the God of St. Thomas and liberty without necessity in the God of William of Ockham.[73]

We must remember that in speaking of any necessity in the will of God we have to distinguish whether the object of his will is himself or some creature. The divine will wills its own goodness necessarily and absolutely. God is not free in this but he wills his goodness just as

---

[72] *Quodl.*, VI, 2: "...dico quod duplex est necessitas: scilicet absoluta, et ex suppositione. Necessitas absoluta est quando aliquid est simpliciter necessarium, ita quod eius oppositum esse verum includit contradictionem. Et sic haec est absolute necessaria 'homo est risibilis,' 'Deus est' et huiusmodi, quia contradictio et quod haec sint falsa et eorum opposita sint vera. Necessitas ex suppositione est quando aliqua condicionalis est necessaria, quamvis tam antecedens quam consequens sit contingens. Sicut haec est necessaria 'si Petrus est praedestinatus Petrus salvabitur,' et tamen tam antecedens quam consequens est contingens. Vel quando aliqua talis consequentia est necessaria, tunc dicitur necessitas ex suppositione....dico quod Deus non de necessitate acceptat actum elicitum ex caritate creata, loquendo de necessitate absoluta, sed potest de potentia sua absoluta illum actum non acceptare, accipiendo 'non acceptare' pro non velle dare alicui vitam aeternam. Quod probo, quia secundum Sanctos Deus nihil agit ad extra de necessitate, nec aliquid aliud a se vult necessario; igitur quocumque actu posito in quocumque viatore, Deus non de necessitate naturae vult sibi dare vitam aeternam, et per consequens potest talem actum non acceptare....dico quod de necessitate acceptat actum elicitum ex caritate, loquendo de necessitate ex suppositione, quia haec consequentia est necessaria: Deus ordinavit et instituit per leges iam datas quod talis actus sic elicitus sit acceptandus, igitur Deus illum actum iam elicitum acceptat; quia antecedens non potest esse verum sine consequente, et tamen tam antecedens quam consequens est simpliciter contingens." (OTh IX, 590-91).
See J. Scotus, *Quaestiones in primum librum Sententiarum*, d. 38, q. un., n. 4 in *op. cit.*, tom. X, pp. 604-605. See also E. Iserloh, *op. cit.*, pp. 72-73; P. Vignaux, *op. cit.*, col. 763 ff.

[73] A. Pegis, "Some Recent Interpretations of Ockham," *Speculum*, XXIII (1948), p. 454.

CHAPTER IV

naturally, that is, necessarily, as he knows his goodness.[74] But this type of necessity does not destroy, as a matter of fact, the perfection of liberty in the divine will, even though it is repugnant to liberty in reference to that concerning which there is necessity. But keeping in mind what was said above concerning the absolute identity in God, we should not imagine that liberty is something or other which is real and distinct from the will of God itself. Actually it is a connotative term, signifying the divine will itself, or an intellectual nature, and connoting that something can be done by that will in a contingent manner. Because of this connotation liberty cannot be applied to the divine essence in reference to itself. That is, it is impossible for liberty to be correctly predicated of the divine essence or the divine will as long as the essence or the will only refer to God Himself. It would not be true to say that the will freely wills itself or the divine essence.[75] The will of God is free, but it is not free in reference to everything.[76]

But outside himself (ad extra), in reference to creatures, God does not act freely. In his acts regarding creatures God is free from any necessity of the absolute type.[77] The proposition, however, that God acts

---

[74] Ockham, In I Sent., d. 10, q. 2: "Ad aliud dico quod voluntas divina necessario vult bonitatem suam, non tamen libere, sed ita naturaliter sicut naturaliter intelligit bonitatem suam." (OTh III, 343).

[75] In I Sent., 10, 2: "Ad aliud dico quod firmitas non tollit perfectionem et ideo non tollit libertatem, quamvis repugnet libertati respectu eiusdem respectu cuius est necessitas...Imaginantur enim ac si libertas esset aliquid unum reale distinctum aliquo modo ex natura rei a voluntate, vel non omnino idem cum voluntate, quod tamen non est verum. Sed est unum nomen connotativum importans ipsam voluntatem vel naturam intellectualem connotando aliquid contingenter posse fieri ab eadem. Et ideo repugnat essentiae divinae respectu sui ipsius, hoc est, impossibile est quod vere praedicetur de essentia vel voluntate divina respectu sui ipsius, sic dicendo scilicet 'voluntas libere vult se vel essentiam divinam.'" (OTh II, 344).

[76] In I Sent., 10, 2: "...concedo quod voluntas est potentia libera, non tamen respectu cuiuscumque, sed respectu illius ad quod contingenter se habet." (OTh III, 345).

[77] Quodl., VI, q. 22: "Quidquid Deus agit ad extra, contingenter agit et non necessario...Secundum Sanctos Deus nihil agit ad extra de necessitate." (OTh IX, 589f.). The necessity involved here is "absolute necessity" as is evident from the context. See note 72 of this chapter. There are parallel expressions in Scotus. For example, Ordinatio, I, d. 2, p. 1, qq. 1-2, n. 149 [textus interpolatus]: "Deus est libere et voluntarie agens respectu omnium quae sunt extra ipsum." (ed. Vaticana, II, 215); Ibid., d. 39, qq 1-5 [Appendix A]: "...voluntas divina nihil aliud necessario respicit pro obiecto, ab essentia sua; ad quodlibet ergo aliud contingenter se habet, ita quod posset esse oppositi." (ed. Vaticana, VI, 427); Ibid., II, d. 1, q. 1, n. 14: "...nihil enim aliud a se vult voluntas divina necessario." (ed. Vaticana, VII, 8); Ibid., II, d. 1, q. 2, n. 70: "...Deus causat 'omnia quae sunt ad extra' contingenter." (ed. Vaticana, VII, 39). See also G. Stratenwerth, Die Naturrechtslehre des Johannes Duns Scotus (Göttingen: Vandenhoeck aund Ruprecht, 1951), pp. 6-7; 45-46.

GOD: THE OBJECTIVE NORM OF MORALITY

freely cannot be demonstrated by natural reason alone.[78] In this case it would not be of any help to prove that an agent acts through the will, for this is not the same as proving that he acts contingently and non-necessarily. To prove that God produces creatures through an act of his will is not the same as proving that he produces them freely. The pagan philosophers, for example, held that God produces creatures through an act of his will, but they still held that this was done necessarily.[79] Ockham here criticizes the arguments of St. Thomas.[80] In Ockham's opinion the arguments which St. Thomas used to prove that God acts freely do not really touch the essential point. The third argument of St. Thomas, for example, if it proves anything at all, only proves that God produces creatures by his intellect and will. But from the fact that creatures are produced from the intellect and will of God it does not follow necessarily that he produces them freely.[81] The real point at issue is not whether God acts through his intellect and will, but whether he acts freely. These are clearly different questions. And this can be seen from the fact that St. Thomas himself admits that the divine will acts in a necessary manner toward itself and, moreover, even the human will seeks God naturally, that is, necessarily and not freely. Likewise, when

---

[78] Ockham, *In II Sent.*, 3-4: "Ideo quod Deus sit causa libera respectu omnium, tenendum est tanquam creditum, quia non potest demonstrari per aliquam rationem ad quam non responderet unus infidelis. Persuaderi tamen potest sic..." (OTh V, 55) *In I Sent.*, 42, un.: "Et ita cum non possit ratione naturali probari quod Deus sit causa contingens, non potest ratione naturali probari quod Deus potest causare immediate et se solo omnem effectum producibilem." (OTh IV, 618). A. Pegis points this out in *op. cit.*, p. 454: "Belief is the only ground on which Ockham holds that God is a free creator--a belief which has, as one of its motives, the convictions that the philosophers could refute every argument for God as a free creator." See by the same author, "Necessity and Liberty: An Historical Note on St. Thomas Aquinas," *New Scholasticism*, XV (1941), p. 29. See also G. De Lagarde, *op. cit.*, p. 54.

[79] Ockham, *In I Sent.*, 43, 1: "Sed non est probatum quod omne agens per voluntatem tamquam per principium agendi contingenter agit et non naturaliter. Igitur per istam rationem non est probatum quod Deus non producit creaturas per necessitatem naturae....Igitur ista consequentia non valet, secundum istos [philosophos infideles], 'Deus producit per voluntatem, igitur non producit de necessitate naturae..'..Igitur probare quod Deus producit creatuas per voluntatem, non est probare quod non producit de necessitate naturae." (OTh IV, 625-26).

[80] St. Thomas, *De potentia*, q. 3, a. 15, gives four principal arguments to discuss the question: "Utrum res processerint a Deo per necessitatem naturae vel per arbitrium voluntatis." For a further explanation of the controversy between St. Thomas and Ockham consult A. Pegis' article, "Necessity and Liberty," pp. 18-45.

[81] Ockham, *In I Sent.*, 43, 1: "Similiter tertia ratio [argumentum S. Thomae] non valet. Quia si aliquid probat, praecise probat quod Deus producit illas per intellectum et voluntatem. Sed ex hoc non sequitur evidenter quod non producit eas per necessitatem naturae." (OTh IV, 627).

the intellect judges, the will must necessarily follow its judgment. All this serves to indicate the difference between the question of whether God acts through his will and the question of whether God acts freely.[82]

Though he holds that we cannot demonstrate that God acts freely, Ockham does present this argument by way of persuasion. Suppose we have a non-impedible cause which equally considers all or an infinite number of possibilities. Now this cause acts concerning one of these possibilities but not regarding another of them. Such a cause is contingent and free. From the fact that it is not impeded and that it equally considers all the possibilities, there would be no other reason except its freedom to explain why the cause would produce one rather than the other possibility. God is this kind of cause in regard to all things that he produces.[83] Therefore, in all his acts regarding creatures God acts freely.

Thus Ockham admits, by way of persuasion, that God is free from necessity--absolute necessity--regarding creatures.[84] God is not bound or obligated to anyone or to anything.[85] Whatever God wills concerning creatures is not only willed freely but justly.[86] And as he creates any

---

[82] *In II Sent.*, 3-4: "Quaestio non quaerit utrum Deus agat per intellectum et voluntatem, sed utrum libere, et hoc non est idem quaerere. Quia per eum [S. Thomam] voluntas divina et nostra vult Deum naturaliter, et sic quando aliquid iudicatur ab intellectu, voluntas necessario vult illud. Igitur non est idem quaere unum et aliud. Item Philosophus tenet quod producit per intellectum et voluntatem, et tamen necessario et non libere." (OTh V, 52-53.

[83] *In II Sent.*, 3-4: "Persuaderi tamen potest sic: omnis causa non impedibilis aequaliter respiciens multa sive infinita si agat unum illorum in aliquo instanti et non aliud, est causa contingens et libera. Quia ex quo non est impedibilis et aequaliter respicit omnia et aeque primo, non videtur ratio quare plus producit unum quam aliud nisi propter libertatem suam. Sed Deus est huiusmodi causa respectu omnium producibilium ab eo ab aeterno, igitur etc." (OTh V, 55-56).

[84] *In I Sent.*, 35, 6: "...tamen in potestate voluntatis divinae est producere creaturam contingenter, et omnia alia facere circa creaturas est in potestate voluntatis divinae. Ideo ista productio potest aliquo modo dici praxis, quia scilicet contingenter est a voluntate divina..." (OTh IV, 512).

[85] *In II Sent.*, 3-4: "...obligatio non cadit in Deo, quia ipse ad nihil faciendum obligatur." (OTh V, 59). *In II Sent.*, 15: "...Deus autem nulli tenetur nec obligatur tanquam debitor, et ideo non potest facere quod non debet facere nec facere quod debet facere." (OTh V, 343). *Quaest. Variae*, q. 1: "...quia [Deus] nullius debitor est." (OTh VIII, 26). *Ibid.*, q. 8: "...quia voluntas divina non tenetur velle oppositum eo quod ad nihil obligatur." (OTh VIII, 435). *In IV Sent.*, qq. 3-4: "Et ratio est quia Deus nullius est debitor..." (OTh VII, 55). *Ibid.*, qq. 10-11: "Deus autem ad nihil faciendum vel non faciendum obligatur." (OTh VII, 226).

[86] *In I Sent.*, d. 14, q. 2: "...Deus multa agit per plura quae posset facere per pauciora, nec est alia causa quaerenda. Et ex hoc ipso quod vult, convenienter fit et non frustra."

GOD: THE OBJECTIVE NORM OF MORALITY

creature that he wills to create, so also he can do anything he wishes concerning creatures. By the very fact that God does anything, it is done justly and well.[87] How important these ideas are for an ethics which is fundamentally based on the will of God is immediately evident. The absolute freedom of an omnipotent God certainly has to be given serious consideration in examining the role of this God as the supreme lawgiver for the human race.[88] These statements, therefore, lead to a more detailed discussion of another fundamental idea in Ockham's thought: the question of God's omnipotence.

The doctrine of divine omnipotence occupies a prominent position in Ockham's writings, but whether it constitutes the starting point of his philosophy with the result that we can legitimately characterize that philosophy as a "philosophy of divine omnipotence" is another question. The author of the *Tractatus de principiis theologiae* takes as his starting point the principle of divine omnipotence.[89] L. Baudry in his publication of the critical edition of the above work notes:

(OTh III, 432). *Ibid.*, d. 17, q. 3: "...eo ipso quod ipse [Deus] vult, bene et iuste factum est." (OTh III, 478). *Quaest. Variae*, q. 8: "...voluntas divina non indiget aliquo dirigente quia ipsa est prima regula directiva et non potest male agere." (OTh VIII, 410); *In IV Sent.*, qq. 10-11: "...et ideo eo ipso quod Deus vult hoc, [hoc] est iustum fieri." (OTh VII, 198). See G. Biel, *Repertorium...super quattuor libros Sententiarum* (Tuebingen, 1527), lib. I, d. 14, q. 2, F. See also P. Boehner, *Ockham. Selected Writings*, p. xlix; A. Garvens, *op. cit.*, p. 262; O. Suk, *op. cit.*, pp. 27-28; S. Tornay, *Ockham: Studies and Selections* (LaSalle, Ill.: Open Court Publ., 1938), pp. 73-74; P. Vignaux, "Occam," *Dictionnaire de théologie catholique*, t. XIa (Paris: Letouzey et Ané, 1931), col. 879-880.

[87] Ockham, *In IV Sent.*, qq. 3-4: "...sicut Deus creat creaturam quamlibet ex mera voluntate sua, ita ex mera voluntate sua potest facere de creatura sua quidquid sibi placet...Et ratio est quia Deus nullius est debitor...Et ideo eo ipso quod Deus aliquid facit, iuste factum est." (OTh VII, 55). See H. Meyer, *Geschichte der abendländischen Weltanschauung*, III. *Die Weltanschauung des Mittelalters* (Paderborn: Schoeningh, 1948), p. 318: "Der göttliche Wille bedarf keiner Direktion und Determination, er ist schlechthin die oberste Regel für Sittlichkeit und Recht." See also J. Scotus, *Reportata Parisiensia*, IV, d. 46, q. 4, n. 8 in *op. cit.*, tom. XXIV, p. 584: "Ex hoc enim quod aliquid competit voluntati divinae est rectum, et quamcunque actionem Deus possit habere absolute est recta; sed quodlibet, quod non includit contradictionem, non repugnat voluntati divinae absolute; igitur quidquid Deus faciat, vel agat, erit rectum et justum."

[88] See L. Baudry (ed.), *op. cit.*, pp. 37; 39-40; 42-43; R. Guelluy, *Philosophie et théologie chez Guillaume d'Ockham* (Louvain: Nauwelaerts, 1947), p. 365; H. Meyer, *op. cit.*, p. 317.

[89] L. Baudry (ed.), *op. cit.*, p. 45: "Deus potest facere omne quod fieri non includit contradictionem. Nota quod non dico quod Deus potest facere omne quod non includit contradictionem quia tunc posset facere se; ipse enim non includit contradictionem; sed potest facere omne quod fieri non includit contradictionem, id est, omne illud de quo ad hanc propositionem: ipsum fit, non sequitur contradictio."

CHAPTER IV

According to the author of the Tractatus two principles are dominant in Ockham's philosophy. The first: God can do anything which does not involve a contradiction in his doing it. This is a clear, simple statement of the doctrine of God's omnipotence...[90]

Baudry's own view of Ockham's philosophy and, particularly, the place of the doctrine of divine omnipotence within it, corresponds with that of the author of the *Tractatus de principiis theologiae*. Opposing this view A. Pegis states that "it is not at all clear that this doctrine of omnipotence was...the starting point of Ockham's philosophical activity."[91] On this occasion P. Boehner was "happy to agree with Professor Pegis," while disagreeing with L. Baudry's view of Ockham's philosophy as a philosophy of divine omnipotence.[92] At any rate, apart from the controversial aspects of the position of the doctrine of divine omnipotence--whether it is the starting point or not of Ockham's philosophy--all authors agree that it does play an important part, at least, in his philosophical thought. This is made abundantly clear from the amount of attention paid to the doctrine of divine omnipotence by commentators on Ockham.[93] Divine omnipotence and its consequences are without doubt the most discussed items of Ockham's writings.

---

[90] *Ibid.*, pp. 18-19: "Pour l'auteur de *Tractatus* deux principes dominent la philosophie de Guillaume d'Occam. Le premier: Dieu pour faire tout ce qui peut être fait sans contradiction, est tout simplement l'énoncé du dogme de la tout-puissance divine..."

[91] A. Pegis, "Concerning William of Ockham," *Traditio*, II (1944), p. 466. See also *Ibid.*, p. 478 and A. Pegis, "Some Recent Interpretations of Ockham," p. 452.

[92] P. Boehner, "In Propria Causa: A Reply to Professor Pegis' 'Concerning William of Ockham'," *Franciscan Studies*, V (1945), p. 38: "He [Pegis] imputes to me that I accept Baudry's interpretation of Ockham's philosophy...I can only state that I do not accept the views of this excellent Ockhamist scholar *in toto*; certainly not as to the particular interpretation of Ockham's philosophy 'as the philosophy of divine omnipotence.' Hence I am happy to agree with Professor Pegis: 'But it is not at all clear that this doctrine of omnipotence was, in fact, the starting point of Ockham's philosophical activity.'"

[93] See, for example, the following authors: É. Bréhier, *La philosophie du moyen âge* ("L'evolution de l'humanité Synthèse Collective," XLV; Paris: Michel, 1949), p. 411; E. Bonke, *op. cit.*, p. 60; G. Buescher, *The Eucharistic Teaching of William Ockham* ("Franciscan Institute Publications; Theology Series," No. 1; St. Bonaventure, N.Y.: Franciscan Institute, 1950), p. 156; F. Copleston, *op. cit.*, pp. 94-95; 116; S. Day, *Intuitive Cognition: A Key to the Significance of the Later Scholastics* ("Franciscan Institute Publications; Philosophy Series," No. 4; St. Bonaventure, N.Y.: Franciscan Institute, 1947), pp. 176-177; A. D'Entrèves, *op. cit.*, pp. 68-69; A. Garvens, *op. cit.*, pp. 262 ff.; E. Gilson, *La philosophie au moyen âge*, p. 653; E. Gilson and P. Boehner, *Chrsitliche Philosophie*, pp. 619-620; 622-623; J. Hirschberger, *op. cit.*, pp. 459-460; E. Hochstetter, *Studien zur Metaphysik und Erkenntnislehre Wilhelms von Ockham* (Leipzig: de Gruyter, 1927), p. 17; E. Iserloh, *op. cit.*, p. 67; E. Iserloh, "Um die Echtheit des

GOD: THE OBJECTIVE NORM OF MORALITY

But let us turn to Ockham himself. That God is omnipotent means that everything which does not include a manifest contradiction must be attributed to the divine power.[94] More precisely, it does not refer to everything simply, but to everything that can be made or done (*omne factibile*) without contradiction. For the simple term "everything without contradiction" would also include God. Hence the clearer formulation of the principle would be in terms of everything that can be made or done without contradiction.[95]

There is another distinction to be made: the distinction between God's absolute power and his ordered power. This is also a question which is discussed very frequently by commentators on Ockham's writings.[96] God can do, and does, certain things by his ordered or ordained

---

'Centiloquium.' Ein Beitrag zur Wertung Ockhams und zur Chronologie seiner Werke," *Gregorianum*, XXX (1949), p. 330; A. Maurer, "Scotism and Ockhamism," *History of Philosophical Systems*, ed. V. Ferm (New York: Philosophical Library, 1950), pp. 221-222; H. Meyer, *op. cit.*, pp. 303; 317-320; R. Scholz, *Wilhelm ckham als politischer Denker und sein Breviloquium de principatu tyrannico* ("Schriften des Reichsinstituts für ältere deutsche Geschichtskunde"; Leipzig, 1944), p. 21; O. Suk, *op. cit.*, pp. 27-28; P. Vignaux, "Nominalisme," col. 763 ff.; D. Webering, *The Theory of Demonstration according to William Ockham* ("Franciscan Institute Publications; Philosophy Series," No. 10; St. Bonaventure, N.Y.: Franciscan Institute, 1953), p. 151; S. Zuidema, *De Philosophie van Occam in zign Commentar de Sententiën* (Hilversum: Schipper, 1936), p. 512. For a different approach to the problem of divine omnipotence, see A. Wolter, "Ockham and the Textbooks: On the Origin of Possibility," *Franziskanische Studien*, XXXII (1950). pp. 70-96, in which the question is posed: Are things possible because God can create them, or can God create them because they are possible?

[94]Ockham, *Quodl.*, VI, 6: "Quodlibet est 'divinae potentiae attribuendum quod non includit manifestam contradictionem..." (OTh IX, 604). Cf. *In I Sent.*, 20, un. (OTh IX, 586). See also Scotus, *Ordinatio*, I, d. 20, q. un., n. 17: "...omnipotentia est ad omne illud quod non includit contradictionem." (ed. Vaticana, V, 310). *Ibid.*, n. 33: "...licet in ipso sit omnipotentia quae dicit potentiam ad omnia possibilia." (ed. Vaticana, V, 317). P. Boehner, *Ockham. Philosophical Writings*, p. xix: "*All things are possible for God, save such as involve a contradiction*. In other words, God can do (or make or create) everything which does not involve a contradiction; that which includes a contradiction is absolute non-entity." *Ibid.*, p. xlix.

[95]*In I Sent.*, 20, un.: "...dico quod omnipotentia, sicut modo loquimur, non respicit omne illud quod non includit contradictionem, hoc est dictu, omnipotens non potest efficere omne illud quod non includit contradictionem, quia non potest efficere Deum. Omnipotens tamen potest efficere omne factibile quod non includit contradicitionem...." (OTh IV, 36). *Ibid:* "...omnipotens idem est quod potens facere omnia factibilia..." *In II Sent.*, 15 (OTh V, 342). See L. Baudry (ed.), *Tractatus de principiis theologiae*, p. 45; G. Biel, *op. cit.*, Lib. I, d. 20, q. 1, B.

[96]See the following, for example: P. Boehner, "The Spirit of Franciscan Philosophy," *Franciscan Studies*, II (1942), p. 221; F. Copleston, *op. cit.*, p. 105; J. Hirschberger, *op. cit.*, p. 459; E. Hochstetter, *Studien zur Metaphysik und Erkenntnishlehre Wilhelms von Ockham*, p. 16; E. Iserloh, *Gnade und Eucharistie in der philosophischen Theologie des Wilhelm von Ockham*, p. 72; W. Kölmel, "Das Naturrecht bei Wilhelm Ockham," *Franziskanische Studien*, XXXV (1953), p. 58; E. Gilson and P. Boehner, *Christliche Philosophie*, pp. 619-620; G. Stratenwerth, *op. cit.*, pp. 46-47; O. Suk, *op. cit.*, pp. 28-30; S. Tornay, *op. cit.*, pp. 75-76; P. Vignaux, "Nominalisme," col. 763 ff.

CHAPTER IV

power (*potentia ordinata*); and he can do certain things by his absolute power (*potentia absoluta*). In discussing this division for God's omnipotence we should, of course, keep in mind the fact that the absolute identity in God prevents us from interpreting the distinction of absolute and ordered power in the sense that there are really two powers in God; there is only one power in God and this power is indistinct from God Himself. Nor should we interpret ordered and absolute power in the sense that God does some things in an orderly fashion and other things in an unorderly way. God does not do anything in an unorderly fashion. The phrase "something can be done by God" may be interpreted as "done according to the laws and ordinations already set down by God Himself"-- and these things God is said to do in virtue of his ordered or ordained power. In another sense the phrase "something can be done by God" can be interpreted to mean that God can do anything which would not involve a contradiction in being done; and he can do this whether he has already ordained that he will do it or whether he has already ordained that he will not do it. For there are many things which God could do which he does not, however, actually carry out. These things, therefore, do not pertain to God's ordained power; but they are called possible in virtue of God's absolute power.[97]

---

[97] *Quodl.*, VI, 1: "Circa primum dico quod quaedam potest Deus facere de potentia ordinata et aliqua de potentia absoluta. Haec distinctio non est sic intelligenda quod in Deo sint realiter duae potentiae quarum una sit ordinata et alia absoluta, quia unica potentia est in Deo ad extra, quae omni modo est ipse Deus. Nec sic est intelligenda quod aliqua potest Deus ordinate facere, et aliqua potest absolute et non ordinate, quia Deus nihil potest facere inordinate. Sed est sic intelligenda quod 'posse aliquid' quandoque accipitur secundum leges ordinatas et institutas a Deo, et illa dicitur Deus posse facere de potentia ordinata. Aliter accipitur 'posse' pro posse facere omne illud quod non includit contradictionem fieri, sive Deus ordinaverit se hoc facturum sive non, quia multa potest Deus facere quae non vult facere, secundum Magistrum Sententiarum, lib. I, d. 43; et illa dicitur Deus posse de potentia absoluta." (OTh IX, 585-86). For Scotus' explanation of the distinction between God's absolute and ordained power, see *Ordinatio*, I, d. 44, q. un., n. 3: "In omni agente per intellectum et voluntatem, potente conformiter agere legi rectae et tamen non necessario confirmiter agere legi rectae, est distinguere potentiam ordinatam a potentia absoluta; et ratio huius est, quia potest agere conformiter illi legi rectae, et tunc secundum potentiam ordinatam (ordinata enim est in quantum est principium exsequendi aliqua confirmiter legi rectae), et potest agere praeter illam legem vel contra eam, et in hoc est potentia absoluta, excedens potentiam ordinatam...ideo dicunt iuristae quod aliquis hoc potest facere de facto, hoc est de potentia sua absoluta,--vel de iure, hoc est de potentia ordinata secundum iura." (ed. Vaticana, VI, 363f.). For pertinent comments on this passage, see G. Stratenwerth, *op. cit.*, pp. 46-47. A parallel passage in St. Thomas, *S. ThI*, q. 25, a. 5 ad 1, reads: "Quia voluntas non determinatur ex necessitate ad haec vel illa, nisi forte ex suppositione...neque sapientia Dei et iustitia determinatur ad hunc ordinem; nihil prohibet esse aliquid in potentia divina, quod non vult et quod non continetur sub ordine quem statuit rebus. Et quia potentia intelligitur ut exequens, voluntas autem ut imperans, et intellectus et sapientia ut dirigens, quod attribuitur potentiae secundum se consideratae, dicitur Deus posse secundum potentiam absolutam; et huiusmodi est omne illud in quo potest salvari ratio

GOD: THE OBJECTIVE NORM OF MORALITY

For the purpose of illustrating this type of division in God's power Ockham points out that we often speak of the same kind of distinction of powers on the part of the Pope. There are many things which, absolutely speaking, the Pope could do, but he is prevented from doing them because of laws he has already made. Another example would be in connection with the necessity of baptism for salvation. As there was a time prior to the institution of the sacrament of baptism by Our Lord when baptism was not required for salvation, so God, whose power has certainly not diminished in the meantime, could still admit unbaptized persons into heaven in virtue of his absolute power. But because of the laws enacted in the New Testament, such an arrangement is not possible in virtue of God's ordained power, although it is possible absolutely speaking.[98] Quite a number of other applications of the distinction between God's absolute and ordained power occur throughout Ockham's writings, perhaps most frequently in connection with his treatment of original sin, merit, and the supernatural virtue of charity.[99]

God's power, then, is not limited by any absolute necessity in reference to creatures. But he is bound by conditional necessity, and to this conditional necessity corresponds his ordained power. Thus, "If Peter is predestined, he will be saved." But such conditional necessity is necessity only in virtue of a prior absolutely free ordination of Almighty God--"if Peter is predestined"--a provision which is contingent and dependent on the completely free will of God. Radically creatures

---

entia...quod autem attribuitur potentiae divinae, secundum quod exequitur imperium voluntatis justae, hoc dicitur Deus posse facere de potentia ordinata." Cf. G. Biel, *op. cit.*, II Sent., d. 17, q. 1, H.

[98] *Quodl.*, VI, 1: "Sicut Papa aliqua non potest secundum iura statuta ab eo, quae tamen absolute potest. Ista distinctio probatur per dictum Salvatoris, Ioannis 3: *Nisi quis* inquit *renatus fuerit ex aqua et Spiritu Sancto, non potest introire in regnum Dei.* Cum enim Deus sit aequalis potentiae nunc sicut prius, et aliquando aliqui introierunt regnum Dei sine omni baptismo, sicut patet de pueris circumcisis tempore Legis defunctis antequam haberent usum rationis, et nunc est hoc possibile. Sed tamen illud quod tunc erat possibile secundum leges tunc institutas, nunc non est possibile secundum legem iam institutam, licet absolute sit possibile." (OTh IX, 586).

[99] *Quodl.*, III, 10: "...dico quod potuit fieri per potentiam Dei absolutam quod peccatum originale nullius diceret carentiam..." (OTh IX, 240-41). *In I Sent.*, 17, 2: "Ita de potentia sua absoluta posset acceptare eundem motum voluntatis etiam si non infunderet caritatem." (OTh III, 472); *Ibid.*: "Unde idem actus qui modo elicitur ab habente caritatem et est meritorius, posset Deus de potentia Dei absoluta non acceptare eum." (OTh III, 472); *Ibid.*: "...de potentia sua absoluta posset statuere quod quicumque diligeret Deum super omnia et non faceret scienter contra rectam rationem, quod mereretur vitam aeternam." (OTh III, 475); *In I Sent.*, 17, 1: "...ad actum beatificum non requiritur de potentia Dei absoluta aliquis habitus talis [caritas]." (OTh III, 446). *Ibid.*: "...adhuc est in potentia Dei absoluta acceptare illam animam vel non acceptare." (OTh III, 449). *Ibid.*: "Sed Deus de potentia absoluta potuit fuisse numquam incarnatus." (OTh III, 450). *Ibid.* (OTh III, 453f.).

and everything that properly pertains to creatures are contingent. And from the very fact that God does anything, it is done justly and well.[100] God is not bound or obligated to anyone or to anything, and therefore it is impossible to speak of his doing anything which he must not do or of his not doing what he ought to do.[101] Whatever God wills concerning creatures is not only willed freely but also justly; God always acts reasonably and most wisely.[102]

3. WILL WHAT HE WILLS

Granting that whatever God wills, he wills justly and well, is the human will obliged to conform to and fulfill the decrees of the divine will? What does it mean to conform to the divine will, to will what God wills? This is the third part of our formula, "Love God and will what he wills." Here we will examine how the human will can fulfill the divine will and under what conditions it is obliged to do so. The following treatment will involve, therefore, an understanding of the nature of conforming to the will of God, the possibility of doing so, and the necessity or obligation on the part of the creature to will what God wills.

In a certain sense the will of God is always fulfilled. No one can frustrate the will of God. If we keep in mind that all the following terms refer in reality to the one, absolutely simple, will of God, then we may say that God's will is always fulfilled at least as far as the consequent will of good pleasure (*voluntas beneplaciti*) is concerned; but if we speak of the antecedent will of good pleasure and the will of expression (*voluntas signi*), there are human acts which can be against or contrary to the will of God.[103] Thus the antecedent will of God--the will by which God provides the necessary help or antecedent conditions for someone to act, the will whereby God co-acts with the creature--is required for any meritorious act on the part of any creature. God is ready

---

[100] *In I Sent.*, 17, 3: "...eo ipso quod ipse vult, bene et iuste factum est." (OTh III, 478).

[101] *In II Sent.*, 15: "Deus autem nulli tenetur nec obligatur tanquam debitor, et ideo non potest facere quod non debet facere nec non facere quod debet facere." (OTh V, 343).

[102] *In I Sent.*, 35, V: "...dicitur [Deus] rationabiliter operans....Et ex hoc ipso quod Deus est Deus, Deus cognoscit omnia. Nec aliter esset rationabiliter operans nisi cognosceret illa quae operatur." (OTh IV, 504 and 506). See E. Gilson and P. Boehner, *Christliche Philosophie*, p. 622: "Nun ist aber Gott ein vernünftig wirkendes und darum such vernünftig wollendes Wesen: [Deus] dicitur rationabiliter operans.'"

[103] For a development of the meaning of these distinctions see A. Tanquerey, *op. cit.*, pp. 287-288. In this place the author also remarks, "Quidquid Deus vult simpliciter, absolute et consequenter, semper impletur...Sed illud quod Deus vult antecedenter vel conditionate, aliquando non fit." Cf. St. Thomas, *S. Th.*, I, q. 19, a. 6.

to co-act with anyone in a meritorious act; but, unfortunately, not everyone elicits meritorious actions. Many not only omit these acts but elicit acts of a contrary nature, acts which are demeritorious. Therefore, these demeritorious omissions and commissions are contrary to the antecedent will of God. And it is likewise evident that these acts are contrary to the divine will of expression; they are violations of divine precepts and prohibitions.

What is involved in conformity to the will of God? This is the question Ockham seeks to answer in the First Book of the Sentences, distinction 48, question 1: Is the created will bound to conform to the divine will?

Ockham first presents this argument which is really contrary to his intended thesis: one could say that if the created will must conform to the divine will, then it would be a sin whenever the created will did not conform, because it does not do what it is obliged to do. Consequently, if a person would honor his parents when God wills them not to be honored, he sins. The consequence, that a person sins by honoring his parents, is false; therefore, the antecedent is false also. Against this argument Ockham says that every created will must conform to its norm. But the will of God is the norm for any created will. Therefore, every created will is obliged to conform to the divine will.[104] Later, in reference to this same argument presented above, Ockham concludes with the words: you say that the human will must never be in deformity with the divine will and that, therefore, someone who honors his parents whom God does not wish to be honored has a will which is not in conformity with the divine will, consequently he intends to sin in honoring his parents. And from this you conclude that since the consequence is false, the antecedent must be false also. But actually the consequence is true. For I answer, says Ockham, that if God would will that the parents should not be honored, neither by this man nor by that one, then both would sin in honoring their parents. However, if God does not will them to be honored by this man, but wills them to be honored by that one, then the latter does not sin by honoring his parents, although the former would. For

---

[104] Ockham, *In I Sent.*, 48, un.: "...utrum quaelibet voluntas creata teneatur se conformare voluntati divinae....Praeterea si sic, voluntas quandocumque non conformaret se voluntati divinae peccaret, quia non faceret illud ad quod tenetur, et per consequens honorans parentes, quos Deus non vult honorare, peccaret. Consequens falsum, igitur antecedens. Ad oppositum: Quaelibet voluntas creata tenetur se conformare regulae suae; sed voluntas divina est regula cuiuslibet voluntatis creatae; igitur quaelibet voluntas creata tenetur se conformare voluntati divinae." (OTh IV, 686). See D. Scotus, *Reportata Parisiensia*, II, d. 6, q. 2, n. 10 in *Opera omnia* (ed. Vivès) tom. XXII, p. 622: "Iste [appetitus] naturalis rectus est, si sit per se; sed appetitus liber non est rectus ex hoc, quod conformatur alicui inferiori recto, sed ex hoc, quod vult illud, quod vult Deus eam velle." See also G. Biel, *op. cit.*, I Sent., d. 48, q. 1.

CHAPTER IV

the former, by honoring his parents, would be acting contrary to the divine will; the latter, by honoring his parents, would conform to the divine will.[105]

But before Ockham reached this conclusion he developed several related topics in explanation of what conformity to the will of God would imply. It is mainly these ideas which are of greater interest here. Some rearrangement of his ideas may make them more adaptable for our purposes in this chapter. Let us begin with the notion that conforming to the will of another can be an actual or habitual conformity. A concrete act of love and reverence for our parents as a fulfillment of the divine command to honor our parents would be an example of actual conformity to the will of God. A further distinction will be useful in the case of habitual conformity. Habitual conformity can be either immediate or mediate. Habitual conformity is called immediate if it proceeds from a habit which immediately inclines the will to a certain concrete action. A habit of this type would be acquired through the repeated performance of the concrete act in question. For example, the habit of attending Mass may be acquired and incline the will to the repeated performance of attending Mass. On the other hand, a habit may have a mediate influence in the performance of a concrete action. The term "remote" influence could be used if it is not conceived as involving, necessarily, any lessening of the influence of the habit in reference to the particular concrete act. An example of a habit which exercises a mediate influence would be a habit in the intellect regarding general principles which only mediately lead to an act which is specified in the conclusion drawn from these principles.[106] If we take the same example presented above, the attendance at Mass, then we may describe the mediate habit as consisting in

---

[105] Ockham, *In I Sent.*, 48, 1: "Et si dicatur quod voluntas numquam debet esse difformis voluntati divinae, sed iste qui vult honorare parentes, quos Deus non vult honorari, habet voluntatem difformem voluntati divinae, igitur peccat in honorando: Dicendum est quod si Deus vult eos non honorari, nec ab isto nec ab alio, iste peccat in honorando parentes suos. Si tamen Deus vult eos non honorari ab alio, sed vult eos honorari ab isto, iste in honorando non peccat, nec est difformis voluntati divinae, sed est conformis voluntati divinae..." (OTh IV, 690-691). Cf. *In II Sent.* 15 (OTh V, 353). See also E. Bonke, *op. cit.*, p. 68; O. Fuchs, *op. cit.*, pp. 85-86; A. Garvens, *op. cit.*, p. 266; E. Iserloh, *Gnade und Eucharistie in der philosophischen Theologie des Wilhelm von Ockham*, p. 68.

[106] *In I Sent.*, 48, un.: "...quaelibet istarum conformitatum potest esse actualis vel habitualis. Et si sit habitualis, vel est habitualis propter habitum aliquem immediate inclinantem ad talem actum. Sicut aliquis dicitur habitualiter velle vel diligere aliquid quando habet habitum generatum ex actibus circa illud, vel alium ita immediate inclinantem sicut inclinat habitus generatus ex actibus illis. Vel dicitur habitualis propter habitum mediate inclinantem quo modo in intellectu habitus principiorum inclinat mediate ad actum conclusionis, quia scilicet mediante actu principiorum." (OTh IV, 687). See O. Fuchs, *op. cit.*, pp. 86 ff.

GOD: THE OBJECTIVE NORM OF MORALITY

following a general principle such as "God is to be honored." In this case "Mass should be attended" is a particularization of this general principle relating to the honor of God. But the habit of the general principle would only mediately incline the will to the act of attending Mass. Although this example expresses the idea of mediate influence of a habit, it is somewhat misleading, because the mediate influence is even more mediate than Ockham would require in his notion of mediate conformity. It seems that Ockham has in mind a very remote habit which, as it were, influences actual conformity only through several intermediary stages. This, in brief, is what he presents as an answer to the question: "What is this habit inclining the human will to will what God wills?" For Ockham it is the habit of the human will to agree with everything willed by God.[107] Hence the habit is said to incline the will mediately to conformity in a concrete act. In fact, the habit first inclines to some other act which afterwards causes the habit of actually willing what God wills. Hence this habit inclines mediately because it first inclines the will to an act of being pleased with everything that God does.[108] If we now apply what has just been said to the example previously given, we may draw it out in this series: first there is the general habit which inclines the will to agree with everything in general that God wills. This general will of God would include the notion that he is to be honored. One particular way of honoring God is by attending Mass. The actual attendance at Mass is then mediately influenced by the general habit of conforming to everything that God wills. In other words, the general habit does not incline the will immediately to the concrete or particularized act of attending Mass. Immediately, the general habit of willing what God wills inclines the human will to the general act--or intention--of fulfilling whatever God wills. It is through this act of the will that the general habit exercises its influence; but such an influence, though real and effective, is only mediate.

The habit of willing what God wills must be in everyone who has attained the use of reason, at least as soon as he obtains, or could ob-

---

[107] *Ibid.*: "Et si quaeratur quis est ille habitus qui inclinat ad volendum omnia a Deo volita? Dicendum est quod aliquis talis quo complacet voluntati omne quod placet divinae voluntati....Iste autem habitus non inclinat immediate ad omne volitum a Deo. Nam oportet praesupponere cognitionem qua sciatur hoc esse volitum a Deo, et mediante illa inclinat ad actum." (OTh IV, 688).

[108] *Ibid.*: "Et sic etiam iste habitus inclinat mediate, quia primo inclinat ad actum quo complacet voluntati omne quod fit a Deo." (OTh IV, 689).

CHAPTER IV

tain, some knowledge of God.[109] But not everyone is bound to conform to the divine will by willing in an habitual and immediate manner everything willed by God. Since everyone cannot be bound to know everything willed by God, he is not bound to will everything habitually and immediately. This would be obliging everyone to the impossible. But if a person does know that a certain thing is willed by God by his will of good pleasure, he would be bound to will what God wills, that is, be pleased in it actually, or at least habitually, and immediately. But what is to be said about those things which are willed by God by his will of expression? The answer is that if it is a precept or prohibition and willed by God as such by his will of expression, then the created will is bound to conform to the will of God. If, however, it is willed by the signified will of God merely as a divine counsel, then the will of the creature is not obliged to conform, since a counsel does not impose any obligation.[110]

Not everyone is bound always to conform actually, however, to the divine will in willing those things, and all those things, which the divine will wills. This is true because not everyone is obliged to know everything willed by the divine will, and also because he is not obliged always to fulfill the affirmative divine precepts. The affirmative precepts oblige always, but not for all times (*semper sed non pro semper*).[111] From the reason given why actual conformity is not necessary, we can conclude that the created will is bound in those cases not covered by the reasons. This would include the condition that the precept is known as commanded, and that it be a negative precept, a prohibition to which the created will is obliged always and for all times (*semper et pro semper*). The affirmative precepts would be included in so far as they obliged a person always but not for all times.

A second distinction should be made. God wills some things absolutely, others he wills only conditionally. God wills those things which

---

[109] *Ibid.*: "qui [habitus mediante inclinans] debet esse semper in omni habente usum rationis postquam ad aliqualem Dei cognitionem attingerit vel potuit attingere." (OTh IV, 688).

[110] *Ibid.*: "...non quilibet tenetur se conformare voluntati divinae volendo volitum a Deo habitualiter immediate, quia non tenetur scire illud esse volitum a Deo, et per consequens non tenetur velle illus habitualiter immediate. Tamen si sciat illud esse volitum a Deo voluntate beneplaciti, tenetur illus velle, hoc est, in illo complacere vel habitualiter vel actualiter. Sed quid dicetur de illis quae sunt volita a Deo voluntate signi? Dicendum quod si sit praeceptum et ita volitum a Deo voluntate signi, tenetur se voluntas conformare. Si autem sit volitum voluntate signi quia est consilium divinum, non tenetur." (OTh IV, 689).

[111] *Ibid.*: "...non quilibet tenetur se semper conformare actualiter voluntati divinae volendo omne illud quod est volitum a voluntate divina, tun quia non tenetur cognoscere omne volitum a voluntate divina, tum quia non tenetur semper implere praecepta divina affirmativa."

GOD: THE OBJECTIVE NORM OF MORALITY

we call good in themselves. These he wills absolutely. But God also wills, for example, punishment and physical evils. These God wills only conditionally, dependent on the demeritorious acts of creatures. If the creature commits a certain act, then God wills that a certain punishment or a certain physical evil will be inflicted.[112]

First it should be mentioned that every created will is bound to conform at least habitually and mediately to the divine will in so far as God wills something absolutely. The created will must also then absolutely will those things, not willing the opposite, even conditionally.[113] Secondly, the things that God wills conditionally must also be willed by the creature. The creature can, however, in this case also conditionally will the contrary or deny what God wills. Hence, absolutely speaking, the created will would be obliged to will that an evil-doer be justly punished by Almighty God; but conditionally we may will that this person will not be punished--under the condition, for example, that he repents of his evil deeds.[114]

More important, however, is the following distinction. There are two ways in which a will can conform to another will. First by willing the same thing that is willed by the other will. And secondly, by willing what the other will would will it to will.[115] In Ockham's opinion it is this second way, and only the second way, that constitutes true conformity to the will of God. As a general principle he holds that the human will is obliged to conform to the divine will by willing those things which the divine will wills it to will. This is true regarding those things willed by the divine will of good pleasure; it is also true regarding those things willed by the divine will of expression in so far as precepts are concerned. It does not, however, oblige concerning the will of expression in so far as the counsels are concerned, as mentioned

---

[112] *Ibid.*: "...quaedam sunt volita a Deo quasi absolute, cuiusmodi sunt omnia bona quae nec sunt mala culpae nec poenae; quaedam sunt volita a Deo propter malum culpae praecedens in alio cuius est poena." (OTh IV, 687).

[113] *Ibid.*: "...quaelibet voluntas creata...tenetur se conformare habitualiter mediate voluntati divinae...quantum ad volita primo modo [i.e., absolute] dicta, et haec absolute ea volendo et non volendo opposita sub condicione." (OTh IV, 687-88).

[114] *Ibid.*: "...alia volita a Deo debet voluntas absolute velle; potest tamen condicionaliter velle contrarium et illud nolle. Et ideo absolute debet voluntas velle aliquem puniri iuste a Deo, tamen condicionaliter potest velle ipsum non puniri." (OTh IV, 688).

[115] *Ibid.*: "...sciendum est quod voluntas potest alteri conformari...vel quia vult volitum ab alia voluntate, vel quia vult illud quod alia voluntas vult ipsum velle..." (OTh IV, 687).

CHAPTER IV

above.[116] Therefore, the person who would not conform to the divine will wherever and whenever he is bound for the necessity of his salvation, sins mortally. But here it should be mentioned again that while the affirmative precepts oblige always but not for all times, the negative precepts oblige always and for all times.[117]

The created will, it must be emphasized, is not always right when it is in conformity with the divine will regarding the willed object itself. That is, the created will would not always conform to the divine will by willing what God wills or by willing the same thing that God wills. For sometimes God wills something and at the same time wills that the creature is not to will this same thing. For example, from all eternity God willed the death of Christ; but he did not will the Jews to will his death or to put him to death by crucifixion. Likewise, Ockham refers to an example given by St. Augustine that God wills the death of my father; but he does not will that I wish my father to die. Therefore, when I will something that God wills me not to will and I know that he wills me not to will it, then I sin even though this thing itself is willed by God. For even though I will what God wills, I knowingly difform from the norm to which I am bound to conform, because I will what God does not will me to will.[118]

That a created will can do wrong by willing what God wills can also be shown in the following way. Granted that God is the immediate cause of any act, a cause that is necessarily required for any act of a creature, then God can be said to will an act even though the creature would sin by performing that act. Now in this case God would will that act by immediately and partially concurring with the created will. The created will would then will what God wills (that is, the act in this case), even

---

[116] *Ibid.:* "...voluntas tenetur se conformare voluntati divinae volendo ea quae voluntas Dei vult eam velle, et hoc si velit eam velle illud voluntate beneplaciti vel voluntate praecepti. Sed si vult eam velle voluntate consilii, non oportet, sicut dictum est prius." (OTh IV, 698-90). See F. Copleston, *op. cit.*, p. 103.

[117] *Ibid.:* "...non conformans se voluntati divinae pro loco et tempore quo tenetur de necessitate salutis, peccat mortaliter. Sed dictum est prius quod non quilibet pro omni tempore ad hoc tenetur, maxima quantum ad praecepta affirmativa, quamvis ad praecepta negativa pro semper teneatur." See A. Garvens, *op. cit.*, pp. 265-266.

[118] *Quaest. Variae.*, q. 8: "...dico quod voluntas non semper est recta quando conformatur voluntati divinae in obiecto volito. Nam aliquando vult Deus aliquid et tamen vult creaturam velle oppositum. Exemplum: Deus ab aeterno voluit mortem Christi et tamen voluit Iudaeos nolle mortem eius eo modo quo mortuus est ab eis. Similiter ponit Augustinus exemplum, quia Deus vult patrem meum mori et tamen vult me nolle mortem patris mei. Nunc autem quando volo aliquid quod Deus vult me nolle, licet illud sit volitum a Deo, tunc pecco, maxime si scirem Deum me nolle illud, quia tunc scienter discordo a regula cui me teneor in actibus meis conformare, et per consequens pecco." (OTh VIII, 434f.). See O Fuchs, *op. cit.*, p. 85.

GOD: THE OBJECTIVE NORM OF MORALITY

though God also wills the act to be other than it is. God would not sin, but our will sins. For the divine will is not obliged to will the opposite of the act, because the divine will is not obliged to anything. But the created will is bound to will the opposite, because it is bound to will what God wills it to will. But now when God wills this act of sin to take place, he also wills that the created will should turn away from this act which is a sin. And consequently, the created will would sin by willing this act to take place, because the created will is obliged to the opposite. Of course, God does not will this act to take place absolutely, but only by his consequent or conditional will. That is, God wills this act to take place if the creature wills to perform it; but he wills the creature not to will it in the first place. Thus, concludes Ockham, it is evident that the created will is not always bound to conform to the divine will in what the divine will wills. And moreover, by conforming to the divine will in what God wills, the created will may sin, as we have seen in the case just presented. But the created will is bound to conform to the divine will by willing what God wills it to will and in the way that God wills it to be willed.[119]

It is this obligation that makes someone a sinner or not. Suppose that God would command one person to do a certain thing and not command another person regarding the same thing. The first would then sin in not doing this act, but the second would not. And the reason for this is that the second is not obliged as the first is.[120] Therefore, the deformity of a sin does not consist in a lack of justice or rectitude in the

---

[119] *Quaest. Variae*, q. 8: "Ex hoc potest patere,--secundum illam viam quae ponit quod Deus est causa immediata cuiuslibet actus nostri volendo illum actum esse--, quomodo nos in actu aliquo peccamus, licet Deus velit illum actum esse immediate ab eo partialiter concurrente voluntate. Quia licet voluntas creata velit idem quod Deus vult,--quia Deus vult illum actum esse, aliter non fieret--, tamen [Deus] non peccat, sed voluntas nostra peccat [quando obligatur ad oppositum], quia voluntas divina non tenetur velle oppositum eo quod ad nihil obligatur. Sed voluntas creata tenetur velle oppositum quia tenetur velle quod Deus vult eam velle. Nunc autem quamvis Deus velit actum peccati esse, tamen Deus vult voluntatem creatam nolle illum actum peccati, vel saltem non velle. Et per consequens voluntas creata, volendo illum actum quem Deus vult, peccat quia obligatur ad oppositum. Tamen nec etiam Deus vult istum actum esse absolute, sed tantum voluntate consequente sive condicionata, quia Deus vult illum actum esse si creatura velit, sed vult creaturam non velle illum actum si placeat sibi. Sic igitur patet quod voluntas non tenetur se semper conformare voluntati divinae in volito. Immo frequenter, conformando se illi voluntati in volito, peccabit propter causam dictam." (OTh VIII, 435f.).

[120] *In IV Sent.*, 10-11: "...Si esset aliquis superior respectu duorum, et praecipiat uni facere aliquid et alteri non, unus in non faciendo peccaret et alter non, quia secundus non aequaliter obligatur sicut primus. Obligatio igitur facit aliquem peccatorem vel non peccatorem." (OTh VII, 198); *In II Sent.*, 15: "...dico quod aliquis actus ab una causa potest fieri bene, et si fieret ab alia, non posset fieri nisi male. Et tota ratio est quia una causa obligatur ad actum oppositum et alia non." (OTh V, 353).

CHAPTER IV

act that is committed; rather, it is a lack of rectitude which ought to be in the will of the sinner. This means nothing else than that the creature's will is obliged to elicit some act according to the law of God and that the creature does not elicit this obligatory act.[121]

But it is also necessary to state that what is important is that what is willed is willed precisely because God wills it. Or more exactly, that which is willed is willed precisely because God wills it to be willed. Hence in the case frequently mentioned in medieval writings concerning the Israelites who despoiled the Egyptians of their possessions, the Jews did not sin. However, those who took the possessions of the Egyptians with a bad will--and not precisely in obedience to the divine command-- did sin. And they sinned even though they did what God willed them to do, at least in so far as the external act is concerned. That is, they sinned even though they willed what God willed them to will, namely, the spoliation of the Egyptians. But they sinned because they acted with a bad will and not precisely in obedience, or in conformity with the will of God.[122] In so far as the internal act of their wills is concerned, they did not will what God willed them to will. It was in this lack of rectitude in their wills that their sin consisted.

In the formula stated at the beginning of this chapter, "Love God and will what he wills," the phrase "will what he wills" must be understood in the sense and under the conditions outlined above. It must be an actual or an habitual, an absolute or a conditional conformity to the will of God according to the various cases previously discussed. More importantly, the following two modifications of the formula must be taken into account for a more accurate understanding of its correct interpretation. First, it does not mean "willing what God wills" but "willing what God wills willed." Secondly, what is willed must be willed precisely because God wills it to be willed. However, it seems that in Ockham's theory the phrase "because God wills it to be willed" can be interpreted as equivalent to the phrase "out of love of God." The reasons for saying this will be brought out in the following section of this chapter. In any case, it is in the sense and under the conditions developed above that

---

[121] *Quodl.*, III, 15: "Dico igitur quod deformitas non est carentia iustitiae vel rectitudinis debitae inesse actui, sed est carentia rectitudinis debitae inesse ipsi voluntati; quod nihil aliud est dicere nisi quod voluntas obligatur aliquem actum elicere secundum praeceptum divinum quem non elicit." (OTh IX, 261). Cf. *Quaest. variae*, q. 7, a. 4 (OTh VIII, 386).

[122] *In I Sent.*, 47, 1: "...spoliare Aegyptios non fuit malum, immo fuit bonum. Et ideo Deus praecipiendo spoliare Aegyptios non praecepit malum, nec filii Israel peccaverunt in spoliando, nisi illi qui malo animo, non praecise obediendo divino praecepto, spoliaverint." (OTh IV, 685). See St. Thomas, *S. Th.*, I, q. 105, a. 6. See also A. Garvens, *op. cit.*, pp. 264-265; E. Hochstetter, "Viator mundi," p. 14; O. Suk, *op. cit.*, p. 29.

GOD: THE OBJECTIVE NORM OF MORALITY

the formula "Love God and will what he wills" is to be understood as an expression of Ockham's fundamental theory in which the will of God is said to be the highest and the ultimate norm of morality.

4. APPLICATION TO SPECIAL PROBLEMS

We shall now attempt to apply the principles outlined in the preceding section of this chapter to four special problems. I have selected these particular problems not only because they touch the basic theory of Ockham's ethics, but also because they deal with the "extremes," let us say, to which Ockham's theory can be drawn. I do not think that these problems should in any way be considered the starting points of Ockham's ethics, but rather as problems he was led to bring into consideration in drawing out the conclusions of his fundamental principles. E. Bonke's article, which treats of Ockham's nominalism in ethics, may be somewhat misleading in this regard, starting as it does with the problem of the hatred of God.[123]

The problems to be considered here are these four: 1) An introductory problem on the relation between the love of God and obedience to his will. 2) Can God command that evil be done? 3) Can God cause the hatred of himself in a created will? 4) Can God command that he be not loved and even hated?

1) One of the basic problems in Ockham's ethics is this: Is the love of God, above all and for Himself, a good act because it is prescribed by God; or is it a good act without the prescription or command of God? Texts from the *Third Quodlibet*, question 14, and the *Quaestiones Variae*, question 7, mention that man is bound to love God, that such an act is necessarily virtuous whenever it is elicited; but there is no mention of any command on the part of God.[124] But on the other hand, texts from the *Second Book of the Sentences*, question 19, specifically state that the created will is bound to love God because of the divine precept to do so.[125] Is the divine precept, then, the basis for the obli-

---

[123] E. Bonke, *op. cit.*, p. 60.

[124] Ockham, *Quodl.*, III, 14: "...nam iste actus [quo Deus diligitur super omnia et propter se] sic est virtuosus quod non potest esse vitiosus, nec potest iste actus causari a voluntate creata nisi sit virtuosus; tum quia quilibet pro loco et tempore obligatur ad diligendum Deum super omnia, et per consequens iste actus non potest esse vitiosus..." (OTh IX, 255-56). Cf. *Quodl.*, III, 15 (OTh IX, 258); *In I Sent.*, 1, 4 (OTh I, 447); *Quaest. Variae*, q. 7, a. 4: "...quia non diligit Deum super omnia, quod tamen tenetur facere." (OTh VIII, 390). See also E. Gilson and P. Boehner, *Christliche Philosophie*, p. 622; E. Hochstetter, "Viator mundi," p. 16.

[125] *In II Sent.*, 15: "...voluntas creata obligatur ex praecepto Dei ad diligendum Deum, et ideo stante illo praecepto non potest bene odire Deum....Et hoc quia obligatur ex praecepto Dei ad actum oppositum." (OTh V, 353). Cf. *Ibid.* (OTh V, 352) which speaks of the *odium*

CHAPTER IV

gation to love God? Or on the contrary, is the love of God itself the basis for obeying his precept that he must be loved? It would seem that the second alternative is the only one which can save Ockham from falling into a vicious circle in which the love of God is based on obedience to a divine command, and the obedience in turn is obligatory because man is obliged to love God and what God wills. In other words, the love of God itself cannot in the first instance--or on the first level--be an object of a command, for the love of God is already presupposed. It seems that we can say that there are certain levels of obligation in commands, just as there are levels of truth in propositions. The case of love is here analogous to that of obedience itself, which cannot in the first instance be the object of a legitimate command. For a legitimate command presupposes that, if it is a legitimate command, it must be obeyed. But obedience can in the second instance be the object of a legitimate command. For example, a legitimate superior may command: "Every command that I give must be obeyed." Such a command is unnecessary and superfluous but it can none the less be given. But the obligation of obedience to this command is already presupposed before the command is given. And obedience to the command of God that he must be loved is also presupposed before the command is given. If the love of God would be obligatory out of obedience, why is obedience obligatory? The reason is that obedience means doing what God wills because he wills it; but the phrase "because he wills it" is equivalent to saying "out of love for God," a love of God above all and for Himself. Hence, it is the love of God, above all and for Himself, that is basic--but this is a love which includes the doing of whatever God wills. And since the doing of whatever God wills is obedience, this love includes obedience. So intimately are the notions of love and obedience bound together that we may legitimately regard them as being equivalent notions. To love God is to obey Him.[126]

Dei as evil as long as its opposite falls under the divine precept. See F. Copleston, *op. cit.*, p. 109: "The ultimate and sufficient reason why we ought to follow right reason or conscience is that God wills that we should do so. Authoritarianism has the last word. Again, Ockham speaks of an act 'which is intrinsically and necessarily virtuous *stante ordinatione* divina.' In the same section he says that 'in the present order no act is perfectly virtuous unless it is elicited in conformity with right reason.' Such remarks are revealing. A necessarily virtuous act is only relatively so, that is, if God has decreed that it should be virtuous. Given the order instituted by God, it follows logically that certain acts are good and others bad; but the order itself is dependent on God's choice."

[126] See P. Boehner, *Ockham. Philosophical Writings*, p. xlix: "As soon as a human person knows that a certain command is the will of God, he is bound to obey. To do the will of God or, equivalently, to love God, is the supreme ethical rule." Also see P. Boehner, "A Recent Presentation of Ockham's Philosophy," p. 453: "Ockham admits one absolute norm of Ethics, viz.

GOD: THE OBJECTIVE NORM OF MORALITY

In this connection, E. Hochstetter has pointed out that for Ockham the love of God is the absolute commandment, and while other philosophers may have called it into question, for Ockham the love of God had no need of proof or argumentation.[127]

It also becomes a meaningless question to ask of Ockham: Is this to be done out of obedience to a divine precept or out of love of God? The texts mentioned above, those referring to the divine precept to love God, could be interpreted in the sense that the phrase "out of obedience to the divine command" is understood not as stating the basis for the love of God but as emphasizing one aspect of that love. Thus the love of God and obedience to a divine precept are necessarily virtuous acts; and all other acts are only contingently virtuous, that is, virtuous in so far as they are performed out of love for God, or equivalently, out of obedience to a divine precept.

The separation of love and obedience can bring to light certain difficulties. Arising from this separation is the question: Can God command, so that man must obey, that he be not loved? Although this question is treated at some length by Ockham in the *Third Quodlibet*, question 14, it is, in a sense, a meaningless question.[128] However, we shall give this question more attention later on, since there is a sense in which it can be meaningful. It may be mentioned here that Ockham's treatment of the problem only serves to emphasize how the love of God and obedience to his divine will are inextricably bound together.

There is a famous a frequently quoted passage in the *Fourth Book of the Sentences*, question 14. In this passage Ockham is speaking of the command of God that he be hated:

> Every will can conform to the commands of God. God can, however, command a created will to hate Him. Therefore, the created will can do this. Moreover, any act that can be just on earth could also be just in heaven. On earth the hatred of

---

the obligation to obey God. Ockham has never maintained that anyone, not even God, can dispense from this obligation. However, to obey God means to love God."

[127] E. Hochstetter, "Viator mundi," p. 15: "Dieses diligere Deum super omnia...ist für Ockham absolutes Gebot, das für ihn keiner Begründung bedarf, im Unterschied etwa zu seinem nur wenig jüngeren Zeitgenossen Richard Chillington, in dessen Sentenzenkommentar als erste uns die Quaestio entgegentritt: 'Utrum Deus sit super omnia diligendus.'"

[128] *Quodl.*, III, 14: "Si dicis quod Deus potest praecipere quod pro aliquo tempore non diligatur ipse, quia potest praecipere quod intellectus sit sic intentus circa studium et voluntas similiter, ut nihil possit pro illo tempore de Deo cogitare..." (OTh IX, 256).

CHAPTER IV

God can be just, if it is commanded by God Himself. Therefore, the hatred of God could also be just in heaven.[129]

This passage, it may be noted, led to the formulation of one of the propositions presented for censure at Avignon in 1326.[130] This is obviously a different question than the command of God that he be not loved, although there is some tendency on the part of authors to confuse the two questions.[131] Here Ockham's answer--that if God commands that he be hated the created will can do this morally--cannot at all be reconciled with the interpretation favoring the equivalence of love and obedience given previously. However, the interpretation favoring the equivalence of love and obedience is the only one which I think is possible in the light of all the texts examined in this connection, with the exception, of course, of the text in the *Fourth Book of the Sentences*, question 14, referred to above. Consequently, it appears that here is a genuine contradiction in Ockham's thought. Love and obedience are equivalent; and yet the created will can morally obey the command that God be hated. Obedience to the command of hatred would argue to a distinction and separability of love and obedience, for love and hatred of the same object are certainly mutually exclusive. I do not see any way of denying the contradiction; but I also see no reason for refusing to admit as probable that Ockham underwent a change or modification of this thought. There

---

[129] *In IV Sent.*, 16: "Praeterea, omnis voluntas potest se conformare praecepto divino. Sed Deus potest praecipere quod voluntas creata odiat eum, igitur voluntas creata potest hoc facere. Praeterea, omne quod potest esse actus rectus in via, et in patria. Sed odire Deum potest esse actus rectus in via, puta si praecipiatur a Deo, igitur in patria." (OTh VII, 352). On the use of this text as the basis for calling Ockham a divine moral positivist, see T. Barth, "Wilhelm Ockham im Lichte der neuesten Forschung," *Philosophisches Jahrbuch*, LX (1950), p. 465. See L. Baudry (ed.), *Tractatus de principiis theologiae*, p.1 46: "...ponit quod Deus potest virtuose odiri a voluntate creata. Posset enim una creatura alteri praecipere quod odiret Deum. Deus autem potest omne illud facere quod fieri non includit contradictionem: cum igitur tale preceptum fieri non includit contradictionem, quia creatura hoc facere potest, sequitur quod Deus potest hoc precipere." See also E. Bonke, *op. cit.*, p. 67; A. Garvens, *op. cit.*, pp. 266 ff.; E. Iserloh, *Gnade und Eucharistie in der philosophischen Theologie des Wilhelm von Ockham*, pp. 69-71.

[130] A. Pelzer, "Les 51 articles de Guillaume Occam censurés en Avignon en 1326," *Revue d'histoire ecclesiastique*, XVIII (1922), p. 254: "Item ponit quod odire deum potest esse actus rectus in via et a deo preceptus...Dicimus quod utraque assertio articuli est falsa et erronea, quia odire deum importat deordinationem creature rationalis immediate respectu dei, que non potest esse licita, nec in ea potest dispensari etiam per deum. Unde sicut amare deum est per se bonum nec potest esse illicitum, sic odire deum est de se malum nec potest esse licitum nec per consequens a deo preceptum, quia sic deus esset auctor mali."

[131] See E. Gilson and P. Boehner, *Christliche Philosophie*, p. 622; E. Iserloh, *Gnade und Eucharistie in der philosophischen Theologie des Wilhelm von Ockham*, pp. 48-50.

GOD: THE OBJECTIVE NORM OF MORALITY

seems to be no doubt that of the works of Ockham the *Quodlibeta* were written after the *Reportationes*.[132] And a parallel case, the change from the so-called "fictum theory of universals" to the "intellection theory" is solidly established by P. Boehner.[133] In E. Hochstetter's opinion there is a similar modification in Ockham's thought regarding the highest ethical value, the love of God, so that it is only in his later writings, especially the *Quodlibeta*, that he becomes clear on this question.[134]

I would venture the opinion that it would be better, perhaps, to defer final judgment on the question of a modification by Ockham of his basic ethical theory. Similarly, the apparent contradiction in Ockham's theory is perhaps best left with the words: *qui potest capere, capiat*. One thing, however, is certain: that it is surely a misuse of Ockham's writings to criticize his whole ethical theory solely on the basis of a text found in the *Fourth Book of the Sentences*, question 16, as if this were the only text that Ockham has on the love and hatred of God or as if it were, if I may use the expression, the "genuine" ethical theory of Ockham.[135]

2) The second question is: Can God command that evil be done? In treating this problem Ockham first gives a rather lengthy account of an opinion that he later rejects as false. I will try to summarize this false opinion and then give Ockham's objections to it. Upon analysis we find

---

[132] See the chapter on Ockham's bibliography in P. Boehner, *The Tractatus de Successivis Attributed to William Ockham* ("Franciscan Institute Publications; Philosophy Series," No. 1; St. Bonaventure, N.Y.: Franciscan Institute, 1944), p. 21. P. Boehner, "The Relative Date of Ockham's Commentary on the Sentences," *Franciscan Studies*, XI (1951), p. 307: "...Ockham had lectured on the Sentences and had started his Ordinatio (the first redaction of the first book on the Sentences) and while he was preparing this he started commenting on the philosophical works. If this hypothesis is correct, it follows that the oldest writing of Ockham is the Reportatio (certainly the 2nd-4th books are preserved in this state)." See É. Amann, "Occam," *Dictionnaire de théologie catholique*, t. XIa (Paris: Letouzey et Ané, 1031), col. 873.

[133] P. Boehner, "The Realistic Conceptualism of William Ockham," *Traditio*, IV (1946), pp. 307-335; P. Boehner, "The Relative Date of Ockham's Commentary on the Sentences," pp. 305-316.

[134] E. Hochstetter, "Viator mundi," pp. 15-16: "Zur Klarheit über diese Frage des höchsten sittlichen Wertes ist Ockham allerdings, soweit wir sehen, erst in den *Quodlibeta* gekommen...Auch hinsichtlich des Gebotes des Gotteshasses ist Ockham im Sentenzenkommentar, soweit wir sehen, noch nicht zu voller Klarheit durchgedrungen...In den *Quodlibeta* aber hat er die Unmöglichkeit dieser Position erkannt."

[135] As an example of this type of interpretation we may mention H. Rommen, *The State in Catholic Thought. A Treatise in Political Philosophy* (St. Louis: Herder, 1947), p. 18; H. Rommen, "The Natural Law in the Renaissance Period," *University of Notre Dame Natural Law Institute Proceedings*, Vol. II (Notre Dame, Ind.: College of Law, University of Notre Dame, 1949), pp. 89-124.

CHAPTER IV

that there are really two separate, though related, questions to be considered here. The first is, whether God could will evil; and the second, whether he could command that an evil act be done.[136]

Regarding the first of these questions raised by Ockham, the proposition "God wills evil" is to be conceded as true simply, *de virtute sermonis*. It is true because by the proposition, "God wills evil," nothing more is denoted than the fact that God wills something that is evil. That is, he wills some act, which act is done by someone evil and in an evil way. Consequently, that act is evil and so God can be said to will evil in so far as he wills some act which is evil.[137]

However, it is not true, according to this opinion, that whoever does evil is himself evil any more than whoever does good is thereby good. Here an appeal is made to Aristotle, since Aristotle maintained that not everyone performing a just act is, therefore, necessarily just; but whoever performs a just act justly is just. And thus only he who does evil in an evil way is really evil.[138] Therefore God, although he wills evil, does not will evil evilly because he is not obliged to do, or refrain from doing, any act whatsoever. As a result we cannot say that God wills evil evilly, nor can He, consequently, be called evil Himself.[139] In a similar manner, God can also command evil, but he could not command it evilly; and he could command something unjust, but he could not com-

---

[136] Ockham, *In I Sent.*, 47, un.: "Hic primum videndum est utrum Deus possit velle malum, secundo an possit praecipere malum." (OTh IV, 681) See G. Biel, *op. cit.*, I Sent., d. 14, 1; E. Iserloh, *Gnade und Eucharistie in der philosophischen Theologie des Wilhelm von Ockham*, pp. 68-69.

[137] Ockham, *In I Sent.*, 47, un.: "Circa primum posset aliquis dicere quod de virtute sermonis haec esset concedenda 'Deus vult malum,' quia per istam de virtute sermonis non plus denotatur nisi quod Deus vult aliquid quod est malum. Sicut vult aliquem actum, qui actus fit ab aliquo malo et male, et per consequens ille actus est malus, et ita vult malum, hoc est, vult aliquem actum, qui actus est malus." (OTh IV, 681).

[138] *Ibid.*: "...dicerent--qui vellent opinionem praedictam tenere--quod ista non est vera 'quicumque facit malum est malus,' nec ista 'quicumque facit bonum est bonus.'...Unde sicut, secundum Philosophum, II *Ethicorum*, non quicumque facit opera iusta est iustus, sed qui facit iuste opera iusta est iustus, ita qui facti malum male est malus, non autem quicumque facit malum est malus." (OTh IV, 682-83). The reference to Aristotle is: *Ethica Nichomachea*, II, 1105b,ff.

[139] Ockham, *In I Sent.*, 47, un.: *Ibid*: "Unde Deus, quamvis faciat illud quod est malum, et per consequens facit malum...non tamen Deus facit male malum, quia non facit quod tenetur non facere. Et eodem modo non vult malum male, et ideo non est malus quamvis velit malum." (OTh IV, 683).

GOD: THE OBJECTIVE NORM OF MORALITY

mand it unjustly. This is said in accordance with the same explanation that is given above.[140]

Now regarding this opinion just presented Ockham states that he has merely proposed it as an opinion that some philosophers hold without, however, wishing to decide whether it is true or false, erroneous, Catholic or heretical.[141] But, he hastens to add, whether the opinion is Catholic or heretical, it is manifestly contrary to the traditional teaching of the Saints to say that the proposition "God wills evil" is simply true. For whether we consider this proposition *de virtute sermonis* or not, it is understood by everyone to mean that "God wills something evilly and unjustly." To distinguish between the two propositions, "God wills evil" and "God does not will evil evilly" is hardly a valid procedure, because the proposition, "God wills something evilly" is a completely absurd statement. The statement is absurd because God is not bound to do, or to refrain from doing, any act whatsoever. But the proposition, "God wills something evilly," would have to imply necessarily that God is obliged to the opposite.[142] But we know of Ockham's continual insistence that "God is not obliged to anyone or to anything."[143]

At first sight it might seem that God can command evil because he commanded the Israelites to take the possessions of the Egyptians. Therefore God commanded the Israelites to steal. Stealing is something evil; therefore God commanded that something evil be done.[144] To this argument Ockham replies that the taking of the possessions of the Egyptians was not something evil but something good. "The very fact that God

---

[140] *Ibid.*: "...dicerent illi qui vellent tenere primam opinionem quod Deus potest praecipere malum non tamen male, et potest praecipere iniustum non tamen inuiuste." (OTh IV, 684).

[141] *Ibid.*: "Haec omnia dico tantum recitative, recitando opinionem quae posset esse aliquorum, sive sit vera sive falsa sive erronea sive catholica sive haeretica."

[142] *Ibid.*: "Sed sive praedicta opinio sit catholica sive haeretica, dico quod secundum intentionem Sanctorum non est concedendum quod Deus vult malum, nec quod Deus facit malum. Quia, sive de virtute sermonis sive non, per tales propositiones intelligunt istas 'Deus vult aliquid male et iniuste,' 'Deus facit aliquid male et iniuste,' quae nullum intellectum possunt habere bonum, quia tunc Deus faceret aliquid vel vellet, cuius oppositum teneretur facere vel velle, quod est omnino absurdum."

[143] See footnote 85 of this chapter.

[144] Ockham, *In I Sent.*, 47, un.: "...utrum Deus possit praecipere malum fieri. Quod sic: Quia Deus praecepit filiis Israel spoliare Aegyptios; igitur praecepit furtum; sed furtum est malum, igitur praecepit malum." (OTh IV, 680).

CHAPTER IV

wills something, it is just."[145] Therefore, when God commanded the spoliation of the Egyptians, he did not command something evil. And so the Israelites did not sin by robbing the Egyptians of their possessions--except those who did so with an evil intention, that is, those who took the possessions of the Egyptians, but not precisely in obedience to the divine command to do so.[146]

3) Can God cause the hatred of himself in a created will? In order to answer this question adequately, we will first have to take into account Ockham's statements on the subject of God as efficient cause. There are two aspects of Ockham's tract on divine efficient causality that are of primary interest at this point: first, God as the immediate cause of all things; and secondly, God as the partial cause.

As we have no strict proof from natural reason alone that God acts as a free, rather than a necessary, cause, so we cannot prove from reason alone that God can cause every producible effect immediately and as the sole operating cause.[147] But with a certain measure of probability we can legitimately maintain that God is the cause of every effect and that he could, as the sole operating cause, produce any effect. The persuasive reasons on which this probability is based are developed by Ockham in the *Third Quodlibeta*, question 3.[148] In general terms the

---

[145] *Ibid.*: "...dico quod spoliare Aegyptios non fuit malum, immo fuit bonum." (OTh IV, 685); *Ibid.*: "...dico quod spoliare Aegyptios non fuit malum, immo fuit bonum." *In I Sent.*, d. 17, q. 3: "...eo ipso quod ipse [Deus] vult, bene et iuste factum est." (OTh III, 478).

[146] *In I Sent.*, 47, un.: "Et ideo Deus praecipiendo spoliare Aegyptios non praecepit malum, nec filii Israel peccaverunt in spoliando, nisi illi qui malo animo, non praecise obediendo divino praecepto, spoliaverint." (OTh IV, 685).

[147] *In I Sent.*, 42, un.: "...dico quod non potest ratione naturali demonstrari quod Deus potest immediate se solo omnem effectum producibilem producere, quia non potest naturali ratione demonstrari quod Deus causat se solo omnia de facto....Et ita cum non possit ratione naturali probari quod Deus sit causa contingens, non potest ratione naturali probari quod Deus potest causare immediate et se solo omnem effectum producibilem." (OTh IV, 617-18). See F. Copleston, *op. cit.*, p. 128: "That God can produce every possible effect, even without the concurrence of a secondary cause, cannot be proved by the philosopher; but it is none the less to be believed."

[148] Ockham, *Quodl.*, III, 4: "...dico primo quod Deus est causa omnium mediata vel immediata, licet hoc non possit demonstrari. Tamen hoc persuadeo auctoritate et ratione....per rationem hoc probo primo sic: omnia dependent essentialiter a Deo; quod non esset verum nisi Deus esset causa illorum. Praeterea si non sic, tunc aliquid aliud a Deo esset incausatum, vel esset processus in infinitum in causis. Quia accipio aliquid quod non ponis causari a Deo, et quaero utrum sit causatum aut incausatum; si primo modo, igitur causatur ab aliquo; et de illo quaero, et erit processus in infinitum. Si detur secundum, habetur propositum, quia tale est Deus. Secundo dico quod Deus est causa immediata omnium. Quod probo, quia omne aliud a Deo plus dependet a deo quam aliqua creatura ab alia creatura; sed una creatura sic dependet ab alia quod est causa eius immediata; igitur et Deus." (OTh IX, 215-16). *In I Sent.*,

GOD: THE OBJECTIVE NORM OF MORALITY

arguments are stated in this form: Everything which is not effectively from God is uncaused or uncreated. But everything that is uncaused or uncreated is God. Therefore, everything that is not God is effectively from Him. Longer proofs are developed by Ockham step by step, first proving that God is really the cause, either immediate or mediate, of all things; and secondly, a further step or proof to show that God is the immediate cause of all things.

First, God is the cause, either immediate or mediate, of all things. Ockham's argument for this statement is as follows: Everything depends essentially on God. This general principle would not be true unless God is really the cause of everything. However, if God is not really the cause of all things, then there would be something that is not God and yet is uncreated. This consequence must follow or else we are forced into a position of holding an infinite regression in causes.

Secondly, God is the immediate cause of all things. The proof for this statement is as follows: Everything that is not God must depend on him at least to the extent that one creature depends on another creature. But one creature depends on another immediately in those cases in which the one is the immediate cause of the other. Therefore, God is the immediate cause of all things that are not God.

Negatively speaking, we can advance no really valid reasons to uphold the opinion that God is not an immediately concurring cause in the production of every effect.[149] The non-Christian philosophers held that God is not the immediate cause of the acts of inferior beings. But the Christian philosopher holds that God concurs in every action of his creatures in an immediate manner. God's concurrence is so necessary that if God does not concur with the human will, the will of the creature would be totally incapable of eliciting any act whatsoever.[150] And while it cannot be proved, strictly speaking, that God is the immediate cause of all things, the arguments presented above give us a persuasion, a high

---

42, un.: "...videtur posse probabiliter teneri quod Deus est causa cuiuslibet effectus et quod potest se solo omnem effectum possibilem produci causare." (OTh IV, 620-21).

[149] In I Sent., 42, un.: "...dico quod per nullam rationem efficacem vel multum apparentem potest probari Deum non esse causam immediate concurrentem ad producendum omnes effectus." (OTh IV, 620).

[150] In III Sent. 7: "Et quando dicitur quod actus voluntatis est in potestate voluntatis, si intelligitur sic quod non possit impediri, hoc nullus christianus debet concedere; licet Philosophus habeat eam concedere qui non ponit Deum immediate aliquid causare in istis inferioribus. Sed christianus, qui habet ponere quod Deus concurrit in omni actione immediate, habet ponere quod Deo non coagente cum voluntate, voluntas nullum actum elicit, quia deficit causa partialis necessario requisita." (OTh VI, 206). For a discussion of Ockham's criticism of Aristotle on this point, se A. Pegis, "Necessity and Liberty: An Historical Note on St. Thomas Aquinas," pp. 30-32.

CHAPTER IV

degree of probability, to this effect. Accordingly, Ockham frequently mentions that God is the immediate and partial cause in concurrence with the creature in every act of the creature. He speaks, for instance, in the following terms: "God who immediately causes every act...."[151] "God is the immediate cause of every act;"[152] "If God would cause...as total cause what he now always causes as a partial cause..."[153]

Furthermore, it must be admitted that in whatever act God concurs in the way of, in the manner of, a partial cause, he could produce that same act as the total cause.[154] For if two partial causes would concur in the required manner for the production of a certain desired effect, it would not be necessary for both causes to operate in producing this effect in the case where one of these partial causes is of such a nature that it could produce that same effect as a total cause which it now, *de facto*, produces in cooperation with the other partial cause. If this partial, but potentially total, cause would finally act as a real total cause in producing the effect, then the action of the other partial cause is not required. And such is the situation with respect to God and the human will.[155]

Thus God concurs with the human will so that both God and the human will are partial causes in the production of an act of the will; God could, however, produce as the total cause this same act which he now produces as the partial cause; this act could be produced without the partial causality of the human will. Upon analysis, we find that this is just a more involved way of stating, or explaining, Ockham's general principle: Whatever God produces by means of secondary causes he can

---

[151] *Quaest. Variae*, q. 7, a. 4: "...non tantum voluntas creata est causa efficiens illius actus, sed ipse Deus, qui omnem actum immediate causat, sicut quaecumque causa secunda." (OTh VIII, 389).

[152] *Quaest. Variae*, q. 8: "...Deus est causa immediata cuiuslibet actus nostri..." (OTh VIII, 435).

[153] *In IV Sent.*, 10-11: "Unde si Deus causaret odium in voluntate alicuius sicut causa totalis, sicut semper causat sicut causa partialis..." (OTh VII, 198).

[154] *In II Sent.*, 15: "Item respectu cuiuscumque est Deus causa partialis respectu eius est vel esse potest causa totalis, quia ipse supplere potest omnem causalitatem causae secundae in genere causae efficientis." (OTh V, 342). *Ibid.*: "...quia cuiuscumque potest [Deus] esse causa partialis, potest esse totalis." (OTh V, 350). See A. Garvens, *op. cit.*, p. 273.

[155] Ockham, *Ibid.*: "...dico quod si causae sint approximatae debito modo et effectus ponitur, non requiritur necessario atio omnium causarum. Quia una est partialis quae potest esse totalis respectu cuiuslibet producibilis ab alia causa partiali, et quando illa est causa totalis de facto, tunc non requiritur actio alterius causae. Sic est de voluntate nostra et Deo." (OTh V, 350).

GOD: THE OBJECTIVE NORM OF MORALITY

immediately produce and conserve without them. And consequently, every effect which God can cause by means of secondary causes he can cause immediately by Himself, operating as the total cause.[156] God is, therefore, the first and the immediate cause of all that is produced by means of secondary causes. God is truly called the immediate cause, because that cause is called immediate which, if it is posited, the effect will take place; and if it is not posited, it is impossible for the effect to take place. God is this type of cause.[157]

So although God often acts through the instrumentality of secondary causes, he is not on that account to be designated as a mediate cause. He is frequently the partial cause of those things which he could produce alone as the total cause. But God does not choose to produce everything alone as the total cause; as the partial, though principal, cause God co-acts with many secondary causes. However, God is just as much the immediate cause of all things when he cooperates with secondary causes as he is when he acts without them. The secondary causes, on the other hand, should not be considered as totally superfluous on account of their subordinate position in relation to the principal cause. The secondary causes are only secondary; but they are nevertheless real causes. God remains the principal and immediate cause. He

---

[156] *Quodl.*, VI, 6: "...'quidquid Deus producit mediantibus causis secundis, potest immediate sine illis producere et conservare.' Ex ista propositione arguo sic: omnem effectum quem potest Deus mediante causa secunda, potest immediate per se..." (OTh IX, 604-05). *Quodl.*, VI, 1: "...quidquid Deus potest facere mediante causa secunda in genere causae efficientis vel finis, potest immediate per se..." (OT IX, 587). *In II Sent.* 3-4: "Deus enim est tale agens quod potest esse causa totalis effectus sine quocumque alio" (OTh V, 72). See L. Baudry (ed.), *Tractatus de principiis theologiae*, p. 45: "[Deus] potest in genere causae efficientis quidquid potest causa secunda; quia si potest facere omne quod fieri non includit contradictionem et constat quod nulla causa secunda potest facere aliqua ab illis que contradictionem non includunt, sequitur quod ipse potest quidquid potest causa secunda."...See P. Boehner, *Ockham. Philosophical Writings*, pp. xix-xx: "*Whatever God produces by means of secondary (i.e. created) causes, God can produce and conserve immediately and without their aid* Hence any positive reality which is naturally produced by another created being (not of course without the aid of God who is the first cause) can be produced by God alone without the causality of the secondary cause...This is stated in a more general manner: *God can cause, produce and conserve every reality, be it a substance or an accident, apart from any other reality*." See also G. Biel, *op. cit.*, I Sent., d. 14, q. 2, F; S. Day, *op. cit.*, p. 176; D. Webering, *op. cit.*, pp. 151-152.

[157] Ockham, *In II Sent.*, 3-4: "...Deus est causa prima et immediata omnium quae producuntur a causis secundis. Quod autem sit immediata causa patet, quia illa causa dicitur immediata qua posita potest poni effectus et qua non posita non potest poni. Sed Deus est huiusmodi respectu cuiuslibet creaturae, igitur etc." (OTh V, 60-61). See S. Tornay, *op. cit.*, p. 177.

CHAPTER IV

does not, however, always choose to act with his full power as a total cause.[158]

God as the principal efficient cause, says Ockham, immediately and partially produces every effect that is produced by creatures. Evil acts also, in so far as the acts themselves are something positive, are produced by God immediately, though partially, in cooperation with a creature. But it does not follow that if God produces these acts he sins by this cooperation with a creature. God is not obliged to do, or refrain from doing, any action. God is not bound by any rule or obligation.[159]

God cannot sin. But it does not follow that since sin belongs to the realm of the possible, therefore God cannot do everything that is possible. The reason why God cannot sin is that sin is a connotative term, not only signifying the act that is produced, but also connoting that the act is performed by someone who is under the obligation of performing the opposite of that act which he performs or omits. This connotation of an obligation to the opposite excludes any idea of God sinning. A parallel case would be the connotative term "meritorious." This consequence would not be valid: Since God can do every possible act by himself and a meritorious act is possible, therefore God can perform a meritorious act. Or to take a more familiar example: to die is possible. But God cannot die. The reason that God cannot die is that the term "to die" does not signify, precisely, the destruction of something, but it also connotes the destruction of such a thing which must (or can) die. Hence, although God could destroy anything other than Himself, he cannot die or destroy Himself.[160] The conclusion is that since

---

[158] Ockham, *Ibid.*: "...licet Deus agat mediantibus causis secundis vel magis cum eis, non dicitur Deus mediate agere, nec secundae causae frustra....non vult solus totum producere, sed coagit cum causis secundis tanquam causa partialis, licet sit principalior. Ita quod ipse est causa immediata omnium quando agit cum causis secundis sicut quando agit sine aliis. Nec propter hoc superfluunt causae secundae, quia Deus non agit in qualibet actione secundum totam potentiam suam." (OTh V, 72).

[159] *Quodl.*, III, 4: "...omnis res quae est peccatum, est a Deo; tamen Deus non peccat, quia non tenetur ad oppositum, cum nullius debitor sit." (OTh IX, 219).

[160] *In I Sent.*, 42, un.: "...nego istam consequentiam: 'Deus non potest peccare nec mori, et ista sunt possibilia, ergo non potest facere omnia possibilia.' Sicut ista consequentia non valet 'Deus potest facere omnem actum absolutum et positivum se solo; sed actus meritorius est huiusmodi actus; ergo Deus se solo potest facere actum meritorium.' Sed in omnibus talibus est fallacia figurae dictionis. Quia in prima propositione distribuitur unum simpliciter absolutum, et in minori accipitur sub unum connotativum, et in talibus est fallacia figurae dictionis. Ita est in proposito. Quia 'peccare' non tantum importat illam rem quae producitur, sed etiam importat aliquem obligatum ad oppositum illius quod facit vel omittit. Eodem modo 'mori' non importat pracise destructionem alicuius rei, sed connotat destructionem illius rei quae dicitur mori. Et ideo quamvis possit causare aliquo modo destructionem rei quae moritur, tamen non potest ipse mori." (OTh IV, 621-22).

sin implies an obligation and the violation of that obligation, God, who is subject to no obligations, cannot sin. Only creatures are bound by obligations. Sin is possible only for creatures, who can violate these obligations.

In speaking of sin, however, we must admit that not only is the created will the efficient cause of the act of committing a sin, but God also, who immediately causes every act, is the efficient cause. Does God sin in causing such a sinful act? Ockham uses his same argument again: God is debtor to no one. God is not bound in any way by any obligation to cause this act or its opposite; nor is he obliged not to cause this act. Therefore, no matter if he causes or does not cause this act, he does not sin in any case. The created will, on the other hand, is obliged by the law of God not to cause certain acts. Consequently, the created will would sin in causing these acts for in doing them the creature does what he is obliged not to do. If, however, the creature would be freed from obligation, then there would be no sin. Freed from all obligations, the creature would occupy a position, at least in this respect, similar to that of God who is subject to no obligation.[161]

When God cooperates with the sinner as the partial cause in the production of some sinful act, it must not be said that God himself commits any sin, because he is not obliged to any act. Only the violation of an obligation makes a person a sinner.[162] But whatever act God produces as the partial cause, he can also produce, if he so wills, as the total cause.[163] And God would not sin in doing any action as a total cause, which action he now performs as a partial cause in cooperation with sinners. Because a sin, as we have said, is nothing else but some act which is committed or omitted contrary to an obligation which a person has to the opposite. But God cannot be obliged in any way to act or to refrain

---

[161] *Quaest. Variae*, q. 7, a. 4: "Et si dicis quod tunc Deus peccaret causando talem actum deformem, sicut voluntas creata peccat quia causat talem actum: respondeo: Deus nullius est debitor, et ideo nec tenetur illum actum causare nec oppositum actum, nec illum actum non causare, et ideo non peccat quantumcumque illum actum causet. Voluntas autem creata tenetur per praeceptum divinum illum actum non causare, et per consequens in causando illum actum peccat, quia facit quod non debet facere. Unde si voluntas creata non obligaretur ad non causandum illum actum vel oppositum, quantumcumque causaret illum, nunquam peccaret sicut nec Deus." (OTh VIII, 389f.). *In IV Sent.*, 10-11 (OTh VII, 198); footnote 119 of this chapter. See also E. Bonke, *op. cit.*, pp. 67-68; A. Garvens, *op. cit.*, pp. 404-405; E. Iserloh, *Gnade und Eucharistie in der philosophischen Theolgie des Wilhelm von Ockham*, pp. 65-66.

[162] Ockham, *In IV Sent.*, 10-11: "Obligatio igitur facit aliquem peccatorem vel non peccatorem." (OTh VII, 198).

[163] See footnote 154 and following of this chapter.

CHAPTER IV

from acting; and from the very fact that God wills something, it is done justly.[164]

Having finished these preliminaries, we can now return to our original question: Can God cause the hatred of himself in a created will? It should be evident from what was said above that it is completely impossible for God to sin even if he would cause the hatred of himself in any created will. For God is not obliged to anything or to anyone. God could cause the act of hatred of himself in the sense that he is the total cause of any act of a creature. For God can cooperate with the sinner as the partial cause of the sinful act; and whatever God produces as the partial cause he can also, if he so chooses, produce as the total cause. But it cannot be said that God would sin in producing this act. But neither would the created will sin in this case, because the hatred is caused by God as the total cause of the act, and, therefore, it is not completely or really in the power of the created will.[165] For to quote Ockham's own words again, "A sin is so voluntary that, unless it is voluntary, it is not a sin."[166]

Ockham also deals with this same question of God causing the hatred of himself in the created will in a slightly different way. Abstracting from the sinfulness of the act of hatred in this case--for there is, indeed, no sinfulness in this case--Ockham says that God can cause such an act in its absolute sense in the created will. And this is exemplified by the fact that God can cause every absolute without anything else that is not identical with the absolute itself. But the act of hating God, in so far as its absolute being is concerned, is not the same as the deformity or the malice of the act. Therefore God can cause whatever is absolute in the act of hating God. In regard to whatever God is a partial cause, of that same thing he is, or can be, the total cause. For

---

[164] Ockham, *In IV Sent.*, qq. 10-11: "...Deus non peccaret quantumcumque faceret omnem actum sicut causa totalis quem nunc facit cum peccatore sicut causa partialis Quia peccatum, et dictum est, non dicit aliud nisi actum aliquem commissionis vel omissionis ad quem homo obligatur, propter cuius commissionem vel omissionem obligatur ad poenam aeternam. Deus autem ad nullum actum potest obligari, et ideo eo ipso quod Deus vult hoc, [hoc] est iustum fieri." (OTh VII, 198).

[165] *Ibid.*: "Unde si Deus causaret odium in voluntate alicuius sicut causa totalis, sicut semper causat sicut causa partialis, neuter pecaret: nec Deus, quia ad nihil obligatur; nec alius, quia actus ille non esset in potestate sua." (OTh VII, 198), Cf. *In II Sent.*, 15 (OTh V, 350f.). See F. Copleston, *op. cit.*, pp. 95; 104; E. Iserloh, *Gnade und Eucharistie in der philosophischen Theologie des Wilhelm von Ockham*, pp. 65-66; 69-70; G. De Lagarde, *op. cit.*, p. 58; S. Tornay, *op. cit.*, pp. 180-181.

[166] Ockham, *Quodl.*, III, 14: "Praeterea nullus actus est virtuosus nec vitiosus nisi sit voluntarious et in potestate voluntatis, quia peccatum adeo est voluntarium, etc...." (OTh IX, 254). See Chapter III, pp. 51 ff.

GOD: THE OBJECTIVE NORM OF MORALITY

God himself can supply all the causality usually supplied by the secondary causes with which he cooperates in any given case. But in regard to anything positive or absolute which is produced by creatures, God is always the partial cause. Therefore, he can be the total cause in regard to whatever is absolute. Consequently, he can be the total cause of whatever is absolute in the act of hating God.[167]

Similarly, since God cannot be obliged in any way to cause or not to cause any act whatsoever, he could, therefore, cause any act or its opposite without incurring any guilt. And just as he can cause totally an act of loving God--and this act would not have any goodness or evil attached to it because moral goodness or evil connote that the agent is obligated to perform this act or its opposite--so also he could cause totally an act of the hatred of God without any moral evil attached to the act. The reasons are the same for both cases: namely, that the agent here, God, is under no obligation to cause any act whatsoever.[168]

4) The final problem to be treated here as a conclusion to this chapter is: Can God command that he be not loved, even hated? We must first of all distinguish this problem from the preceding question, which was, "Can God cause the hatred of himself in a created will?"[169] Secondly, we must also distinguish between the command of God that he be not loved and the command that he be hated. As mentioned previously,

---

[167] *In II Sent.* 15: "Et quod Deus possit causare actum odiendi Deum quantum ad omne absolutum in actu in voluntate creata probatur, quia Deus potest omne absolutum causare sine omni alio quod non est idem cum illo absoluto. Sed actus odiendi Deum quantum ad omne absolutum in eo nn est idem cum deformitate et malitia in actu, igitur Deus potest causare quidquid absolutum est in actu odiendi Deum....respectu cuiuscumque est Deus causa partialis respectu eius est vel esse potest causa totalis, quia ipse supplere potest omnem causalitatem causae secundae in genere causae efficientis. Sed respectu cuiuslibet positivi, maxime absoluti producti a creatura, est Deus causa partialis, sicut prius ostensum est. Igitur potest esse causa totalis respectu cuiuslibet absoluti, et per consequens respectu actus odiendi Deum." (OTh V, 342-43). See E. Bonke, *op. cit.*, pp. 67-68.

[168] Ockham, *In II Sent.* 15: "Sed Deus ad nullum actum causandum obligatur, ideo quemlibet actum absolutum potest sine omni malo culpae causare et eius oppositum. Et ideo sicut potest causare totaliter actum diligendi sine bonitate vel malitia morali, quia bonitas moralis vel malitia connotant quod agens obligatur ad illum actum vel eius oppositum, ita potest causare totaliter actum odiendi Deum sine omni malitia morali propter eandem causam, quia Deus ad nullum actum causandum obligatur." (OTh V, 353). See F. Copleston, *op. cit.*, p. 104; E. Hochstetter, "Viator mundi," pp. 15-16; S. Tornay, *op. cit.*, p. 180.

[169] E. Hochstetter, "Viator mundi," p. 15: "Zu dessen Aufhellung muss man zweig Fragen auseinanderhalten: die eine ist die der Verursachung des Gotteshasses durch Gott, die andere ist die der Möglichkeit des Gebotes des Gotteshasses durch Gott selbst."

CHAPTER IV

there is some tendency on the part of authors to confuse these two questions.[170]

Although no one can hate God in an orderly way, what would happen if God would command that he be not loved and even hated? Can God issue such a command; and, if so, can the creature obey? Is the creature even under an obligation to obey in this case?

We have already mentioned the case brought up in the *Fourth Book of the Sentences*, question 14, which deals with the command of God that he be hated. In this text Ockham states that every created will can conform to the divine precepts. But God can command that the created will hate Him; therefore, the created will can do this. And moreover, everything that can be a just act for those living on earth, can also be a just act for those in heaven. But to hate God can be a just act on earth, if such hatred is commanded by God. Therefore, it would also be a just act for those in heaven under the supposition of a command from Almighty God.[171]

Since we have already mentioned the difficulties occasioned by this text of Ockham and have already expressed our viewpoint concerning it, we can pass over that particular aspect of the problem here, and, instead, point out one other important distinction that must be kept in mind if we are to avoid misinterpreting Ockham. The point is, we should distinguish between the possibility of giving the command and the possibility of fulfilling the command once it has been given. The command itself is possible. The reason for this will be seen in a parallel case given below. The fulfillment of the command, however, by the creature seems impossible, as previously stated, because of the equivalence between love and obedience.[172]

In the *Third Quodlibeta*, question 13, Ockham answers the question concerning the command of God that he be not loved. The case he presents to illustrate this command is as follows. Suppose that God would issue the command that a man should occupy himself with studying during

---

[170] E. Iserloh, *Gnade und Eucharistie in der philosophischen Theologie des Wilhelm von Ockham*, p. 49: "Es ist hier vom Gotteshass nicht die Rede, sondern danvon, dass Gott dem Menschen verbieten kann, einen direkten Akt der Gottesliebe zu setzen, weil er seine ganze Kraft und Aufmerksamkeit dem Studium widmen soll." See this chapter, p. 171.

[171] Ockham, *In IV Sent.*, 16: "Praeterea, omnis voluntas potest se conformare praecepto divino. Sed Deus potest praecipere quod voluntas creata odiat eum, igitur voluntas creata potest hoc facere. Praeterea, omne quod potest esse actus rectus in via, et in patria. Sed odire Deum potest esse actus rectus in via, puta si praecipiatur a Deo, igitur in patria." (OTh VII, 352). L. Baudry (ed.), *Tractatus de principiis theologiae*, pp. 46-47: "...voluntas igitur tali precepto a Deo facto obediens mereretur ut beatificaretur."

[172] See E. Gilson and P. Boehner, *Christliche Philosophie*, p. 622.

GOD: THE OBJECTIVE NORM OF MORALITY

a certain period of time and during this time he should not be thinking of God. In other words, God is not to be loved during this period of time when the man's entire attention is supposed to be devoted to study. Now, says Ockham, if God would give such a command--and it seems that he could do so without contradiction--then I say that the will cannot elicit an act of loving God during this period of time. For by the very fact that the human will would elicit such an act he would fulfill the divine precept of loving God; but since to love God above all means to love God and love whatever God wills loved, from this it follows that by eliciting an act of love of God during this time the creature would not be fulfilling the law of God which states that for this particular period of time he is not to be loved. Consequently, in eliciting an act of loving God at this time the creature would love God and not love God; he would fulfill the divine command (of loving God) and not fulfill it (by loving God at this time).[173]

Here again we can break the case down into two separate problems: first, can the command be given; secondly, can the command be fulfilled if it has been given? In so far as the giving of the command is concerned, Ockham states that it seems that God can give the command without contradiction. To explain this, we may say that the command itself is something possible as a command. Anyone who would say that the proposition, "God is not to be loved," is impossible need only read the words between the quotation marks in this sentence to see that it is possible. A created being can, and probably has, as a matter of actual fact, often given this command. But whatever a secondary cause can do with the cooperation of God as the partial cause, God can also cause alone as the total cause. Hence God could be the total cause of the command, "God must not be loved."[174]

---

[173] Ockham, *Quodl.*, III, 14: "Si dicis quod Deus potest praecipere quod pro aliquo tempore non diligatur ipse, quia potest praecipere quod intellectus sit sic intentus circa studium et voluntas similiter, ut nihil possit pro illo tempore de Deo cogitare....Respondeo: si Deus posset hoc praecipere, sicut videtur quod potest since contradictione, dico tunc quod voluntas non potest pro tunc talem actum elicere; quia ex hoc ipso quod talem actum eliceret, Deum deligeret super omnia, et per consequens impleret praeceptum divinum, quia hoc est diligere Deum super omnia: diligere quidquid Deus vult diligi; et ex hoc ipso quod sic diligeret, non faceret praeceptum divinum per casum; et per consequens sic diligendo, Deum deligeret et non diligeret, faceret praeceptum Dei et non faceret." (OTh IX, 256-57).

[174] P. Boehner explains the possibility of the command in this way in *Ockham: Philosophical Writings*, p. xlix: "It is well known that Ockham admitted that God can command by his absolute power that a person should hate him or at least not love Him. It is important to note that this possibility is admitted in the purely ontoloical and logical realm. For in this realm there cannot be a contradiction, since it is a fact that creatures can command others to hate God; the command, therefore, is a reality, considered as a mental or spoken sentence, and every reality has God as its primary cause." The same idea is contained in P. Boehner, "A

CHAPTER IV

But, granted that the command that he be not loved can be given by God, there is the second question: can the command be fulfilled? My answer will be that in the case given it is impossible to disobey the command of God by eliciting an act of love during this time. It seems incorrect, as far as I can see, to say "the creature could not obey in this case"; rather, it should be said "the creature cannot disobey in this case."[175] If it were possible for the creature to disobey the command of God by eliciting an act of the love of God, then God would be loved (by the act of loving God) and not loved (by disobeying his command) at the same time. By saying, however, that the creature cannot disobey we avoid the contradiction that God is loved and not loved at the same time.

In explanation of this position, let us suppose that the creature takes either one of two possible alternatives in reaction to the command of God that he is not to be loved during this particular time of study. First, the creature remains intent on studying, does not elicit an act of the love of God, thus fulfilling the particular command of God that he be not loved during this time. Secondly, the creature turns from his studies to elicit an act of the love of God.

In the first alternative, it seems that no difficulty will be encountered. For by following the command not to love God at this particular time, an act which is precisely an act of loving God is not elicited, it is true; but God is loved in the act of being intent on studying since this is in fulfillment of a command of God. At the same time, the obligation to love God is not violated by not loving God by a specific act of love at this time, because the obligation to love God actually, that is, by a specific act of love, is an affirmative precept which obliges always but not at all times (*semper sed non pro semper*). That is, there is no obligation on the part of the creature to be continuously, incessantly, eliciting acts of the love of God. Therefore, by not eliciting an act of the love of God at this particular time no obligation is violated. And following the command not to love God at this time is in fulfillment of a divine command. We find, then, that in this latter alternative God would be loved (by fulfilling the command) and he would not not be loved (by the violation of the command).

P. Boehner's conclusion that "the creature could not obey since in obeying it would love (and not love) Him," it seems to me, if taken in the

---

Recent Presentation of Ockham's Philosophy," pp. 453-454. See also E. Gilson and P. Boehner, *Christliche Philosophie*, p. 622.

[175] P. Boehner, *Ockham: Philosophial Writings*, p. xlix: "If God commanded a creature to hate him or simply not to love Him, the creature would be obliged to obey, but it could not obey since in obeying it would love Him."

GOD: THE OBJECTIVE NORM OF MORALITY

strict sense, cannot be correct.[176] When the creature obeys the command not to love God during this particular period of time, it seems that no difficulty arises. For Ockham is speaking here of a specific act of love--an act which the creature is not to elicit because he is commanded by God to be intent on studying. By obeying the command it is true that the creature would love God, but it would not love God by a specific act of the love of God. It would love God (in the habitual sense, or in the sense of fulfilling the command not to love him by a specific act of love) and it would not love God (in the actual sense, or in the sense of eliciting a special act of love). But to love God and not to love God at the same time would not be a contradiction or an impossibility in this case, because we are speaking of two different kinds of love of God: actual, in the one case; habitual, in the other.

Now let us suppose that the creature would take the second alternative mentioned above: he elicits an act of the love of God. My answer here is that this alternative is not open to the creature; it is simply impossible for him to elicit an act of the love of God in this case. This, I think, is the real meaning of Ockham's words: "I reply: if God could give this command--and it seems that it would not be a contradiction for him to do so--then I maintain that the created will cannot elicit such an act (love of God) during this time."[177] If the creature is commanded by God not to love God (that is, by an act of love at this time), then it is impossible for the creature to elicit an act of love, because in a true act of the love of God must be included the notion that the creature loves God and whatever God wills. But such an act of love is impossible because it falls under the prohibition given by God for this period of time. Thus a genuine act of love--the love of God and what God wills--would be impossible in this case. And we would not have the contradiction, therefore, that God is loved and not loved at the same time.

---

[176] *Ibid.:* "In the ethical realm, however, an antinomy is encountered, the only real antinomy in Ockham's philosophy. If God commanded a creature to hate him or simply not to love Him, the creature would be obliged to obey, but it could not obey since in obeying it would love Him. Since the ethical laws are not propositions (which alone are true or false and between which alone genuine contradictions an occur), but are commands, their ultimate source must be a will, and not any impersonal thing of the ontological sphere, nor any proposition of the logical sphere. Briefly, the command to hate God is not a logical or ontological impossibility, but to fulfill this command is an ethical impossibility." See also P. Boehner, "A Recent Presentation of Ockham's Philosophy," pp. 453-454; E. Hochstetter, "Viator mundi," p. 16; W. Kolmel, *op. cit.*, pp. 58-59.

[177] *Quodl.*, III, 14: "Respondeo: si Deus posset hoc praecipere, sicut videtur quod potest sine contradictione, dico tunc quod voluntas non potest pro tunc talem actum elicere..." (OTh IX, 256).

CHAPTER IV

For the act of love referred to in this case would not be a genuine act of the love of God.[178]

A third alternative appears here. The creature could attempt an act of the love of God. But this is not a real third alternative; it is actually the same case as presented in the second alternative. This attempted act of love is not a genuine act of love at all and does not involve us in the difficulty of explaining how God could be loved and not loved at the same time.

What is impossible, then, in this case is not that the creature can obey the command of God not to love Him, but that it is impossible for the creature to disobey the command by eliciting an act of genuine love of God. The creature could, of course, disobey the command of God by attempting to elicit an act of love, but it still holds true that if God commands that a creature should not elicit an act of the love of God, the creature cannot possibly elicit such an act. It cannot elicit a genuine act of the love of God, in Ockham's words: "the created will cannot elicit such an act during this time." For the love of God as the highest norm of morality, as we have tried to explain at some length in this chapter, means this: Love God and will what he wills.

---

[178] For E. Iserloh's interpretation see *Gnade und Eucharistie in der philosophischen Theologie des Wilhelm von Ockham*, pp. 49-50: "Die Schwierigkeit wird nicht so gelöst, dass Gott ein Verbot des Liebesaktes nicht erlass kann, weil das seinem Wesen oder seiner Weisheit widerspreche, sondern es dem Menschen in dem Falle unmöglich ist, einen solchen Akt hervorzubringen. Der Akt der Liebe kann zwar nicht ethisch schlecht sein, aber der Mensch kann ihn nicht setzen, wenn Gott es ihm verbietet. Das 'voluntas non potest pro tunc talem actum elicere' bezieht sich auf den Akt der Liebe und nicht auf einen Akt gemass dem Gebot, Gott eine Zietlang nicht zu lieben...In *Quodlibet* III q. 14 [13] ist damit lediglich gesagt Ein Akt der Gottesliebe kann vom freien geschöpflichen Willen nur als guter Akt gesetzt werden. Wenn Gott dem Menschen diesen Akt verbietet, dann wird er nicht schlecht, sondern kann er vom Menschen nicht gesetzt werden. Das Handeln Gottes ist also in keiner Weise eingeschränkt." The above work also contains a criticism of P. Boehner's and E. Hochstetter's interpretation of this case in Ockham, pp. 49-50. For E. Iserloh's earlier criticism of P. Boehner's position see "Um die Echtheit des 'Centiloquium'," pp. 334-335.

CHAPTER V

THE NATURE OF MORALITY

In the preceding chapters we investigated the nature of moral science in general as well as the norms, subjective and objective, which govern and direct human acts in the moral sphere. In this final chapter or concluding explanation of Ockham's basic ethical thought it remains to examine the following points in order to give a more detailed picture of Ockham's principles and their application in the field of morals. First, the three types of moral acts will be brought into focus: the necessarily virtuous act, the contingently virtuous act, and the morally indifferent act. Secondly, we will consider an important topic: the nature and source of the rightness of an act and the nature of the evil act, of sin. And lastly, a brief summary of the moral virtues will be presented. It can be seen at a glance that some of these topics have been touched upon already in the previous chapter. Our purpose here is to try to complete the picture, to put in the finishing touches, to clear up, perhaps, some of the points that may still remain somewhat unclear regarding the fundamentals of Ockham's ethics.

Although Ockham himself is not always clear and consistent in his terminology, we can arrive at a distinction of three different types of moral acts mentioned frequently in his writings: the necessarily virtuous act, the extrinsically virtuous act, and the indifferent act. In the *Third Book of the Sentences* Ockham speaks of this division explicitly, distinguishing, first, those acts which are intrinsically good, those which are intrinsically evil, and those which are morally indifferent.[1] This act would be intrinsically good: to will to pray from the motive of honoring God and because it is prescribed by God, because it is according to the dictates of right reason and is in accord with all the other circumstances which the case would require. This act, on the other hand, would be intrinsically evil: to will to pray out of motives of pride against the precept of God or the dictates of right reason. And this act, finally, would be morally indifferent: to will simply to pray

---

[1] Ockham, *Quaest. Variae*, q. 7, a. 2: "...aliquis actus est intrinsece bonus moraliter, aliquis intrinsece malus et vitiosus, aliquis neuter sive indifferens." (OTh VIII, 338).

CHAPTER V

without paying attention to, or abstracting from, any circumstances dictated by right reason and without either a good or an evil intention.[2]

Immediately following the division of moral acts just presented above, Ockham sets down another division: some acts are good or evil of themselves; some acts are good or evil on account of the circumstances which accompany the act; some acts are good because of the supernatural intention which renders them not only good, but also meritorious.[3] This, by the way, agrees with a division offered by Duns Scotus.[4] Examples of these types of acts are given by Ockham. Thus, abstracting from any circumstances which accompany the act, prayer would be a good act of itself, i.e. because it is in reference to a worthy object. In the same way, stealing would be an evil act of itself, i.e. because it has reference to

---

[2] *Ibid.*: "Exemplum primi: velle orare propter honorem Dei et quia praeceptum est a Deo secundum rectam rationem etc. Exemplum secundi: velle orare propter vanam gloriam et quia contra praeceptum Dei et contra rectam rationem. Exemplum tertii: velle simpliciter orare sine aliqua circumstantia dictata a ratione, quia nec propter bonum finem nec propter malum, quia propter nullum finem." (OTh VIII, 338). See O. Suk, "The Connection of Virtues according to Ockham," *Franciscan Studies*, X (1950), pp. 30-31.

[3] Ockham, *Ibid*: "...aliquis actus est bonus ex genere vel malus, aliquis ex circumstantia, aliquis ex principio meritorio." (OTh VIII, 338). See E. Hochstetter, "Viator mundi," *Franziskanische Studien*, XXXII (1950), pp. 9-10.

[4] D. Scotus, *Quaestiones quodlibetales*, XVIII, in *Joannis Duns Scoti opera omnia*, tom. XXVI, ed. Vivès (Paris: 1895), pp. 238-239: "Prima dicitur bonitas ex genere, quae competit volitioni, ex hoc quod transit super obiectum conveniens actui tali, secundum dictamen rectae rationis. Secunda potest dici bonitas virtuosa, sive ex circumstantia, quae competit volitioni ex hoc, quod ipsa elicitur a voluntate cum omnibus circumstantiis dictatis a recta ratione debere sibi competere in eliciendo ipsam. Tertia vero bonitas potest dici meritoria, sive gratuita in acceptatione divina, in ordine ad praemium, quae convenit actui, ex hoc quod praesupposita duplici bonitate, jam dicta elicitur conformiter principio merendi, quod est gratia vel chritas." See P. Vignaux, "Nominalisme," *Dictionnaire théologie catholique*, t. XIa (Paris: Letouzey et Ané, 1931), col. 770: "L'acte méritoire: Les actes humains sont susceptibles de bonté a trois degrés: a) L'acte simplement bon, *actus bonus ex genere*, trouve dans la fin qu'il vise une certaine conformité à la raison; il réalise de l'utile ou de l'agréable, évite un désagrément ou un péril, *propter aliquod bonum utile vel delectabile consequendum aut incommodum vel periculum vitandum.* b) L'acte moralement bon, *actus moraliter bonus*, est accompli en conformité avec la raison, peur cette raison qu'il lui est conforme, *actus secundum dictamen rectae rationis, qui elicitur propter hoc quod ratio sic dictavit.* c) L'acte bon au dégre méritoire, *actus bonus meritorie*, est accompli en vue de Dieu, *propter Deum*, et nous vaut comme récompense la vie éternelle, *de merito virtuous aeternae*. Comme l'acte moralement bon, l'acte méritoire est accompli selon l'ordre de la raison, *secundum dictamen rectae rationis*; c'est un acte verueux, *actus virtuosus*, l'acte verueux parfait, *actus virtuosus perfectus*, par opposition à l'acte moralement bon qui n'est qu'imparfaitment verueux, *actus virtuosus imperfectus.*" See also G. Biel, *Repertorium...super quattuor libros Sententiarum* (Tuebingen, 1527), II Sent., d. 7, q. 1, B, C: Note, however, that at the end of this section Biel makes the following remark: "Licet illa distinctio non in omnibus concordat modo loquendi doctoris nostri [i.e. Ockham]...quia tamen valet ad intelligendum multa dicta doctorum, placuit eam hic ponere..."

an unworthy object. The act of the will regarding these acts would also be good or evil accordingly. However, to will to abstain according to the dictates of right reason and all the other circumstances that would be required in the case--and especially, out of a good intention or motive--would be an act which is good because of the circumstances which accompany it. The motive here, however, is not understood as the love of God, but it is one which even a good pagan could justly intend, such as, of seeking the perfection of human nature or of the personality. The will to steal would be evil because of the accompanying circumstances, if the stealing would be against right reason and for a bad motive. And finally, an act would be good on the basis of its merit, if it is in accordance with the dictates of right reason and all the other required circumstances and, in addition, the purpose intended is the honor of God. For such an act, Ockham notes, is accepted by almighty God as worthy of merit.[5]

For our purposes in this chapter the general distinction of human acts into those which are intrinsically good (or evil), and the morally indifferent acts is sufficient and more convenient for illustrating the points we wish to bring out in this section.

1) The Necessarily Virtuous Act: Concerning the necessarily virtuous act Ockham poses this question in the *Third Quodlibet*, question 13: Is only an act of the will necessarily virtuous? First, it seems the answer should be in the negative, because any act of the will can be elicited with an evil intention. Therefore any act of the will can be evil and thus not necessarily virtuous. Opposing the negative answer, Ockham argues: to love God is an act which is only virtuous and cannot possibly be anything but virtuous. Therefore this act of the love of God is a necessarily virtuous act. Actually the question asked above can be answered by a parallel set of propositions, one of which is nega-

---

[5] Ockham, *Quaest. Variae*, q. 7, a 2: "Exemplum primi quantum ad actum bonum ex genere: sicut orare, dare eleemosynam, sive velle talia facere absolute sine aliqua circumstantia bona vel mala. Exemplum quantum ad actum malum: velle furtum facere, velle fornicari, absolute sine aliqua circumstantia bona vel mala; de quibus dicit Philosophus et Sancti dicunt, quod statim nominata convoluta sunt cum malitia. Exemplum secundi: velle abstinere secundum circumstantias dictatas a recta ratione propter honestatem tamquam propter finem vel propter conservationem naturae vel alium finem quem intenderet philosophus paganus. Exemplum secundi quantum ad actum malum: velle fornicari contra rectam rationem, loco indebito etc., et propter libidinem tamquam propter finem. Exemplum tertii: velle continere secundum rectam rationem et alias circumstantias, et propter honorem divinum quia talis actus est Deo acceptus." (OTh VIII, 339). See E. Bonke, "Doctrina nominalistica de fundamento ordinis moralis apud Gulielmum de Ockham et Gabrielem Biel," *Collectanea franciscana*, XIV (1944), p. 64; A. Garvens, "Die Grundlagen der Ethik Wilhelms von Ockham," *Franziskanische Studien*, XXI (1934), pp. 399-400; E. Iserloh, *Gnade und Eucharistie in der philosophischen Theologie des Wilhelm von Ockham* (Wiesbaden: Steiner, 1956), pp. 93 ff.; O. Suk, *op. cit.*, pp. 31-32.

CHAPTER V

tive in form and the other affirmative. The negative proposition is expressed in these terms: "No act other than an act of the will can be necessarily virtuous."[6]

We have already treated the negative aspect of this question in our third chapter when we attempted to show that only an act of the will can be necessarily virtuous, or, in other words, that no act other than an act of the will is necessarily virtuous but is virtuous only by extrinsic denomination.[7] It was at that time that we indicated, but left unanswered, the further question: Is there some act of the will which is necessarily virtuous? Obviously, from saying that an act of the will can be necessarily virtuous, it does not follow that there is such an act which is necessarily virtuous. Such an inference would proceed, invalidly, from possibility to actuality. It remains legitimate and necessary, then, to raise and to answer the question: Is there any act which is necessarily virtuous? The answer given by Ockham is in the affirmative: There is an act of the will which is necessarily virtuous. But how is this answer to be understood?

First, Ockham reminds us again that in his view the creature and all that the creature does is completely and absolutely contingent.[8] And therefore, if we are going to speak of a necessarily virtuous act, we must still keep in mind the creature's radical contingency. So when we say that a creature's act is necessarily virtuous, the proposition would be false if taken in its simple literal meaning (*de vi sermonis*). The proposition is false in its literal sense, because if no act of the crea-

---

[6]Ockham, *Quodl.* III, 14: "Utrum solus actus voluntatis sit necessario virtuosus. Quod non: Quia omnis actus voluntatis potest elici intentione mala; igitur omnis actus voluntatis potest esse malus. Contra: Diligere Deum est actus solus virtuosus, et non est alius quam virtuosus; igitur ille actus est solus virtuosus. Ad istam quaestionem dico quod illa propositio exclusiva posita in quaestione habet duas exponentes: unam negativam, quae est quod nullus actus alius ab actu voluntatis est necessario virtuosus; et aliam affirmativam, scilicet quod aliquis actus voluntatis est necessario virtuosus." (OTh IX, 253).

[7]See Chapter III, esp. notes 21-23.

[8]P. Boehner, *Ockham: Philosophical Writings* ("The Nelson Philosophical Texts"; London: Nelson, 1957), p. xxii: "*Everything that is real, and different from God, is contingent to the core of its being...*The actual order of creatures remains contingent; the possible order of creatures is above contingency. Hence the tendency of Ockham to go beyond the investigation of the actual order, by asking what is possible regardless of the state of the present universe." F. Copleston, *A History of Philosophy*, Vol. III: *Ockham to Suarez* (Westminster: Newman, 1953), p. 104: "This personal conception of the moral law was closely connected with Ockham's insistence on the divine omnipotence and liberty. Once these truths are accepted as revealed truths, the whole created order, including the moral law, is viewed by Ockham as wholly contingent, in the sense that not only its existence but also its essence and character depend on the divine creative and omnipotent will." See Chapter IV, section 2.

ture is necessary then no act of the creature can be called necessarily virtuous.[9]

Ockham also reminds us of the fact that whatever act the creature performs as a partial efficient cause in cooperation with the causality exercised by God in producing the act, God himself could perform alone as the total cause.[10] Therefore, because any act can be done by God alone, no act is necessarily virtuous since it could be produced by God. In this case, then, since God alone produces the act, it is not a free act as far as the creature is concerned. The act is in no way in the power of the creature. Freedom, as we have seen, is the first condition for a virtuous act.

But there is another way of understanding the phrase that an act is necessarily virtuous. The phrase can mean, correctly, that the act which is necessarily virtuous cannot be evil while the divine precept commanding it remains in force. This means that the act cannot be caused by the created will in such a way that the act will not be virtuous. If we accept this as the meaning of the term "virtuous act," then, Ockham says, there can be an act which is necessarily virtuous. The proof he offers for this conclusion is as follows: it is impossible for some act which is only contingently virtuous--that is, an act which can be said to be indifferently virtuous or vicious--to be determined as virtuous by itself. An act which is only contingently virtuous is determined as virtuous by its conformity with some other act. .Ultimately, the contingently virtuous act can be determined in the category of "virtuous act" only if it is so determined by some act which is itself necessarily virtuous. For instance, the act of walking is not virtuous of itself but only by its relation or conformity to some other act. And then the question arises: What of this other act? Is it necessarily virtuous or only contingently virtuous? If this other act is necessarily virtuous, then our intended thesis is established, namely, that there is some act which is necessarily virtuous. But if this other act, on the other hand, is only contingently virtuous, then it too must be determined as virtuous by some other, a third, act. And the same question can be brought up in reference to this third act: Is it necessarily virtuous or only contingently virtuous? And so the process of questioning would continue ad infinitum as long as we would speak of acts which are not necessarily

---

[9] Ockham, *Quodl.* III, 14: "Circa affirmativam exponentem dico primo quod de virtute sermonis nullus actus est necessario virtuosus. Hoc probatur...quia nullus actus necessario est, et per consequens non est necessario virtuosus..." (OTh IX, 254).

[10] *Ibid.*: "...omnis actus potest fieri a solo Deo, et per consequens non est necessario virtuosus, quia talis actus non est in potestate voluntatis." (OTh IX, 254-55). Cf. G. Biel, *op. cit., III Sent.*, d. 23, q. 1, K.

but only contingently virtuous. Or in other words, we must eventually arrive at some act which in itself is necessarily virtuous.[11]

The act which is necessarily virtuous in the manner stated above must be an act of the will, because only an act of the will can be intrinsically virtuous. And it is the act of the will by which God is loved above all and for himself that Ockham has in mind. This act of the love of God above all and for himself cannot be elicited by a created will without being virtuous. The reason for saying this is that everyone is obliged at the proper time and place to love God above all things. Since everyone is obliged by this obligation, the act of loving God cannot be evil at any time or any place. This act of loving God above all and for himself rightly assumes a place of special prominence in Ockham's writings. He calls it the first, or the source, of all good acts.[12]

That the act of the love of God above all and for himself is the first of all good acts seems to have a special meaning for Ockham. In explanation of this, let us first retrace our steps for a moment back to

---

[11] Ockham, *Quodl.* III, 14: "Tamen aliter potest intelligi actum esse necessario virtuosum, ita scilicet quod non possit esse vitiosus stante praecepto divino; similiter non potest causari a voluntate creata nisi sit virtuosus. Et sic intelligendo actum virtuosum, dico secundo quod sic potest aliquis actus esse virtuosus necessario. Quod probo, quia impossibile est quod aliquis actus contingenter virtuosus, ita quod indifferenter potest dici virtuosus vel vitiosus, fiat determinate virtuosus nisi propter alium actum necessario virtuosum. Hoc probatur, quia actus contingenter virtuosus, puta actus ambulandi, fit determinate virtuosus per conformitatem ad alium actum. Quaero de illo secundo actu: aut est necessario virtuosus modo praedicto, et habetur propositum, quod est aliquis actus in homine necessario virtuosus; aut est contingenter virtuosus, et tunc ille fit determinate virtuosus per conformitatem ad alium actum virtuosum; et de isto est quaerendum sicut prius, et erit processus in infinitum vel stabitur ad aliquem actum necessario virtuosum." (OTh IX, 255). Cf. G. Biel, *op. cit.*, *III Sent.*, d. 23, q. 1, K; L. Baudry (ed.), *Le Tractatus de principiis theologiae attribué à G. d'Occam* ("Etudes de philosophie médiévale," XXIII; Paris: Vrin, 1936), p. 77.

[12] Ockham, *Quodl.* III, 14: "Dico quod ille actus necessario virtuosus modo praedicto est actus voluntatis, quia actus quo diligitur Deus super omnia et propter se, est huiusmodi; nam iste actus sic est virtuosus quod non potest esse vitiosus, nec potest iste actus causari a voluntate creata nisi sit virtuosus; tum quia quilibet pro loco et tempore obligatur ad diligendum Deum super omnia, et per consequens iste actus non potest esse vitiosus; tum quia iste actus est primus omnium actuum bonorum." (OTh IX, 255-56). *Quodl.* III, 15: "...amare Deum propter se et super omnia est actus sic rectus quod non potest fieri deformis." (OTh IX, 260). P. Boehner, "A Recent Presentation of Ockham's Philosophy," *Franciscan Studies*, IX (1949), p. 453: "According to Ockham at least one act is bad in itself, so that it can never be good, viz. to disobey God; and there is one act that is absolutely good, so that it can never be bad, viz. to obey or to love God." P. Boehner's statement is in reply to M. De Wulf, *Histoire de la philosophie médiévale*, t. III (6. ed. rev.; Louvain: Institut supérieur de philosophie; Paris: Vrin, 1947), p. 42: "Il n'y a bien ni mal en soi, la différence entre l'un et l'autre reposant sur un décret de Dieu qui eût pu renverser l'ordre existant. Dieu est un autocrate qui pourrait, sans tenir compte de ce qu'il y a de rationnel ou non dans ses volontés, provoquer chez l'homme des actes d'amour aussi bien que des actes de haine." See also E. Gilson and P. Boehner, *Christliche Philosophie* (Paderborn: Schoningh, 1954), p. 622.

the place where he says that the proposition "an act is necessarily virtuous" can be understood to mean that the act which is necessarily virtuous cannot be evil while the divine precept remains in force--or that it means that the act cannot be caused by the created will in such a way that the act will not be virtuous. Actually, this is not one understanding of the proposition, but it involves two distinct, though related, meanings of the proposition "an act is necessarily virtuous." The first meaning includes the notion of the necessity of the divine precept remaining in force: "the necessarily virtuous act is one which cannot be evil while the divine precept commanding it remains in force." But the second meaning does not include the notion of the divine precept; it simply states that the necessarily virtuous act is one which cannot be caused by a created will without being virtuous. This second formulation regarding the meaning of the necessarily virtuous act, it seems, would indicate a development, or at least a shift of emphasis, in Ockham's thought.[13]

The reason for saying that there was at least a shift in emphasis in Ockham's thought is that in his earlier writings he seems to have favored the first formulation or understanding of the proposition given above. That is, he emphasizes the aspect of the "divine precept remaining in force" even in connection with the necessarily virtuous act. This is brought out more clearly if we consider a parallel text in the *Reportatio* of Ockham, comparing it with the text given above from the *Quodlibeta*. In the *Reportatio* Ockham makes the statement that there is some act which is necessarily and intrinsically virtuous. In proof of this statement he proceeds by way of the same argument that has been presented above from the *Quodlibeta*. That is, it is impossible for any act which is only contingently virtuous to be determined as virtuous except through some other act which is necessarily virtuous in itself. In order, then, to avoid an infinite regress in acts Ockham argues that there must be some act which is necessarily and primarily virtuous, one which is laudable and includes all the required circumstances.[14] But the

---

[13] E. Hochstetter, *op. cit.*, pp. 15-16, points out this transition in Ockham's thought. In conclusion the author remarks: "[Der Akt der Gottesliebe] ist der Akt, so schliesst Ockham, auch hierin über den Standpunkt des Sentenzenkommentars hinausgehend, der 'nullo modo potest elici intentione mala'."

[14] Ockham, *Quaest. Variae*, q. 7, a. 1: "...aliquis actus est necessario et intrinsece virtuosus. Hoc probatur, quia impossibile est quod aliquis actus contingenter virtuosus,--sic scilicet quod potest indifferenter dici virtuosus vel vitiosus--, fiat determinate virtuosus propter novitatem alicuius actus non necessario virtuosi, quia per nullum actum contingenter virtuosum modo praedicto fit alius actus sive denominatur determinate virtuosus. Quia si sic, aut ille secundus actus, qui est contingenter virtuosus, erit determinate virtuosus per aliquem alium actum qui est necessario virtuosus, aut per actum contingenter virtuosum. Si

CHAPTER V

particular point I wish to emphasize is this concluding remark of Ockham: "to do something because it is prescribed by God is an act which is so virtuous that it cannot be evil while the precept of God remains in force." But compare that statement with the concluding remark in the *Quodlibeta*: "an act of the will by which God is loved above all and for himself is so virtuous that it cannot be evil, nor can it be caused by a created will without being virtuous." Here in the *Quodlibeta* there is no reference to any dependence on the precept of God remaining in force.

Does this difference, this omission of the phrase referring to the precept of God, indicate a genuine development of Ockham's thought? It seems on the one hand that he has not completely abandoned his old position regarding the necessity of the divine command remaining in force. This is brought out by the fact that he mentions that one way of understanding the proposition "an act is necessarily virtuous" is that the necessarily virtuous act cannot be evil while the divine precept remains in force. But he immediately adds the second way of understanding the proposition "an act is necessarily virtuous"--it is an act which cannot be caused by a created will without being virtuous. And his concluding remarks in the *Quodlibeta* are in reference to this second understanding of the meaning of a necessarily virtuous act. Thus while his former position is not abandoned completely, Ockham does go beyond it. The divine precept qualification is not mentioned, and he simply states that the act of loving God is necessarily virtuous apart from any consideration of the divine precept. This conclusion is in accordance with the second formulation of the meaning of a virtuous act; it is an act which cannot be caused by a created will without being virtuous.

Perhaps we can interpret Ockham in this way. There is a distinction to be made even among the necessarily virtuous acts. The primary virtuous act is the love of God, understanding this to mean "above all and for himself," a true and genuine love of God as explained in the previous chapter. This act of loving God above all and for himself is virtuous in such a way that it cannot possibly be evil; it cannot possibly be elicited by a created will without being virtuous. And it remains unaffected by any precept of God. This does not at all alter the fact that other acts of the will may also be necessarily virtuous; but they are necessarily virtuous only in a secondary manner. In pointing out the love of God as a necessarily virtuous act, it seems that Ockham's inten-

---

primo modo, tunc eadem ratione esset standum in secundo, et similiter tunc habetur propositum, quod est aliquis actus in homine necessario virtuosus. Si secundo modo, erit processus in infinitum, vel stabitur ad aliquem actum necessario virtuosum, et sic habetur propositum....Ideo dico quod est dare aliquem actum necessario primo virtuosum...qui est ita virtuosus quod non potest fieri vitiosus, sicut velle facere aliquid quia est praeceptum divinum, est ita virtuosus quod non potest fieri vitiosus, stante praecepto divino." (OTh VIII, 327f.).

tion was not to exclude all other acts of the will from the category of the "necessarily virtuous," but merely to select one act to prove his thesis that some act of the will is necessarily virtuous. In other words, there is at least one act which is necessarily virtuous and this is the act of loving God above all and for himself. But it seems he holds that other acts of the will are also necessarily virtuous--but all of these other acts would depend on the condition that the divine precept which commands them remains in force. These other acts are what we have designated as the secondary necessarily virtuous acts. They depend, therefore, on the primary necessarily virtuous act, the love of God. Their goodness is derived from the love of God and obedience to His will. To love God is to obey Him. All other acts of the will except the act of loving God are only secondarily necessarily virtuous. For to love God is "the first of all good acts"--and in this sense the love of God is also the principle or the source of all other good acts.[15]

But it is well to remember that while the love of God is the first of all good acts, other acts of the will may also be necessarily virtuous in the sense described above. That is to say, there are other acts which are necessarily, though secondarily, virtuous. These acts are not virtuous only contingently or by extrinsic denomination. The contingently virtuous acts, acts which are virtuous only by extrinsic denomination, will be the subject of the following discussion.

2) The Contingently Virtuous Act: Any act other than an act of the will immediately under the power of the will is only secondarily virtuous by extrinsic denomination. Such an act can be called virtuous if it is elicited in conformity with a necessarily virtuous act of the will. Of itself, the contingently virtuous act can be determined by an act of the will to be either virtuous or vicious. Therefore, such an act is not necessarily virtuous or necessarily vicious.[16] Such a contingently virtuous act is laudable at first, if it is in conformity with a

---

[15] *Quodl.* III, 14: "...iste actus [quo diligitur Deus super omnia et propter se] est primus omnium actuum bonorum." (OTh IX, 256). T. Barth, "Wilhelm Ockham im Lichte der neuesten Forschung," *Philosophisches Jahrbuch*, LX (1950), p. 465: "Dieser in sich gute Akt der Gottesliebe bildet nämlich die unerlässliche Voraussetzung dafür, dass ein kontingent guter Akt überhaupt gut werden kann...Ockham kennt einen absolut unantastbaren Wert, die Gottesliebe." See also A. Garvens, *op. cit.*, pp. 388-390; E. Iserloh, *op. cit.*, p. 51.

[16] Ockham, *Quaest. Variae*, q. 7, a. 1: "[Actus, qui non sunt a voluntate, non sunt virtuosi] nisi secundario et per quandum denominationem extrinsecam, puta per hoc quod eliciuntur conformiter actui voluntatis. Praeterea quilibet alius actus ab actu voluntatis potest idem manens esse vitiosus vel virtuosus, iste autem solus sic est virtuosus quod non potest fieri vitiosus..." (OTh VIII, 329). Cf. *Ibid.* (OTh VIII, 329 f.). See E. Iserloh, *op. cit.*, pp. 51-52; G. De Lagarde, *Naissance de l'esprit laïque au déclin du moyen âge*, VI: *L'Ockhamisme: La morale et le droit* (Paris: Presses Universitaires de France, 1946), pp. 76-77.

CHAPTER V

virtuous act of the will; but it could become worthy of blame by being in conformity with an evil act of the will.[17] And what has been said of virtuous acts also holds concerning the goodness of habits.[18] We have spoken sufficiently of the extrinsically virtuous acts in Chapter Three when we treated the morality of external acts, intellectual acts, commanded acts of the will, and the acts of the sensitive appetites. We can pass over any further detail at this time.

3) The Indifferent Act: Is there any indifferent act of the will? And if so, can such an act become intrinsically virtuous, extrinsically virtuous, or must it remain morally indifferent?[19] An act of the will can be called indifferent if it is elicited concerning a suitable object, but without being in conformity to or contrary to the required circumstances of the act. In this case, then, the act would be neither good nor evil. For example, if I would love someone without any good or evil intention, neither according to or contrary to any dictate of right reason, without regard to any of the required circumstances, this act would not be morally good nor morally evil. It would be morally neutral or indifferent.[20]

We can ask, then, concerning this morally indifferent act whether it can become intrinsically virtuous. From what has already been said of the intrinsically virtuous act--that it is an act which is necessarily good so that it cannot be evil or indifferent--it is immediately evident that the indifferent act of the will cannot become intrinsically good. We are, of course, speaking here of the impossibility of numerically the same act being at first indifferent and later intrinsically good. For in order to become good it is necessary for this act to be elicited according to all the circumstances required by right reason in the particular

---

[17] Ockham, *Quaest. Variae*, q. 7, a. 1: "...nullus alius actus ab actu voluntatis est intrinsece virtuosus vel vitiosus, tum quia quilibet alius idem manens potest indifferenter esse laudabilis et vituperabilis." (OTh VIII, 329).

[18] *Ibid.*: "...nullus alius habitus ab habitu voluntatis est intrinsece et perfecte virtuosus, quia quilibet alius inclinat indifferenter ad actus laudabiles et vituperabiles." (OTh VIII, 330).

[19] Ockham, *In III Sent.*, 11: "Sed adhuc est dubium, utrum sit aliquis actus indifferens in voluntate sicut in appetitu sensitivo qui potest dici bonus vel malus denominatione extrinseca vel neuter..." (OTh VI, 383). Cf. G. Biel, *op. cit.*, III Sent., d. 23, q. 1, N.

[20] Ockham, *In III Sent.*, 11: "...actus ille voluntatis est indifferens qui elicitur circa obiectum conveniens tali actui, sine tamen circumstantiis requisitis ad bonitatem et malitiam actus. Puta si diligam aliquem hominem, non propter aliquem finem bonum vel malum, nec secundum rectam rationem nec contra, nec loco nec tempore debito nec non [debito], et ita de aliis circumstantiis virtuosis et vitiosis, iste actus nec est bonus moraliter nec malus sed neuter et indifferens." (OTh VI, 384).

case. To use the example given previously, I would have to love this person with a good intention, according to right reason, and so forth. But since the circumstances are nothing else but partial objects of the virtuous act, by any variation in the circumstances the act itself is also necessarily changed. For this reason no act of the will, numerically one, can be indifferent at first and intrinsically virtuous later. And *a fortiori*, no act, numerically one, can be virtuous at first and vicious later, nor vice versa. For there cannot be a change in the morality of the act except by a change in the circumstances of the act. But a change in the circumstances necessarily involves a change in the act itself, so that it is no longer the same act. In a similar fashion no act, numerically one, can be only imperfectly virtuous at first--because it lacks some of the circumstances required for a perfectly virtuous act-- and afterwards become perfectly virtuous because it fulfills all the required circumstances. The reason for saying this is that it is always the case that by the addition or subtraction of anything which is an object of the act, the act itself is changed.[21] When this occurs we cannot any longer speak of the act as being numerically one and the same act.

There is a second question which can be asked: Can an indifferent act of the will become contingently virtuous? Here Ockham's answer is in the affirmative. But his answer is based on the hypothesis that two acts of the will can exist simultaneously, meaning, of course, two distinct acts of the will for the same person at the same time. Ockham is inclined to believe that such a situation is not impossible. However, if the hypothesis is not correct, so that only one act of the will can exist at any given time, then it is obvious that the indifferent act of the will cannot become contingently virtuous. The reason for this is that an act can be contingently virtuous only by conforming to an intrinsically virtuous act. And since an intrinsically virtuous act must be an act of the will, and since under the hypothesis only one act of the will can exist at any

---

[21] *Ibid.*: "Ad hoc igitur quod [actus indifferens] fiat bonus vel malus, oportet eum circumstantionari circumstantiis virtuosis vel vitiosis, puta quod voluntas diligat illum hominem propter finem talem, et tempore debito, et sic de aliis. Sed sic diligendo habet alium actum quia, sicut dictum est prius, circumstantiae non sunt nisi obiecta partialia actus voluntatis virtuosi ad quorum variationem variatur necessario actus. Et propter eandem causam non potest aliquis actus voluntatis primo esse virtuosus intrinsece et post vitiosus- -idem dico actus numero--quia non potest esse mutatio nisi per mutationem circumstantiarum, puta quia nunc actus bene circumstantionatur et post male, et hoc non potest esse sine mutatione actus. Et hoc semper tenet, quia circumstantiae sunt obiecta actus ad quorum variationem sequitur variatio in actibus. Nec--propter eandem rationem--potest esse unus actus primo imperfecte virtuosus, puta quia habet aliquas circumstantias requisitas ad actum perfecte virtuosum, et secundo perfecte virtuosus, puta quando habet omnes circumstantias requisitas. Quia sempter per additionem vel subtractionem alicuius circumstantiae quae est obiectum et causa partialis respectu actus, variatur actus." (OTh VI, 384-85).

CHAPTER V

given time--it must be this intrinsically virtuous act which exists in the will. But this does not at all imply that the indifferent act has changed into a necessarily virtuous act. The necessarily virtuous act is actually a new act of the will, specifically distinct from the indifferent act, because by any variation in the objects (circumstances) of the act, the act itself is changed, as explained previously.[22]

However, if two acts can exist at the same time in the will, then it is possible for the indifferent act to become extrinsically virtuous without any change in the act itself. For example, if I love someone without any good or evil circumstances connected with the act, then the act is neither good nor evil; it is neutral or indifferent. And while this act of love remains in my will I would elicit another act of loving this person, but now out of a good motive, according to the dictates of right reason and all the other required circumstances. But according to the present hypothesis both acts exist at the same time in my will. The second act is perfectly and intrinsically virtuous, and in virtue of this act the first act can also be called virtuous by extrinsic denomination, since it is in conformity with the second act of love for this person. So the first act, an act which was at first morally indifferent, now, while remaining unchanged in the will, is elicited in conformity with an act which is intrinsically virtuous.[23]

We can also note that it is in this way that exterior acts also become virtuous by extrinsic denomination. And furthermore, acts of the sensitive faculties and of the intellect can also be called indifferent in the above manner. But they can become good by extrinsic denomination. There does not seem to be any special difficulty in including these acts here. For example, if the intellect would dictate that I should study at some particular time, and the will now commands that the intellect should

---

[22] *Ibid*: "...dico quod si quaeratur utrum aliquis actus voluntatis possit esse indifferens primo ad bonitatem et malitiam et post fieri bonus vel malus denominatione extrinseca...tunc distinguendum est. Quia aut ponitur quod in voluntate possunt esse simil duo actus volendi naturaliter, aut non. Si non, tunc in voluntate non potest esse aliquis actus indifferens dicto modo, quia non posset sic ese indifferens nisi quatenus posset conformari alteri actui perfecte et intrinsece virtuoso...." (OTh VI, 385).

[23] *Ibid*: "Si autem duo actus volendi possunt simul esse naturaliter in voluntate, quod credo esse verum...tunc in voluntate potest esse aliquis actus indifferens modo praedicto. Exemplum: si enim diligam aliquem hominem absolute, terminando actum volendi ad illum hominem et non ad qliquam circumstantiam bonam vel malam, tunc iste actus non est bonus nec malus moraliter, sed est neuter. Si tunc, stante illo actu, eliciam alium actum quo volo diligere illum hominem propter Deum, secundum rectam rationem et secundum omnes alias circumstantias requisitas, iste secundus actus est perfecte et intrinsece virtuosus. Et primus, qui prius fuit indifferens, nunc est virtuosus denominatione extrinseca quatenus elicitur conformiter actui perfecte virtuoso et recto dictamini." (OTh VI, 385-86). See E. Iserloh, *op. cit*., pp. 52-53.

study for the motive of honoring God and according to all of the other required circumstances, then the act of studying can be called good by extrinsic denomination in so far as it is elicited in conformity with a virtuous act of the will.[24]

It is also worthy of mention at this time that there is also another way in which an act of the will may be called morally indifferent. And this is, if it is caused by God alone as the total cause. For in this case the first condition of a good act or an evil act, the condition that states that the act must be willed freely by the creature, is entirely absent. The terms "morally good" and "morally evil" do not signify the act precisely, but also connote that the act is freely willed, just as the term "meritorious" connotes the activity of a created will.[25]

Having considered the nature of the intrinsically good act, the contingently good act and the morally indifferent act, we are now in a position to turn to Ockham's theory of the exact nature of morality. What, precisely, is meant by saying that an act has moral goodness or moral malice? In what does the rightness of acts consist, or what is meant by the deformity of an act? Do these, rectitude and deformity, inhere somehow in the act itself, adding something to it or taking something from it? These are some of the questions we will attempt in the following paragraphs to find an answer from the standpoint of Ockham's moral theory. Once again Ockham's main opponent, at least by explicit mention, is Duns Scotus. The answers to the above questions are dependent in the majority of cases on the dispute between Ockham and Scotus on the question of the intrinsic goodness and on the role of prudence in morality--topics which were treated in some detail in connection with the role of right reason in the third chapter of this work.[26]

In considering these questions we may start, as it seems advisable in this case, with a question Ockham raises in the *Third Quodlibet*, question 14: Does the rectitude or deformity of an act differ from the substance of the act itself? And Ockham's answer is that the act and its

---

[24] Ockham, *Ibid.*: "Et dico ultra quod tam actus partis sensitivae quam intellectus quam voluntatis potest dici indifferens modo praedicto et denominari bonus vel malus denominatione extrinseca. Nec hoc est plus inconveniens de actu intellectus quam appetitus sensitivi vel voluntatis, puta si intellectus dictet quod tali tempore est studendum, et voluntas imperet intellectui quod studeat propter honorem Dei et alias circumstantias, dicitur tunc actus studendi bonus denominatione extrinseca." (OTh VI, 389).

[25] *Ibid.*: "Alio modo potest dici quod aliquis actus sit indifferens in voluntate si causetur totaliter a Deo, quia tunc nec dicetur bonus moraliter nec malus, quia ista nomina connotant activitatem voluntatis sicut meritorius actus." See L. Baudry (ed.), *Tractatus de principiis theologiae*, p. 81.

[26] See Chapter III, section 2.

CHAPTER V

rectitude never differ.[27] The act of which we are speaking may be either an act of the will or an act other than an act of the will. Accordingly, we will distinguish between these two questions: First, in what does the rectitude of an act of the will consist? And secondly, what is meant by the rectitude of an act other than an act of the will?

First let us outline the answers to these questions in general terms. In answer to the first question, we must first point out that since we are dealiung with the rectitude of an act of the will--understanding the act as immediately in the power of the will--we are speaking of a necessarily virtuous act. But such an act, if it is a virtuous act, cannot be performed by a creature without being virtuous. The act is necessarily good; it is good in itself. In a manner of speaking, the act and its rectitude are inseparable. The rectitude of the act consists in the act itself.[28]

On the other hand, an act which is not an act of the will is called right only by extrinsic denomination. In this case it is called right because it is caused--or continued--by an act which is essentially virtuous to which the extrinsically virtuous act conforms. But on account of this conformity we cannot conclude that something positive is added to the extrinsically good act. Rectitude does not attach itself, as it were, to such an act; the act is only called right by extrinsic denomination.[29] These general statements also hold true, *mutatis mutandis*, for the deformity of an act, whether it is an act of the will or an act which is not of the will.

In clarification of the general statements presented above, let us consider several doubts or questions that could be raised concerning Ockham's opinion. 1) How are rectitude and deformity related to acts? 2) Since deformity is commonly called "a lack of rectitude that should be in the act," does it not follow that the rectitude of the act is distinct from the act itself? 3) It is also commonly said that there are two elements in sin: a material element, the substance of the act; and a formal

---

[27] Ockham, *Quodl.* III, 15: "Utrum rectitudo actus et deformitas differant a substantia actus....Ad istam quaestionem dico universaliter quod numquam actus et sua rectitudo differunt..." (OTh IX, 257-58). See G. Biel, *op. cit.*, III Sent., d. 23, q. 1, JJ; A. Garvens, *op. cit.*, pp. 400-402; E. Iserloh, *op. cit.*, p. 62.

[28] Ockham, *Ibid.*: "...omnis actus rectus aut est rectus essentialiter, aut per denominationem extrinsecam. Si primo modo, tunc substantia actus est sua rectitudo, quod patet ex hoc quod impossibile est quod talis actus sit a voluntate creata nisi sit rectus." (OTh IX, 258).

[29] *Ibid.*: "Si secundo modo, tunc ille actus dicitur rectus quia causatur vel continuatur ab actu essentialiter virtuoso, ad cuius conformitatem dicitur rectus; sed propter talem causalitatem vel conformitatem nihil positum recipit actus exterior..."

element, the lack of justice which should be in the act. If this be true, does it not follow that the substance of the act is distinct from its deformity, just as the material and formal elements of sin are distinct?[30]

1) How are rectitude and deformity related to acts? Ockham answers that a right act and an evil act are related to acts in general in the same way that "an inferior is related to a superior." That is, they are related to the general classification of acts as two individual things are related to a class or as two classes are related to a higher class. A right act and an evil act are included in the general category or classification, act, as two singular whitenesses are related to whiteness in general, or in the way that Peter and Paul are related to the general class, "man". In Ockham's words: "A right act and an evil act are two singular acts of which "act" in general is predicated as a superior to inferiors."[31] And this is how rectitude and deformity are related to acts in general: a right act is an act; and an evil act is an act.

But rectitude and deformity are not only related to acts in general but are also related to particular acts. In what does this relation to particular acts consist? Here we must make a distinction in order to treat the question adequately. Some particular acts are of such a kind that rectitude and deformity can be related to them successively, though not, of course, both rectitude and deformity at the same time. In other words, there are some particular acts of which "right act" and "evil act" can be successively predicated, so that at one time it will be true to say "this act is a right act" and at another time it will be true to say "this act is an evil act."[32] For example, if I abstain from food without any consideration of the accompanying circumstances, this act can be either a right act or an evil act. Now if I continue this act of abstaining with a good intention or out of obedience to a divine precept, then it can be said that abstaining from food is a good act. And this proposition will

---

[30] *Ibid.:* "Sed hic sunt dubia: unum, quomodo deformitas et rectitudo se habent respectu actus. Secundum, quia videtur quod rectitudo sit aliquid distinctum ab actu, quia communiter dicitur quod deformitas est carentia rectitudinis quae debet inesse actui; et per consequens rectitudo, ex quo inest actui, distinguitur ab actu. Praeterea in peccato sunt duo: materiale, puta substantia actus; et formale, puta carentia iustitiae debitae inesse actui; igitur distinguuntur, sicut materiale et formale." (OTh IX, 259).

[31] *Ibid.:* "Ad primum istorum dico quod se habent ad actum in communi sicut inferiora ad suum superius, puta sicut duae singulares albedines se habent ad albedinem in communi; quia actus rectus et actus turpis sive deformis sunt duo singulares actus, de quibus praedicatur actus in communi sicut superius de inferioribus." Cf. also *In III Sent.*, 11 (OTh VI, 387-88).

[32] *Quodl.* III, 15: "sed ad actus particulares et singulares diversimode se habent, quia ad aliquem actum particularem sic se habent quod possunt successive convenire eidem per praedicationem, et hoc propter assistentiam vel non-assistentiam alicuius alterius actus." (OTh IX, 259-60).

CHAPTER V

be true because the act of abstaining is continued in conformity with an act of the will which is necessarily virtuous--obedience to a divine command. But the act of abstaining may continue while the act of the will changes, so that now I am abstaining out of human respect or pride. And now it can be said that "abstaining is an evil act," and the propositon will be true. So the terms "right act and "evil act" are predicated successively of the particular act of abstaining. Rectitude and deformity, then, are related to some particular act of abstaining in this successive manner. And this will also hold for other particular acts of the same class. But the particular acts of which we are speaking here will always be acts which are good only by extrinsic denomination, acts which are good or evil only contingently.[33]

There are, however, other kinds of particular acts to which the singulars, "right act" and "evil act," cannot be related successively. For some particular acts are not contingently good or evil. For example, to love God above all and for himself is a particular act of the will which is always good and cannot be evil. The particular acts of which we are speaking here are those which are necessarily good or necessarily evil, in such a way that they cannot be otherwise.[34] So in answer to the question which was asked above: How are rectitude and deformity related to acts? Ockham emphasizes again that some acts are only contingently good or evil and others are necessarily so.

This gives rise to the further question: What, then, does the goodness or the deformity of the act add to the substance of the act itself? In answer to this question Duns Scotus believed that the substance of the virtuous act and of the vicious act can be the same. But the virtuous act would be called virtuous because of its conformity to the required circumstances of the act. For Scotus the circumstances remain merely circumstances and are not partial objects of the virtuous or the evil act. Hence, according to Scotus, the goodness of an act adds to the

---

[33] *Ibid.*: "Exemplum: amare patrem absolute, sine omni circumstantia, quandoque est actus rectus et quandoque deformis; quia propter assistentiam novi actus potest dici rectus, puta si continuet illum amorem bona intentione, puta propter praeceptum divinum; et tunc dicitur rectus propter actum quo vult illum actum continuare propter praeceptum divinum. Et idem actus postea dicitur deformis propter carentiam istius actus necessario vitiosi, puta si velit illum actum continuare propter vanam gloriam." (OTh IX, 260).

[34] *Ibid.*: "Respectu autem alicuius actus non sic se habent rectitudo et deformitas successive, quia amare Deum propter se et super omnia est actus sic rectus quod non potest fieri deformis."

substance of the act a certain relation of conformity to all the required circumstances."[35]

But in Ockham's theory the required circumstances are not merely circumstances at all, but they are the immediate partial causes and partial objects necessarily required for a perfectly virtuous act.[36] So if you ask, from where does an act have its goodness or malice, Ockham answers, from those same things from which it has its substance. That is, the act's morality is derived from its common object and from all the circumstances as from multiple partial causes which together form one total cause. As partial causes and partial objects the circumstances are included in the total cause of the act and pertain to the substance of the act itself.[37] And, as already mentioned, the virtuous and the vicious act are related to act in general just as this whiteness and that whiteness are related to whiteness in general. So just as this whiteness is this whiteness of itself and not by something extrinsic to it, so also the virtuous act in the primary sense is of itself formally and intrinsically virtuous.[38] It is not virtuous by something extrinsic to the act itself. "The substance of the act is the act's goodness."[39] The same would hold true concerning the evil act: "The substance of the act is the act's malice."[40] And as from this whiteness and that whiteness we are able to abstract the concept of whiteness in general, so do this virtuous act and

---

[35] *In III Sent.* 11: "Ex istis patet quid bonitas moralis vel malitia addit super substantiam actus; quia aliter est dicendum secundum istam viam, aliter secundum viam Ioannis [Duns Scoti]. Ioannes enim ponit quod substantia actus virtuosi et vitiosi potest esse eadem, sed dicitur virtuosus propter conformitatem ad actus virtuosi. Ideo per eum bonitas addit super substantiam actus respectum conformitatis ad omnes circumstantias." (OTh VI, 387). See a. Garvens, *op. cit.*, pp. 400 ff.

[36] Ockham, *Ibid.*: "sed secundum istam viam [auctoris] quae ponit quod omnes circumstantiae requisitae ad actum sunt causae immediatae partiales necessario requisitae ad actum perfecte virtuosum..." (OTh VI,388).

[37] *Ibid.*: "Si quaeras unde actus habet bonitatem suam vel malitiam, dico quod ab eisdem a quibus habet substantiam actus, quia ab obiecto communi et omnibus circumstantiis tamquam a causis multis partialibus quae omnes simul positae faciunt unam causam totalem."

[38] *Ibid.*: "...actus virtuosus et vitiosus se habent ad actum in communi sicut haec albedo ad albedinem in communi. Quia sicut haec albedo est de se haec et non per aliquid extrinsecum sibi, formaliter et intrinsece virtuosus..." (OTh V, 388).

[39] *Ibid.*: "...haec substantia actus est haec bonitas actus..."

[40] *Ibid.*: "...haec substantia actus est haec malitia actus."

CHAPTER V

that evil act provide us with the foundation for abstracting the notion of act in general.[41]

The above statements refer, of course, to the virtuous act which is intrinsically good. Does the goodness or malice of the act add anything to the substance of the act which is called good only by extrinsic denomination? Ockham's answer is that it adds nothing absolute, either positive or relative, distinct from the act itself. But here goodness is a connotative term, signifying the act itself principally but also signifying secondarily the virtuous act of the will and the dictates of right reason in conformity to which things this act is elicited. And, therefore, the act is termed virtuous only by extrinsic denomination.[42]

We must add at this time, at the risk of repeating some of the ideas expressed earlier, a few comments about the power of God in producing acts which are, when produced with the requisite conditions by the created will, either moral or immoral. For to say that the rectitude of the act consists in the act itself is not to imply that the act cannot be considered apart from its requisite conditions and thus apart from its moral connotations. Ockham calls this "considering the act absolutely." Those things which by their presence or absence render an act virtuous or evil can be abstracted from and the act in its absolute sense considered. Although God cannot, for example, totally cause an act so that it is elicited freely by the creature--for the term "freely" means that the act is in the power of the creature--he can produce any act in its absolute sense. So here Ockham goes so far as to say that God could cause whatever is absolute in the act of hatred of himself. And he can do this without causing any deformity or malice in the act of hatred. For the act of hating God, in so far as its absolute sense is concerned, is not the same as the deformity or malice of the act. Just as moral goodness can be separated from the act of loving God in the absolute sense, as, for instance, when the act is produced by God as the total cause and is, therefore, not a free act of the creature, so also the act of hating God can be separated from its malice or deformity. God can do anything which does not involve a contradiction in being done. And in regard to what-

---

[41] *Ibid.*: "Et ab istis duobus potest abstrahi conceptus actus in communi, sicut ab hac albedine et illa potest abstrahi conceptus albedinis."

[42] *Ibid.*: "Si autem quaeras quid addit bonitas actus vel malitia super substantiam actus qui dicitur bonus solum denominatione quadam extrinseca...dico quod nihil positivum absolutum vel respectivum distinctum ab illo actu quod habet esse in ipso actu per quamcumque causam. Sed tantum est bonitas illa nomen vel conceptus connotativus, significans principaliter ipsum actum sic neutrum, connotans actum voluntatis perfecte virtuosum et rectam rationem quibus conformiter elicitur. Ideo denominatur virtuosus talis actus denominatione extrinseca." (OTh VI, 388-89). See E. Iserloh, *op. cit.*, pp. 62-63.

ever God is a partial cause, in regard to that same thing he is, or can be, the total cause. Since God can supply the causality of a secondary cause in the line of efficient causality, so any act, considered absolutely, which is produced by creatures in cooperation with God as the partial cause, can be produced by God as the total cause. Since God could be the total cause of the hatred of himself, there would be no sin. As explained previously, since God can be the total cause regarding anything absolute, consequently he could be the total cause of the hatred of himself.[43] There would be no sin in this case because the creature would not sin because the act is not freely within his power; God would not sin because he is not obliged to anyone or to anything.[44]

So although the hatred of God, stealing, adultery and the like have an evil circumstance connected with them, in so far as they are done by someone who is obliged to the contrary by the commandments of God, still, in so far as they can be considered absolutely, these acts can be done by God without any accompanying evil circumstances. And here Ockham goes a step further, saying that these acts could also be performed meritoriously by a creature if they would happen to fall under the divine precept in the same way as their opposites now fall under the prohibition of almighty God. It is certain, however, that as long as the present laws of God remain in force no one can perform these acts meritoriously or well.[45]

---

[43] Ockham, *In II Sent.*, 15: "Et quod Deus possit causare actum odiendi Deum quantum ad omne absolutum in actu in voluntate creata probatur, quia Deus potest omne absolutum causare sine omni alio quod non est idem cum illo absoluto. Sed actus odiendi Deum quantum ad omne absolutum in eo non est idem cum deformitate et malitia in actu, igitur Deus potest causare quidquid absolutum est in actu odiendi Deum vel nolendi, non causando aliquam deformitatem vel malitiam in actu, igitur etc. Item, non minus potest separari deformitas ab odio Dei quam bonitas moralis a dilectione Dei... Et tunc omne quod non includit contradictionem, nec malum culpae, potest fieri a Deo solo, igitur odium Dei, etc. Item respectu cuiuscumque est Deus causa partialis respectu eius est vel esse potest causa totalis, quia ipse supplere potest omnem causalitatem causae secundae in genere causae efficientis. Sed respectu cuiuslibet positivi, maxime absoluti producti a creatura, est Deus causa partialis....Igitur potest esse causa totalis respectu cuiuslibet absoluti, et per consequens respectu actus odiendi Deum." (OTh V, 342-41). See A. Garvens, *op. cit.*, pp. 272-73; E. Iserloh, *op. cit.*, pp. 68-69.

[44] Ockham, *In IV Sent.*, 10-11: "Unde si Deus causaret odium in voluntate alicuius sicut causa totalis, sicut semper causat sicut causa partialis, neuter peccaret: nec Deus, quia ad nihil obligatur; nec alius, quia actus ille non esset in potestate sua." (OTh VII, 198). Cf. *In II Sent.*, 15 (OTh V, 343, 350-51). See A. Garvens, *op. cit.*, pp. 263-64.

[45] Ockham, *In II Sent.*, 15: "...dico quod licet odium, furari, adulterari et similia habeant malam circumstantiam annexam de communi lege, quatenus fiunt ab aliquo qui ex praecepto divino obligatur ad contrarium, tamen quantum ad omne absolutum in illis actibus possunt fieri a Deo sine omni circumstantia mala annexa. Et etiam meritorie possunt fieri a vi-

CHAPTER V

But here we come upon an important point. The terms "stealing," "adultery," "hatred" and so forth do not signify the act only in its absolute sense, but also connote the violation of a divine precept. By using these terms we understand that the acts to which they refer are performed by someone who is bound by the commandments of God to do the opposite. In other words, the substance of the act is signified, the act with all its attendant evil circumstances, by the terms "stealing," "adultery," etc. Therefore, it follows that if such acts, considered absolutely, would fall under the divine precept in such a way that they would be obligatory, then we could no longer use the terms "stealing," "adultery," "hatred," or the like, to signify these acts. For these terms signify that the acts are forbidden, while in the hypothetical situation we are considering the acts are obligatory.[46] Therefore it would not be true to say (as Ockham is sometimes accused of doing) that God could permit adultery, stealing, the hatred of himself. For the very terms "adultery," "stealing," "hatred of God," signify connotatively that these things are not permitted by God. To say that God could permit them would then involve the contradiction that God can permit what he does not permit at the same time. But even for Ockham God cannot do anything involving a contradiction.

In this same connection, Ockham again mentions that it is possible that some particular act be good if it is done by one cause, but if it is done by another cause this same act would be evil. And the whole reason for this is that the first cause is not obliged to the opposite, while the second cause is obliged. Thus, for instance, the created will is obliged by divine precept to the love of God and as long as this precept stands the creature cannot hate God in a right way. The hatred of God would be necessarily evil because the creature is under the obligation to love God. Nor can God, as long as the first precept holds, prescribe the opposite. However, God himself is not obliged to cause any act whatsoever. Therefore, God can cause any act whatsoever, or its opposite, considering

---

atore si caderent sub praecepto divino, sicut nunc de facto eorum opposita cadunt sub praecepto. Sed stante praecepto divino ad eorum opposita non posset aliquis tales actus meritorie nec bene exercere..." (OTh V, 352). See E. Bonke, *op. cit.*, pp. 60; 67-68; F. Copleston, *op. cit.*, p. 105; A. Garvens, *op. cit.*, pp. 269-71; E. Iserloh, *op. cit.*, pp. 68-69; S. Tornay, *Ockham: Studies and Selections* (LaSalle, Ill.: Open Court, 1938), pp. 75, 180-81.

[46] Ockham, *Ibid*: "Sed si sic fierent a viatore meritorie, tunc non dicerentur nec nominarentur furtum, adulterium, odium etc., quia ista nomina significant tales actus non absolute sed connotando vel dando intelligere quod faciens tales actus per praeceptum divinum obligatur ad oppositum. Et ideo quantum ad totum significatum quid nominis talium nominum signifcant circumstantias malas. Et quantum ad hoc intelligunt Sancti et philosophi quod ista statim nominata convuluta sunt cum malitia. Si autem caderent sub praecepto divino, tunc faciens tales actus non obligaretur ad oppositum, et per consequens tunc non nominaretur furtum, adulterium, etc." (OTh V, 352-53). See E. Iserloh, *op. cit.*, pp. 68-69.

THE NATURE OF MORALITY

the act in its absolute being. Since God can cause totally an act of love without any moral goodness or evil being attached to the act--since moral goodness or evil connote that the agent is obliged to this act or to its opposite--so also God could cause, operating as the total cause, an act of hatred of himself without any moral malice. And this is true for the same reason as for above. It seems that Ockham always tries to keep this principle clearly in mind: God is not obliged to anyone or to anything.[47]

2) The second question to be discussed is in connection with the commonly held opinion that the deformity of an act consists in its lack of rectitude which should be in the act. Again it is Duns Scotus' opinion that Ockham criticizes here.[48] Scotus held that the sin or deformity in an act of sinning is nothing else than the lack of rectitude which should be in the act which is elicited by the will, that rectitude which the will

---

[47] Ockham, *Ibid.*: "...dico quod aliquis actus ab una causa potest fieri bene, et si fieret ab alia, non posset fieri nisi male. Et tota ratio est quia una causa obligatur ad actum oppositum et alia non...voluntas creata obligatur ex praecepto Dei ad diligendum Deum, et ideo stante illo pracepto non potest bene odire Deum nec causre actum odiendi, sed necessario male causat malitia moris. Et hoc quia obligatur ex praecepto Dei ad actum oppositum. Nec stante primo praecepto potest sibi Deus oppositum praecipere. Sed Deus ad nullum actum causandum obligatur, ideo quemlibet actum absolutum potest sine omni malo culpae causare et eius oppositum. Et ideo sicut potest causare totliter actum diligendi sine bonitate vel malitia morali, quia bonitas moralis vel malitia connotant quod agens obligatur ad illum actum vel eius oppositum, ita potest causare totaliter actum odiendi Deum sine omni malitia morali propter eandem causam, quia Deus ad nullum actum causandum obligatur." (OTh V, 353). *Ibid:* "...Deus autem nulli tenetur nec obligatur tanquam debitor, et ideo non potest facere quod non debet facere nec non facere quod debet facere.: (OTh V, 343). *Ibid.*: "...dico quod Deus potest esse causa totalis respectu actus in voluntate, puta respectu dilectionis Dei et odii, sicut potest esse causa totalis respectu lapidis vel hominis, quia cuiuscumque potest esse causa partialis, potest esse totalis....dico quod si causae sint approximatae debito modo et effectus ponitur, non requiritur necessario actio omnium causarum. Quia una est partialis quae potest esse totalis respectu cuiuslibet producibilis ab alia causa partiali, et quando illa est causa totalis de facto, tunc non requiritur actio alterius causae. Sic est de voluntate nostra et Deo." (OTh V, 350). Cf. *In II Sent.*, 3-4 (OTh V, 58-63). See F. Copleston, *op. cit.*, p. 104; A. Garvens, *op. cit.*, pp. 271-72.

[48] D. Scotus, *Quaestiones in secundum librum Sententiarum*, d. 37, q. 1, n. 6 in *op. cit.*, tom. XIII, pp. 356-57: "Hoc enim modo peccatum est formliter corruptio rectitudinis in actu secundo, quae opponitur illi rectitudini, vel privatio habitui, non quidem rectitudini, quae inest, quia tunc opposita simul inessent, nec quae prius infuit illi actui, quia actus non manet, ut possit alterari ab opposito in oppositum, quae deberet inesse. Voluntas enim libera debitrix est ut omnem actum suum eliciat conformiter regulae superiori, scilicet secundum divinum praeceptum, et ideo quando agit discorditer ab illa regula, caret justitia actuali debita. Haec est justitia quae deberet inesse actui et non inest, et haec carentia inquantum est actus voluntatis deficientis...est formaliter peccatum actuale."

is bound to give to the act.[49] Now, Ockham asks, what does Scotus really mean by the phrase "the lack of rectitude"? If he understands this to mean that there is a lack of rectitude which should be in the will of the sinner, then he is correct. For in sinning the will elicits an act which it should not elicit because the act is against the divine will and command; or else the will does not elicit an act which it should elicit according to the command of God. However, it seems that Scotus does not understand the phrase "the lack of rectitude" in the sense just explained. For Scotus "the lack of rectitude" applies to the act itself rather than to the will of the sinner. So the deformity in the act of sin is a lack of rectitude that should be in the act of the sin itself. But this way of understanding "the lack of rectitude," says Ockham, is impossible.[50]

In Ockham's view rectitude consists in the act itself which is elicited by the will according to the dictates of right reason and all the other required circumstances. It is a right act of the will. Therefore, deformity is not a lack of justice or rectitude which should be in the act, but a lack of justice or rectitude which should be in the will of the creature. Lack of rectitude would be equivalent, then to the lack of an act which should be elicited by the will. This is only saying that the will is obliged to elicit some act according to and in conformity with the will of God, which act the creature's will, however, does not elicit. Rectitude is nothing else than the act of the will itself. This act must be elicited according to right reason and all the other required circumstances. And on the other hand, the lack of rectitude, or deformity, is

---

[49] Ockham, *Quaest. Variae.*, q. 7, a. 4: "...dicit [Scotus] in secundo, ubi tractat de peccato originali, quod peccatum sive deformitas in actu peccati non est nisi carentia rectitudinis, non quidem quae inest actui nec quae aliquando infuit, quia actus idem est et per consequns non alteratur ab opposito in oppositum, sed solum est carentia rectitudinis quae debuit inesse actui tali, quam rectitudinem tenebatur voluntas sibi dare." (OTh VIII, 380).

[50] *Ibid.*: "...quaero quid intelligit [Scotus] per rectitudinem debitam inesse. Aut intelligit quod peccatum et deformitas in actu est carentia rectitudinis debitae inesse voluntati peccanti, et tunc verum dicit, quia voluntas elicit actum quem non debuit elicere quia contra voluntatem et praeceptum divinum...Aut intelligit quod deformitas in actu peccati est carentia rectitudinis debitae inesse actui illius peccati vel quae potest sibi inesse in posterum. Sed hoc est impossibile." (OTh VIII, 383). For a rather lengthy argument against Scotus' position confer parallel texts in Ockham, *Quodl.* III, q. 15 (OTh IX, 258-61) and *Quaest. Variae*, q. 7, a. 4 (OTh VIII, 380-85). In general Ockham argues that rectitude cannot be any absolute or relative quality of the act, neither a habit nor a species, an act of the intellect, a relation to prudence or any other kind of relation. See E. Bonke, *op. cit.*, pp. 65-66.

nothing else but the absence of this act which ought to be elicited by the will of the creature.⁵¹

In not eliciting an act which it is obliged to elicit, the created will would sin by omission. In this case it seems clear that the lack of rectitude is nothing else but the absence of the act of the will. It is the will which lacks this act; the lack of rectitude is not in the act itself--which does not even exist--but it is in the will which fails to elicit this act. The lack of rectitude cannot be applied to the act when the act itself does not exist. In other words, since the rectitude of an act is equivalent to the act itself, the lack of rectitude is equivalent to the lack of the act itself. And in the same manner, if the will elicits an act which it is obliged by divine precept not to elicit, then there would be a sin of commission. For instance, someone elicits an act contrary to right reason and the commandments of God. If the created will would be bound at the same time to an opposite act, then the deformity is nothing else but the lack of the opposite act which the created will would be under obligation to elicit.⁵²

3) The third question concerns the distinction between the material element in sin (the substance of the act) and the formal element (the lack of justice). Ockham maintains that such a way of speaking is simply false. A sin is a sin of commission, a sin of omission, or of both together. Now in the case of a sin of commission the will elicits an act against the dictates of right reason and against the prohibition of Almighty God, while not being bound in a positive way to elicit an opposite act. All that we have here is the act itself of sin, without any lack of rectitude or justice which should be in the act. For instance, in the act of stealing a person sins. But his sin does not consist in any lack

---

⁵¹*Quodl.* III, 15: "Dico igitur quod deformitas non est carentia iustitiae vel rectitudinis debitae inesse actui, sed est carentia rectitudinis debitae inesse ipsi voluntati; quod nihil aliud est dicere nisi quod voluntas obligatur aliquem actum elicere secundum praeceptum divinum quem non elicit. Et ideo rectitudo actus non est aliud quam ipse actus qui debuit elici secundum rectam ratione." (OTh IX, 261). Cf. *Quaest. Variae*, q. 7, a. 4 (OTh VIII, 384-8). See E. Iserloh, *op. cit.*, p. 65.

⁵²Ockham, *Quaest. Variae*, q. 7, a. 4: "...peccatum in actu..est carentia rectitudinis debitae inesse voluntati; quod nihil aliud est dicere nisi quod voluntas tenetur et obligatur aliquem alium actum elicere secundum praeceptum divinum quem non elicit, et sic peccat peccato omissionis; et ita rectitudo nihil absolutum vel respectivum est aliud quam ipse actus qui debuit elici secundum rectam rationem et voluntatem Dei....Et ideo carere rectitudine in actu est carere tali actu. Et similiter voluntas elicit aliquem actum quem tenetur non elicere quia elicit contra rectam rationem et praeceptum Dei, et sic peccat peccato commissionis; et si voluntas teneatur ad actum oppositum, tunc deformitas in isto actu est carentia rectitudinis debitae inesse voluntati, quia est carentia alterius actus oppositi quem voluntas tenetur elicere." (OTh VIII, 387). See A. Garvens, *op. cit.*, pp. 403-404; E. Iserloh, *op. cit.*, p. 65; S. Tornay, *op. cit.*, pp. 75, 180-181.

of justice in the act of stealing. Justice is not required in the act of stealing; there is not lack of rectitude which should be in the act. But according to the dictates of right reason and the prohibition of God concerning stealing, the act of stealing should not exist at all. In other words, by stealing the created will elicits an act which is prohibited, an act which it is under an obligation not to elicit. From this consideration Ockham draws the following conclusion: In a sin of commission the material element, the substance of the act, is present; but the formal element, the lack of justice which should be in the act, is not present.[53]

In the case of a sin of omission, on the other hand, just the opposite would be true. In a sin of omission the formal element is present; but the material element is absent. The creature sins by omission when he is under an obligation to elicit some act which actually he fails to elicit. And since no act is elicited, we can say that there is a lack of justice, the formal element; but since no act is elicited, we cannot say that the material element is present, that is, the substance of the act. And the reason for this is that the act simply does not exist.[54]

Finally, there can also be the case of a sin of both commission and omission. For example, the will elicits some act against the law of God while it is at the same time bound to elicit an opposite act. The sin of commission consists in the act against the law of God; the sin of omission is the lack of the other act which should be in the will. Consequently, to speak of the material and formal elements of sin, all that is indicated is that the sin of commission is the material element and the sin of omission is the formal element. Therefore, when we have the case of a sin of commission alone, then the material and formal elements are not both present, but only the material element; and if we speak of the act as being omitted, the sin of omission, then only the formal element of sin is present.[55]

---

[53] Ockham, *Quaest. Variae*, q. 7, a. 4: "...non bene dicitur quod actus positivus est materiale in peccato, et carentia iustitiae debitae inesse est formale; quia aut est peccatum commissionis, aut omissionis in volutate, aut utrumque simul. Si primum solum, puta si voluntas eliciat aliquem actum contra rectam rationem et praeceptum divinum, et non teneatur elicere oppositum actum, tunc solum est ibi in voluntate actus peccati sine omni carentia rectitudinis vel iustitiae debitae inesse, et per consequens carentia non est ibi formale." (OTh VIII, 387)

[54] *Ibid.*: "Si secundum solum sit in voluntate, puta quia voluntas tenetur aliquem actum elicere quem non elicit, tunc solum est ibi carentia rectitudinis sine omni materiali, quia sine omni actu elicito." (OTh VIII, 387 f.).

[55] *Ibid.*: "Si tertium detur, puta quando voluntas elicit aliquem actum contra praeceptum Dei, et ad oppositum tenetur, tunc est ibi duplex peccatum: commissionis et omissionis. Peccatum commissionis est actus ille positivus solum, peccatum omissionis est carentia alterius actus debiti inesse. Et per consequens nihil aliud erit dicere quod in peccato sunt

THE NATURE OF MORALITY

We will conclude this section with some further remarks on the nature of sin. First of all we must emphasize again that sin is necessarily a voluntary act. Sin is so voluntary that unless it is voluntary it cannot be a sin.[56] A sin exists in no act unless it exists in the power of the will.[57] No act is liable to blame unless it is under the power of the will.[58] Secondly, sin involves the violation of an obligation. No one sins unless he is obliged to do what he does not do, or does what he is obliged not to do.[59] Sin is nothing else but doing the opposite of what is obligatory.[60] It is in the observance or the violation of an obligation, therefore, that a person becomes a sinner or a non-sinner. Hypothetically, there could be the case in which one person who performs an external act actually fulfills an obligation, while another person who performs the same external act as the first would violate an obligation. Suppose that a legitimate superior obliges one of his subjects to do a certain act while at the same time forbidding another of his subjects from doing the same act. The first would fulfill the command of the superior by performing the act; the second would violate the command of

---

talia duo, materiale et formale, quam quod peccatum commissum est materiale et omissum est formale." (OTh VIII, 388).

[56] *Quodl* III, 14: "...nullus actus est virtuosus nec vitiosus nisi sit voluntarius et in potestate voluntatis, quia peccatum adeo est voluntarium etc." (OTh IX, 254). *In III Sent.*, 11: "...dico quod vitium proprie non est nisi in voluntate, quia secundum Augustinum, peccatum adeo est voluntarium quod si non sit voluntarium, non est peccatum." (OTh VI, 390); *Quaest. Variae*, q. 8: "...nullus peccat in eo quod vitare non potest. Nam peccatum adeo est voluntarium quod si non sit voluntarium non est peccatum, secundum Augustinum." (OTh VIII, 438).

[57] *In III Sent.* 7: "...in nullo actu consistit peccatum nisi exsistat in potestate voluntatis." (OTh VI, 210).

[58] *In III Sent.* 7: "Et tunc excusatur peccatum, quia in nullo actu consistit peccatum nisi exsistat in potestate voluntatis, sicut nec meritum quod non potest esse nisi eliciatur a voluntate, saltem partialiter." (OTh VI, 210). *In III Sent.*, 11: "...sed solus actus voluntatis est virtuosus. Probatur: quia solus actus voluntatis est laudabilis vel vituperabilis; igitur solus ille est virtuosus....Conformatur per Philosophum, III *Ethicorum* ubi dicit quod nullus actus est vituperabilis nisi sit in potestate nostra. Nullus enim culpat caecum natum quia est caecus. Sed si sit caecus per peccatum proprium, tunc est culpabilis." (OTh VI, 366; *Quaest. Variae*, q. 8: "...solus actus voluntatis sit virtuosus vel vitiosus." (OTh VIII, 439); *Ibid.*, q. 6, a. 9 (OTh VIII, 162 ff.). See E. Iserloh, *op. cit.*, p. 47.

[59] *In II Sent.*, 15: "...nunquam homo peccat nisi quia tenetur facere quod non facit vel quia facit quod non debet facere." (OTh V, 343). Cf. *Ibid.* (OTh V, 353); *In III Sent.*, 11 (OTh VI, 388-89).

[60] *In II Sent.*, 3-4: "...malum nihil aliud est quam facere aliquid ad cuius oppositum faciendum aliquis obligatur." (OTh V, 59); *Quaest. Variae*, q. 8: "...semper peccat voluntas peccato commissionis quando elicit aliquem actum ad cuius oppositum obligatur..." (OTh VIII, 428); *Ibid.*: "...nullus peccat nisi quia tenetur ad oppositum illius quod fcit." (OTh VIII, 431). See F. Copleston, *op. cit.*, p. 103.

CHAPTER V

the superior by acting. For each of the subjects is obliged in a different way.[61] We also spoke of this case in connection with conforming to the will of God, a question discussed in the last chapter. So a sin is nothing else than acting or omitting an act in a matter of obligation.[62] The will commits a sin of commission when it elicits an act to whose opposite it is obliged by divine command.[63] And as no one sins by a sin of commission except by eliciting an act which he is obliged not to elicit, so also no one sins by a sin of omission except by omitting an act which he is under an obligation to elicit.[64]

The violation of an obligation is a vicious or an evil act; the fulfillment of an obligation is a virtuous act. But the obligation can be fulfilled in ways which are specifically distinct. The whole act which fulfills the obligation must be taken into consideration. Though two acts may both be a fulfillment of an obligation, the circumstances, which form partial objects of the act, may differ. Since the circumstances are distinct specifically, the acts are also specifically distinct. Thus, as we have indicated previously, the virtues of the Christian are specifically distinct from those of the pagan philosophers.[65] As a matter of fact, Ockham sets up a scale of five distinct grades of moral virtue:[66]

1) The first grade of moral virtue: Someone wills to perform a just act in conformity with the dictates of right reason requiring that such an act is to be performed with all the requisite circumstances. But here special regard is given to the act itself. For instance, right reason dictates that a certain act is to be performed at a certain time and

---

[61] Ockham, *In IV Sent.*, qq. 10-11: "...si esset aliquis superior respectu duorum, et praecipiat uni facere aliquid et alteri non, unus in non faciendo peccaret et alter non, quia secundus non aequaliter obligatur sicut primus. Obligatio igitur facit aliquem peccatorem vel non peccatorem." (OTh VII, 198). See A. Garvens, *op. cit.*, p. 271; G. Lagarde, *op. cit.*, pp. 58, 69.

[62] Ockham, *Ibid.*: "Peccatum...non dicit aliud nisi actum aliquem commissionis vel omissionis ad quem homo obligatur." (OTh VII, 198).

[63] *Quaest. Variae*, q. 8: "...quia semper peccat voluntas peccato commissionis quando elicit aliquem actum ad cuius oppositum obligatur." (OTh VIII, 428).

[64] *Ibid.*: "...sicut nullus peccat peccato commissionis nisi quando elicit actum quem tenetur non elicere, ita nullus peccat peccato omissionis nisi omittendo actum quem tenetur elicere." (OTh VIII, 439 f.). See L. Baudry (ed.), *op. cit.*, p. 147.

[65] See the latter portion of Chapter III.

[66] *Quaest. Variae*, q. 7, a. 2: "...iustitia et quaelibet una virtus moralis, secundum quod non est alia virtus nec formaliter nec aequivalenter, habet quinque gradus, non quidem eiusdem speciei, sed distinctarum specierum." (OTh VIII, 334). See L. Baudry (ed.), *op. cit.*, pp. 74, 83 ff.

place because it is a just act; the will then elicits an act of willing this act in conformity with the dictates of right reason.[67]

2) The second grade of moral virtue: In the second grade of moral virtue we must presuppose all the conditions mentioned above in the first grade of virtue. Besides these conditions we add the intention of the will to fulfill its obligations, even to the point of undergoing death if such be required.[68]

3) The third grade of moral virtue: The distinguishing characteristic of this grade of moral virtue lies in the intention of the will to fulfill its obligations according to the dictates of right reason and all of the other required circumstances precisely in virtue of the fact that right reason dictates that this particular act should be performed.[69]

4) The fourth grade of moral virtue: Here the person wills to perform an act according to all the conditions already mentioned, and besides them, he wills to perform the act precisely out of the love of God. For example, the intellect dictates that a certain act should be elicited by the will out of the love of God. It is important to note that it is only in this grade of moral virtue that we find the truly perfect virtuous act. The fourth grade of moral virtue is moral virtue in the proper sense.[70]

5) The fifth grade of moral virtue: This grade includes the familiar notion of "heroic virtue." Hence it involves an act which exceeds

---

[67] *Ibid.*: "Primus gradus est quando aliquis vult facere opera iusta conformiter rationi rectae dictanti talia opera esse facienda secundum debitas circumstantias respicientes praecise ipsum opus propter honestatem ipsius operis sicut propter finem, puta intellectus dictat quod tale opus iustum est faciendum tali loco tali tempore propter honestatem ipsius operis vel propter pacem vel aliquid tale, et voluntas elicit actum volendi talia opera conformiter iuxta dictamen intellectus." (OTh VIII, 335).

[68] *Ibid.*: "Secundus gradus est quando voluntas vult facere opera iusta secundum rectum dictamen praedictum, et praeter hoc cum intentione nullo modo dimittendi talia pro quocumque quod est contra rectam rationem, etiam non pro morte, si recta ratio dictaret tale opus non esse dimittendum pro morte; puta si homo velit sic honorare patrem secundum rectum dictamen praedictum loco et tempre etc., cum intentione et voluntate non dimittendi illum honorem pro morte, si immineret." (OTh VIII, 335).

[69] *Ibid.*: "Tertius gradus est quando aliquis vult tale opus facere secundum rectam rationem praedictam cum intentione praedicta, et praeter hoc vult tale opus secundum circumstantias praedictas facere praecise et solum quia sic est dictatum a recta ratione." (OTh VIII, 335).

[70] *Ibid.*: "Quartus gradus est quando vult tale opus facere secundum omnes condiciones et circumstantias praedictas, et praeter hoc propter amorem Dei praecise, puta quia sic dictatum est ab intellectu, quod talia opera sunt facienda propter amorem Dei praecise. Et iste gradus solum est perfecta et vera virtus moralis de qua Sancti loquuntur." (OTh VIII, 335 f.).

CHAPTER V

the common capabilities of human nature, or an act which is at least strongly against our natural inclinations.[71]

That these grades of moral virtue are numerically distinct, says Ockham, is evident from the fact of their separability. They are also specifically distinct. These virtues concern specifically distinct partial objects. For Ockham, as has been explained, those things which others call merely circumstances of a virtuous act, are really the partial and secondary objects of the act. Therefore, when these objects are specifically different, the acts or the habits in relation to them are also specifically distinct. Now as we ascend in the scale of the grades of virtue, we find that for each higher grade there is an object or "circumstance" which is not found in any of the lower grades.[72] For example, the fourth grade, the grade of perfect moral virtue, has this specific object, that the act is performed with the motive of loving God. It is this "circumstance" of the act or of the virtue which distinguishes it from all the other grades.

If a person possesses any particular virtue on the fourth level, the possession of this one virtue also inclines the person to elicit an act of any other virtue on this level. The reason is that on the fourth level the person is motivated by the love of God, which includes not only the idea of loving God above all and for himself, but also the willingness to do whatever God wills. The willing of whatever God wills cannot be restricted, it is universal in its scope. A person, therefore, who possesses the virtue of justice in a perfect degree, a justice that is possessed on the basis of the love of God, will also possess the virtue of temperance or any of the other moral virtues. The possession of any particular moral virtue tends to lead to the possession of all the moral virtues. The reason, as mentioned, is seen in the intention which forms the partial object of any particular moral virtue. For if a person out of the motive of loving God wills whatever right reason dictates, he cannot limit himself to any particular dictate of right reason, or to any particular virtue. He must will whatever right reason dictates. For the love

---

[71] *Quaest. Variae*, q. 7, a. 2: "Et si tunc velit actu imperativo formaliter facere vel pati aliquid quod ex natura sua excedit communem statum hominum et est contra inclinationem naturalem...talis inquam actus imperativus formaliter talis operis est generativus virtutis heroicae vel elicitus a virtute heroica." (OTh VIII, 336).

[72] *Ibid.*: "Distinctio numeralis istorum habituum et actuum patet per separabilitatem ipsorum. Distinctio specifica patet, primo per distinctionem specificam obiectorum partialium, quia pono quod illa quae ponuntur circumstantiae virtutum ab aliis, sunt obiecta partialia et secundaria ipsius actus virtuosi, et ideo quando talia obiecta variantur secundum speciem, actus et habitus istorum variantur secundum speciem; sed actus cuiuslibet gradus ascendendo habet aliquod obiectum et circumstantiam distinctam specie quod non habet alius gradus inferior." (OTh VIII, 337).

of God includes the notion of willing whatever God wills. Therefore, potentially at least, all the virtues would be included.[73]

The fourth grade of moral virtue, the level of perfect moral virtue, is also necessarily connected in the present order established by God with the theological virtues. The distinguishing characteristic of the fourth level of virtue is that the acts are performed out of the love of God. No one can perform acts out of the love of God unless he loves God, understanding this love of God as above all and for Himself. But such a love of God, at least in the present order, cannot exist without the virtues of faith, hope, and charity.[74] The theological virtues are not, of course, necessarily connected with the lower levels of moral virtue, for on the lower levels acts are elicited apart from any consideration of God or the love of God. Therefore, an unbeliever could be virtuuos on any of the first three levels of virtue without possessing the theological virtues of faith, hope, and charity.[75]

The theological virtues are necessarily connected with the fourth grade of moral virtue. They also exclude any moral evil in the strict sense. One who loves God above all cannot be evil. The evil-doer loves something else more than he loves God. For anyone who loves God above all also loves whatever God wills him to love; and he hates whatever God wills him to hate. But the sinner does not love whatever God wills him to love, because the sinner does not love virtue. And by sinning, the sinner actually seeks something that God does not will him to seek.[76]

---

[73] *Quaest. Variae*, q. 7, a. 3: "...una virtus perfecta sufficienter cum voluntate et recta ratione sive prudentia inclinat ad primum actum alterius virtutis qui est generativus illius virtutis; et intelligo per virtutem perfectam virtutem in tertio et quarto gradu....Quia si aliquis vult aliquid solum quia dictatum est a recta ratione quantum ad tertium gradum, vel quia solum dictatum est a recta ratione et propter honorem divinum, tunc vult omne dictatum a recta ratione." (OTh VIII, 347f.). See O. Suk, *op. cit.*

[74] *Ibid.*: "...virtus moralis in quarto gradu necessario coexigit virtutes theologicas, et hoc de potentia Dei ordinata. Hoc patet, quia non potest esse amor creaturae vel alicuius creati propter Deum nisi talis amet Deum super omnia...talis autem amor de potentia Dei ordinata non potest esse sine fide, spe et caritate..." (OTh VIII, 356). See L. Baudry (ed.), *op. cit.*, p. 86.

[75] Cf. Ockham, *Quaest. Variae*, q. 7, a. 3 (OTh VIII, 357). L Baudry (ed.), *op. cit.*, pp. 85-86: "Ex hoc sequitur quod virtus in quinto gradu distinguitur in fideli a virtute in quinto gradu in infideli quia una habet Deum pro obiecto, alia, non."

[76] *Ibid.*: "...virtutes theologicae nullum vitium morale compatiuntur...Patet tertio, quia qui recte diligit Deum, diligit omne quod Deus vult diligi, et odit omne quod Deus vult ordiri; sed si sit vitiosus, tunc non diligit omne quod Deus vult diligi, quia non virtutem, quam Deus vult diligi; similiter diligit aliquod quod Deus non vult diligi, quia vitium..." (OTh VIII, 358f.). See L. Baudry (ed.), *op. cit.*, pp. 75, 86.

CHAPTER V

We have completed the circle, and again the love of God comes to the fore. The love of God, the virtue of charity, is intimately connected with any perfect virtue, because charity itself forms a partial object of that virtue. Charity, therefore, would immediately incline the will to an act of any kind of virtue. Here Ockham also appeals to Gregory who says that all the precepts are one, since they are rooted in charity. In this sense, then, all the virtues are connected in and by the virtue of charity. Without charity no one can be perfectly virtuous nor is any act perfectly meritorious.[77] In the words of the Gospel: "Thou shalt love the Lord thy God...This is the greatest and the first commandment."[78]

---

[77] Ockham, *In IV Sent.*, qq. 3-4: "...caritas inclinat immediate ad actum cuiuslibet virtutis. Et ideo dicit Gregorius quod omnia praecepta sunt unum in radice caritatis. Et isto modo omnes virtutes sunt connexae in caritate. Unde caritas inclinat ad actum cuiuscumque virtutis....Et ideo nullus actus est perfecte virtuosus vel meritorius sine actu caritatis." (OTh VII, 57f.).

[78] St. Matthew, XXII, 37-38.

CHAPTER VI

CONCLUSION

There have been many attempts made to summarize Ockham's basic ethical theory. More importantly, these attempts have also sought to construct a general framework within which the fundamental ethical ideas of Ockham could be located and discussed.[1] Often, however, the discussion digresses into a comparison between Ockham's system of ethics and the philosophy which underlies his system with that of another leading philosopher--Plato or Aristotle, St. Augustine, St. Thomas Aquinas or Duns Scotus. The result is a criticism of Ockham in predominantly negative tones. Moreover, the examination of Ockham's basic theory is thus often abandoned at a very superficial level. For this reason our purpose here is to attempt a more positive criticism of Ockham's theory of ethics by concentrating our attention on Ockham's thought rather than on the systems of his predecessors, contemporaries, or successors. At the same time we shall also try to fashion a framework consistent with Ockham's fundamental theory which will in a sense "characterize" Ockham's theory in the field of ethics.

At first reading it might appear that in Ockham's writings there are really two ethical systems proposed and that these two systems are separate and distinct. Ockham, of course, does not develop systematically

---

[1] See, for example, the following: T. Barth, "Wilhelm Ockham im Lichte der neuesten Forschung," *Philosophisches Jahrbuch*, LX (1950), pp. 465-66; P. Boehner, "A Recent Presentation of Ockham's Philosophy," *Franciscan Studies*, IX (1949), pp. 443-45; P. Boehner (ed.), *Ockham. Philosophical Writings* ("Nelson Philosophical Texts"; London: Nelson, 1957), pp. xlviii-l; E. Bonke, "Doctrina nominalistica de fundamento ordinis moralis apud Gulielmum de Ockham et Gabrielem Biel," *Collectanea franciscana*, XIV (1944), pp. 57-83; A. Garvens, "Die Grundlagen der Ethik Wilhelms von Ockham," *Franziskanische Studien*, XXI (1934), pp. 243-73; F. Copleston, *A History of Philosophy*. Vol. III. *Ockham to Suarez* (Westminster: Newman, 1953), pp. 103-10; J. Hirschberger, *Geschichte der Philosophie*. I. *Altertum und Mittelalter* (Freiburg, 1949), pp. 459-60; E. Hochstetter, "Ockham-Forschung in Italien," *Zeitschrift für philosophische Forschung*, I (1947), pp. 575-76; E. Hochstettr, "Viator mundi," *Franziskanische Studien*, XXXII (1950), pp. 1-20; E. Iserloh, *Gnade und Eucharistie in der philosophischen Theologie des Wilhelm von Ockham* (Wiesbaden: Steiner, 1956), pp. 44-79; W. Kolmel, "Das Naturrecht bei Wilhelm Ockham," *Franziskanische Studien*, XXXV (1953), pp. 39-85; J. Rubert y Candáu, "Los principios básicos de la Etica en el Ockhamismo y en la via moderna de los siglos XIV y XV," *Verdad y vida*, XVIII (1960), pp. 97-116; S. Tornay, *Ockham. Studies and Selections* (La Salle, Ill.: Open Court, 1938), pp. 54-76; 173-180.

CHAPTER VI

his ethical theory to the extent that we can speak of a complete and explicit system which he proposes. But at least there are definite and clear ideas expressed which form the foundations of an ethical system. It is upon analysis of these fundamental ideas that the idea of two ethical systems appears; the one system based on the will of man and his right reason as the norm of morality, and the second system resting on the will of God as the highest ethical norm.

Without doubt there is a dual viewpoint to be found in Ockham's ethical theory.[2] And this dual aspect is, I believe, fundamental to the understanding of and the characterization of Ockham's basic theory of ethics. But the study of this dual character of Ockham's ethics is open to two dangers. First, there is the danger of completely separating the two theories. The separation may be made to the extent that the two theories are viewed as completely exclusive, perhaps even contradictory. To characterize Ockham's norms of morality as contradictory would be a misreading and misunderstanding of his intention and purpose. Even to say that the two theories, though not contradictory, are exclusive and independent or are completely unrelated to each other, would also be an erroneous interpretation of Ockham's writings. For, as will be shown, if it is not already clear from the preceding chapters, the two systems are related and there is a dependence in a very close and intimate way of the one system upon the other.

Secondly, there is the danger of considering Ockhams twofold system of ethics as one, of identifying and merging the two theories to the degree that each loses its own special character. This viewpoint is exemplified in F. Copleston's characterization of Ockham's ethics in terms of a "substructure" (the will and right reason of man as the norm of morality) and a "superstructure" (the will of God as the norm). In Copleston's view the superstructure is conceived as erected upon the substructure which thus forms the foundation upon which the former depends. The superstructure is looked upon as an added element, an "ultra-personal conception of the moral law," built upon the substructure of "the Christian-Aristotelian tradition."[3] In Copleston's view, then, the two structures together form one complete and integrated system of ethics.

---

[2] F. Copleston, *op. cit.*, p. 107: "It would seem, then, at least at first sight, that we are faced with what amounts to two moral theories in Ockham's philosophy...That there is truth in the contention that two moral theories are implicit in Ockham's ethical teaching can hardly, I think, be denied."

[3] *Ibid*: "He [Ockham] built on the substructure of the Christian-Aristotelian tradition, and he retained a considerable amount of it, as is shown by what he says about the virtues, right reason, natural rights and so on. But he added to this substructure a superstructure which consisted in an ultra-personal conception of the moral law..."

CONCLUSION

The integration of the two systems can, of course, be achieved only with great difficulty, if at all. Based on such a view of Ockham's systems it is no wonder that Copleston concludes that Ockham "does not seem fully to have realized that the addition of this superstructure demanded a more radical recasting of the substructure than he actually carried out."[4]

F. Copleston's viewpoint on the two theories of Ockham's ethics is certainly not without considerable merit. By keeping in mind the dual character of Ockham's ethics Copleston is able to present an uncommonly fair and penetrating analysis of Ockham's thought in this field. But the attempt to analyze Ockham's twofold viewpoint in terms of "structures" tends, at least, to blur the lines between the two aspects of Ockham's theory. And more importantly, it also tends to obscure the fundamental ideas which led to the construction of his dual theory of ethics. In the present author's viewpoint, therefore, an examination of the leading ideas upon which the dual aspect of Ockham's theory of ethics is founded will lead us away from both the danger of considering the two theories as completely separate as well as the danger of merging the two theories into one. Ockham's dual system of ethics is then not interpreted or expressed either in terms of two parallel, unrelated and often contradictory, systems or in terms of a combination of a substructure and a superstructure. The dual character of Ockham's ethics can perhaps be better characterized in general as a presentation of two sides of the same coin. In explanation of this we must turn to the fundamental ideas which underlie each side or each aspect of Ockham's dual theory of ethics. Such an explanation should also be able to serve as a summary and synthesis of the leading ideas presented in the preceding chapters of this dissertation.

It will prove expedient in this connection to borrow a page from the American philosopher, William James, who distinguished the "tender-minded philosophers" from the "tough-minded philosophers" and formulated a list or box-score of their chief characteristics.[5] In a similar style we can draw up a list of the leading characteristics of each of Ockham's theories of ethics and by this means indicate the fundamental ideas upon which each theory is based. Such a listing of basic ideas should include the following items; but we do not pretend that the list is exhaustive, nor that the items are necessarily arranged in the order of importance.

---

[4] *Ibid.*

[5] W. James, *Pragmatism* (New York: Longmans, Green, 1914), p. 12.

CHAPTER VI

The will of God as the norm of morality	Right reason as the norm of morality
Based on:	
1. God's absolute power,	1. God's ordered power,
2. his omnipotence and free will,	2. his intelligence, etc.
3. the moral order's necessity	3. the moral order's contingency
4. an absolute moral code..	4. a provisional moral code
5. the law's relation to God	5. the law's relation to man.
6. known through revelation.	6. known by natural reason.
7. with absolute certitude.	7. with practical certitude.
8. The moral law is personal	8. The moral law is impersonal
9. and the ethics one of love.	9. and the ethics one of reward.

As previously mentioned, the above list is not meant to be exhaustive. Many other items could also be explicitly brought to our attention here. However, I believe that the above enumeration expresses adequately in summary form the ideas which are basic to each of Ockham's viewpoints in ethics. Further examination of the items in each list will reveal more clearly the interrelations which exist among them.

It can hardly be denied that the key to the correct understanding of Ockham's view on the will of God as the norm of morality is contained in the notion of the absolute power of God. The will of God is viewed in terms of his absolute power. By his absolute power God is able to do anything that does not involve a contradiction in its being done. The question brought into focus here is not "What does God do?" but "What can God do?" Ockham, for the moment, is not interested in the real world as it exists here and now, the nature and present condition of man, the actually existing moral order. He is interested only in determining the limits of God's absolute power in virtue of logical contradictions, if, indeed, these can be called limitations at all. Applied to the realm of ethics, the only contradiction that Ockham seems to discover is in the fulfillment of the command of God that he be hated. For the actual fulfillment of this command would imply obedience to God and, consequently, the love of Him. But love and hate are mutually exclusive.[6]

By appealing to the absolute power of God Ockham is conducting a mental experiment. The tool of this experiment is the notion of the absolute power of God. In virtue of God's absolute power his will and omnipotence are set aside and isolated from his intellect and other at-

---

[6] See the discussion of this and related problems in Chapter IV of this dissertation.

CONCLUSION

tributes. The absolute freedom of God's will is under consideration, not his purpose in acting, his wisdom, infinite goodness, justice or mercy. Everything that God does, however, is done justly and well. God is under no obligation to anyone or to anything.[7]

But there is another side to the coin. Turning the coin over we find that Ockham's view of the present order is made according to the ordained power of God. Here he investigates what God does or has done rather than what God can or could do. God always acts reasonably; He is the wise Creator, governing with providential justice and mercy. In this realm the reader of Ockham must be struck by his acceptance of the traditional viewpoint on the existence and content of the moral order. Nowhere do we find him attempting to justify what was condemned by the traditional moral code in the present order: stealing, adultery, lying, or any other immoral act. Very significantly, Duns Scotus, whom Ockham frequently criticizes, never comes under attack on these grounds. Ockham seems to accept Scotus' view under the aspect of the ordered power of God. He upholds rather than destroys the moral code based on man's nature and the nature of those institutions—family, state, society—by which the major objectives of man are attained in this life.[8]

Ockham's acceptance of the existing moral order, however, did not prevent him from asking how necessary it actually is. Scotus had raised the same question before Ockham and clearly distinguished in the Decalog those commandments necessarily connected with man's nature and those which are only in harmony with or are agreeable to man's nature.[9] Ockham saw that it would only be by using the notion of the absolute power of God as a strong starting-point that he could arrive at a determination of what was necessarily the content of the moral order. And only by establishing the necessary content of the moral law could he construct an absolute moral code. He realized that there must be at least one nec-

---

[7] See Chapter IV, footnotes 85 and 86 for references.

[8] G. Biel, for example, did not interpret Ockham's ethics as opposed to the natural law theory.

[9] D. Scotus, *Quaestiones in tertium librum Sententiarum*, d. 37, q. un., n. 5 in *Joannis Duns Scoti opera omnia*, tom. XV, ed. Vivès (Paris: 1895), p. 825: "Ad quaestionem igitur dico quod aliqua possunt dici esse de lege naturae dupliciter: Uno modo tanquam prima principia practica nota ex terminis, vel conclusiones necessario sequentes ex eis; et haec dicuntur esse strictissime de lege naturae." *Ibid*, n. 8, p. 826: "Alio modo dicuntur aliqua esse de lege naturae, quia sunt multum consona illi legi, licet non sequantur necessario ex principiis practicis, quae nota sunt ex terminis, et omni intellectui apprehendenti sunt necessario nota; et hoc modo certum est omnia praecepta etiam secundae tabulae esse de lege naturae, quia eorum rectitudo valde consonat primis principiis practicis necessario notis." See G. Budzik, *De conceptu legis ad mentem Joannis Duns Scoti* (Burlington, Wis.: 1954), pp. 37-42.

essarily virtuous act from which all contingently virtuous acts receive their morality. The act which has an absolute value: to love, or equivalently, to obey God. This command is absolute not because it is always true in the present order, but because it would hold in any possible order. For this command is based on the relation of creature to Creator, a relation that holds as long as any creature exists. In this sense, then, the moral code is grounded on an objectively absolute command. Ockham cannot be charged with divine moral positivism which maintains that the morality of every human act is determined solely by the will of an almighty God expressing a certain precept or prohibition.[10]

It remains true, however, that Ockham saw the will of God as the highest norm of morality. Through a consideration of God's will, omnipotence and absolute power, Ockham sought the basis for necessity in the moral order and the establishment of a foundation for an absolute code of ethics. This view, it seems to me, concentrates its attention on the relation of God to the moral order. This could also be expressed in terms of a dynamic rather than a static view of the moral order, as is done by E. Bonke.[11] Man's relation to the moral law is better seen in the light of God's ordered power, his wisdom and other attributes, in virtue of which the present moral order is established. But here man is confronted not with an absolute code (except the love of God which is always a good act) but with a provisional code only.[12] Outside of the present moral order or under special circumstances within this order God

---

[10] See T. Barth, *op. cit.*, 465-66; P. Boehner, "A Recent Presentation of Ockham's Philosophy," pp. 453-54; J. Hirschberger, *op. cit.*, p. 460.

[11] E. Bonke, *op. cit.*, p. 57: "Aspectus staticus [ordinis moralis] fautores suos habuit apud philosophos graecos, praesertim vero apud Aristotelem, et apud S. Thomam eiusque scholam. Hi philosophi attentionem specialem dirigentes ad relationem quae intercedit inter ordinem moralem et naturalem, obligationem moralem ex ipsa notione boni et mali deduci posse putabant. Aspectus autem dynamicus apud S. Augustinum et in schola franciscana praevalebat. Hi totam creationem considerantes in eius directa dependentia a Deo magis ad relationem inter Deum et ordinem moralem attendunt speciatim quoad ultimum fundamentum obligationis moralis. Non negant quidem relationem intrinsecam inter ordinem moralem et naturam, at illam coarctant ad naturam intrinsecam boni et mali."

[12] F. Copleston, *op. cit.*, p. 14: "By making the moral law dependent on the free divine choice he [Ockham] implied, whether he realized it or not, that without revelation man can have no certain knowledge even of the present moral order established by God. The best that man could do, unaided by revelation, would presumably be to reflect on the needs of human nature and human society and follow the dictates of his practical reason, even though those dictates might not represent the divine will. This would imply the possibility of two ethics, the moral order established by God but knowable only by revelation, and a provisional and second-class natural and non-theological ethic worked out by the human reason without revelation. I do not mean to say that Ockham actually drew this conclusion from his authoritarian conception of the moral law; but it was, I think, implicit in that conception."

CONCLUSION

could by his absolute power command the opposite of what he now commands. Ockham found justification for this viewpoint in instances related in Sacred Scripture.[13] But, he concludes, if God would allow such acts as stealing, lying etc., these acts could no longer be called stealing or lying etc., because they no longer fall under divine prohibition.[14]

The exceptions that God makes or could make to the present moral order do not undermine the moral order as such; nor do they destroy the provisional code of ethics derived from the moral order. The provisional code still has value as a guide to man's moral conduct. Man could not know of an exception to the code except by a special act of intervention by God. But until God would make a special dispensation in a particular instance, the code still stands. It is only in this sense, then, that the moral code is to be called provisional or hypothetical.

By the natural light of reason man is capable of acquiring a knowledge of the order established by God in the universe. This includes a knowledge of the moral order. In accordance with his knowledge of the moral order man constructs a code of ethics, a philosophy of right action by which he can guide his life with practical certitude. In following the precepts of his code of ethics man's right reason is the norm which he must follow. The moral goodness or depravity of an act is measured in terms of its conformity with right reason. God's will, however, as manifested in a positive act of revelation, may supersede the demands of the moral order and the commands and prohibitions of a humanly constructed code of ethics, whether this code be constructed by an individual for his own personal guidance or by society for the governing of its legitimate subjects. This is especially true in the light of God's absolute power. And it is only in this connection that it is true that "authoritarianism again has the last word."[15]

The way in which man's knowledge of the moral order and his knowledge of the will of God are related raises an important issue. At first sight it would appear that: 1) by his natural reason man discovers the principles and precepts which have right reason as the norm of morality;

---

[13] An example of this was treated earlier, in Chapter IV: the taking of the possessions of the Egyptians by the Israelites at the command of God.

[14] *In II Sent.*, 15: "Sed stante praecepto divino ad eorum opposita non posset aliquis tales actus [odium Dei, furari, adulterari] meritorie nec bene exercere, quia non possent [exerceri] meritorie nisi caderent sub praecepto divino. Sed opposita non possunt simul cadere sub pracepto divino. Sed si sic fierent a viatore meritorie, tunc non dicerentur nec nominarentur furtum, adulterium, odium, etc., quia ista nomina significant tales actus non absolute sed connotando vel dando intelligere quod faciens tales actus per praeceptum divinum obligatur ad oppositum." (OTh V, 352).

[15] See F. Copleston, *op. cit.*, p. 109.

CHAPTER VI

2) man discovers the will of God only through a divine revelation in positive law. If such were actually the case, then right reason is simply and clearly a philosophical norm of ethics, while the will of God, on the other hand, is the norm for a moral theology.[16] As a matter of fact, however, this formulation of the way in which the twofold system of Ockham's ethics operates is an oversimplification. For it is exactly at this point that the two systems merge and overlap to a considerable extent. If we were to represent the two theories of Ockham by a set of parallel vertical lines, it would be at this point that we should insert a connecting horizontal line to indicate the unity in the two systems. The two systems are not completely distinct and, much less, contradictory in foundation or contents.

The merging of the two theories at this point is evident from several aspects. For example, we say that the precepts of right reason can be discovered by man's natural power of reason. But this does not necessarily imply that right reason has no role at all to play in the case of a divinely revealed command. As a matter of fact, right reason would also in the case of a divinely revealed command demand that the command of God be obeyed. Right reason is not lost or denied; the fulfillment of the command of God is certainly in conformity with right reason, its non-fulfillment, contrary to right reason. Though superseded by the command of God as the highest norm of morality, right reason as a more proximate norm coincides with the will of God, if His will is manifested by positive revelation. Secondly, it is said that the will of God is knowable only by revelation. But this should not be understood only in the sense in which a purely positive decree of God, unknowable except through some kind of divine communication, is revealed to us by a special act of God. For from the aspect of God's ordered power, can we not also speak of a "natural revelation" made from God to man? From its knowledge of created things the human mind "begins its journey" to the mind of God.[17] From the order of creation we glimpse the wisdom of almighty God; we learn of his goodness and providence. And so it is that from the moral order, discoverable and discovered by right reason, we learn the will of God.

The divinely established order governing the morality of man's acts is an order which Ockham accepted. Though it is not expressed in terms of purely positive precepts, the moral order is, we may say, just as much an expression of God's will as is a positive divine decree. The "law

---

[16] *Ibid.*, pp. 107-108.

[17] See St. Bonaventure, *Itinerarium mentis in Deum* in *Tria opuscula Sancti Bonaventurae* (ed. 5; Florence: Quaracchi, 1938), pp. 287 ff.

CONCLUSION

written in our hearts" is just as much the law of God as the law written by God on Moses' tablets of stone. The fulfillment of the unwritten law is the fulfillment of the will of God. Behind the moral law Ockham sees the hand of God which fashioned it; behind the moral code he sees the will of God which enforces it. Our knowledge of the moral law progresses. If we can speak of this progress, along with a dynamic development of human nature in self-perfection, there is also a progressive and dynamic aspect of this natural revelation. The unfolding of nature and our awareness of its development implies an unfolding of the mind and will of God toward man, a continuous revelation. And part of this unfolding and development involves the natural moral law.

The principles and precepts discovered by human reason in the natural order are the natural, non-positive, commands of God. The fulfillment of the precepts of right reason is the fulfillment of the commands of God. For the Christian this means that his morally good acts are performed out of obedience to God and out of love of Him. I cannot see in Ockham's writings any restriction of this love of God to the fulfillment of only his positive commands. It must include the whole moral order, comprising both the positive and the non-positive commands of God. This is a most significant but often overlooked point in Ockham. However, it is exactly this point that leads us to an understanding of how his two systems or ethical theories can be integrated and how they are meant to complement one another.[18]

The above consideration also leads us to a fuller understanding of the Christian's position in this world. We have already indicated how the

---

[18] Strangely enough, F. Copleston finds this to be a major obstacle in the integration of Ockham's ethics. See F. Copleston, *op. cit.*, pp. 109-110: "One can, then, sum up Ockham's position on more or less the following lines. The human being, as a free created being which is entirely dependent on God, is morally obliged to conform his will to the divine will in regard to that which God commands or prohibits. Absolutely speaking, God could command or prohibit any act, provided that a contradiction is not involved. Actually God has established a certain moral law. As a rational being man can see that he ought to obey this law. But he may not know what God has commanded; and in this case he is morally obliged to do what he honestly believes to be in accordance with God's commands. To act otherwise would be to act contrary to what is believed to be the divine ordinance; and to do this is to sin. It is not clear what Ockham thought of the moral situation of the man who has no knowledge of revelation, or even no knowledge of God's existence. He appears to imply that reason can discern something of the present moral order; but, if he did mean this, it is difficult to see how this ideas can be reconciled with his authoritarian conception of morality. If the moral law is dependent simply on the divine choice, how can its content be known apart from revelation? If its content can be known apart from revelation is simply a provisional code of morality, based on non-theological considerations. But that Ockham actually had this notion clearly in mind, which would imply the possibility of a purely philosohic and second-rank ethic, as distinct from the divinely-imposed and obligatory ethic, I should not care to affirm."

CHAPTER VI

virtues of the Christian differ from those of the pagan. The love of God, which impresses itself on every virtuous act of a Christian and gives those acts their absolute value, is impossible for the pagan or atheist. The loss of value is evident in the case of positive commands of God, for these are either unknown or opposed by the pagan or atheist. But the loss of value also extends to the whole moral order, for here, too, the pagan or atheist is blind to the will of God. This does not imply that the atheist or pagan is incapable of virtuous acts; but it does mean that these acts do not have the specific value conferred upon them in virtue of the fact that they are performed out of love of God by the Christian. The atheist or pagan is, in this sense, a moral cripple.

In view of the Christian's position in the world as contrasted with that of the pagan, we will shift our point of emphasis in briefly analyzing the remaining items which were listed above as basic to the understanding of Ockham's twofold theory of ethics. This shift of emphasis is made intentionally. We can speak now of the will of God as the norm in the sense of including the whole range of morality for the Christian. In this sense, the will of God can be termed a "personal" norm, expressing, as it does, the intimate relation between Creator and creature. The Christian confronts God, the will of God. He is not obeying some blind force, an impersonal nature, a created "moral order" of some kind. The pagan, left without God, can only obey something; the Christian obeys Someone. And this Someone is the highest Good. The unbeliever can only seek limited, short-range, self-satisfying goods in following the dictates of his reason in the realm of morality. The Christian following his right reason sees his actions as a mode of conforming to the will of Him who is the only true good. The Christian sees his own good actions as an expression of his love of God operating in and through his obedience to His holy will. The Christian bases his conduct on an ethics of love; he is moved to act out of the motive of love. The unbeliever can have at most an ethics of natural reward, whether this reward be expressed in terms of utility, pleasure, self-perfection of his personality, or whatever other motives he may conjure up.[19] This difference certainly points out the sublimity and grandeur of Ockham's thought in the realm of ethics.

---

[19] See E. Hochstetter, "Viator mundi," p. 10. *Ibid.*, p. 14-15: "Hieraus ist ersichtlich, dass zwar Inhalt der Gebote Gottes positiv ist, weil er de potentia absoluta auch anderes, ja Entgegengesetztes befohlen hat, also befehlen kann, dass aber der eigentliche sittliche Wert in der Gesinnung liegt, aus der heraus sie befolgt werden. Dieser Wert aber ist absolut. Er ist hier der frei Gehorsam gegenüber Gott, und dieser hat seinen tiefsten Grund in der Liebe zu Gott, denn dieser ist, wie gezeigt, das letzte Ziel jeder guten Tat...Denn trotz der Positivität aller Gebote....steht für Ockham der viator letztlich doch zwischen zwei äussersten Möglichkeiten, zwischen denen er unbedingt wählen muss: dem absoluten Wert der Liebe zu Gott und dem absoluten Unwert der höchsten Selbstliebe."

CONCLUSION

Ockham's philosophy has been aptly called and concernedly defended as a philosophy of a believer.[20] I think that this is perhaps no more clearly evident and no more highly important than in his teaching in the field of ethics. His mention of the love of God is not casual; he insists on the love of God emphatically. For it is in the love of God that he sees all our worthy actions transformed and purged, tried as if by fire. There is but one absolute commandment given to creatures: Love God. There is only one basis for the absolute worth of all our moral conduct: the love of God. The love of God is the "first and greatest commandment." The love of God is the norm and motive for morality. It is, in short, the very purpose of our existence.

---

[20] See L. Baudry (ed.), *Le Tractatus de principiis theologiae attribué à G. d'Occam* ("Etudes de philosophie médiévale," XXIII; Paris: Vrin, 1936), pp. 34-37.

BIBLIOGRAPHY

BIBLIOGRAPHY

ANCIENT AND MEDIEVAL WORKS

Anselm, St. *De conceptu virginali et de originali peccato* in *S. Anselmi opera omnia*, tom. II, pp. 135-173. Ed. Franciscus S. Schmitt. Edinburgh: Nelson, 1946.

Aristotle. *De anima* in *The Basic Works of Aristotle*, pp.533-603. Ed. Richard McKeon. Trans. J. A. Smith. New York: Random House, 1941.

_____. *Ethica Nicomachea* in *The Basic Works of Aristotle*, pp. 927-1112. Ed. Richard McKeon. Trans. W. D. Ross. New York: Random House, 1941.

Augustine, St. *De civitate Dei* in *Patrologiae cursus completus: Patrologiae latinae*, tom. XLI. Ed. J. P. Migne. Paris, 1861.

Biel, Gabriel. *Repertorium generale...Gabrielis Biel super super quatuor libros Sententiarum*. Tuebingen, 1527.

Bonaventure, St. *Itinerarium mentis in Deum* in *Tria opuscula S. Bonaventurae*, pp. 287-361 (ed. 5) Quaracchi: Collegium S. Bonaventurae, 1938.

Ockham, William. *Guillelpmi de Ockham Breviloquium de potestate papae*. Ed. Leon Baudry. ("Etudes de philosophie médiévale," XXIV) Paris: Vrin, 1937.

_____. *Guillelmi de Ockham opera philosophica et theologica* (Editiones Instituti Franciscani Universitatis S. Bonaventurae, St. Bonaventure N.Y.). *Opera philosophica*, Vol. I-VII (1974-86): *Opera theologica*, Vol. I-X (1967-86).

_____. *Guillelmi de Ockham opera politica*. Vol. I-III. Mancunii: E typis Universitatis, 1940-63.

Scotus, John Duns. *Ioannis Duns Scoti Tractatus de Primo Principio*. Ed. Marianus Mueller. Freiburg im Breigau: Herder, 1941.

_____. *Ordinatio* in *Ioannis Duns Scoti opera omnia*. Civitas Vaticana: Typis Polyglottis Vaticanis, 1950 .

_____. *Quaestiones quodlibetales* in *Obras del Juan Duns Escoto: Cuestiones cuodlibetales*. Ed. F. Alluntis. Madrid: Biblioteca de Autores Cristianos, 1968. Also in *Joannis Duns Scoti opera omnia*, tom XXV-XXVI. Parisiis: Apud Ludovicum Vivès, 1894.

BIBLIOGRAPHY

_____. *Reportatio Parisiensia* in *Joannis Duns Scoti opera omnia*, tom. XII-XXIV. Parisiis: Apud Ludovicum Vivès, 1893-94.

Thomas Aquinas, St. *Quaestiones disputatae: De potentia* in *D. Thomae Aquinatis opera omnia*, tom XIII. Parisiis, Apud Ludovicum Vivès, 1875.

_____. *Summa theologica* in *D. Thomae Aquinatis opera omnia*, tom. I-VI. Parisiis: Apud Ludovicum Vivès, 1871-1873.

Le Tractatus de principiis theologiae attribué à G. d'Occam. Ed. Léon Baudry. ("Etudes de philosophie médiévale," XXIII.) Paris: Vrin, 1936.

BIBLIOGRAPHY

OCKHAM LITERATURE

Amann, Emile. "Occam" in *Dictionnaire de théologie catholique*, t. XIa, col. 864-876; 889-904. Paris: Letouzey et Ané, 1931.

Barth, Timotheus. "Wilhelm Ockham im Lichte der neuesten Forschung," *Philosophisches Jahrbuch*, LX, 1950, pp. 464-467.

Baudry, Léon. "A propos de la théorie occamiste de la relation," *Archives d'histoire doctrinale et littéraire du moyen âge*, IX, 1934, pp. 199-203.

_____. "En lisant Jean le Chanoine," *Archives d'histoire doctrinale et littéraire du moyen âge*, IX, pp. 175-197.

_____. *Guillaume d'Occam. Sa vie, ses oeuvres, ses idees sociales et politiques.* Tom I: *L'homme et les oeuvres.* ("Etudes de philosophie médiévale," XXXIX.) Paris; Vrin, 1950.

_____. (ed.) *Guillelmi de Occam Breviloquium de potestate papae.* ("Etudes de philosophie médiévale," XXIV.) Paris: Vrin, 1937).

_____. *Lexique philosophique de Guillume d'Ockham.* Paris: Vrin, 1936.

_____. "Le philosophie et le politique dans Guillaume d'Ockham," *Archives d'histoire doctrinale et littéraire du moyen âge*, XII, 1939, pp. 209-230.

_____. (ed.) *Le Tractatus de principiis theologiae attribué à G. d'Occam.* ("Etudes de philosophie médiévale," XXIII.) Paris: Vrin, 1936.

Becher, Hubert. "Gottesbegriff und Gottesbeweis bei Wilhelm von Ockham," *Scholastik*, III, 1928, pp. 369-393.

Belmond, Seraphin. "Deux penseurs franciscains: Pierre-Jean Olivi et Guillaume Occam," *Etudes franciscains*, XXXV, pp. 188-197.

Boehner, Philotheus. "In propria causa. A Reply to Professor Pegis' 'Concerning William of Ockham'," *Franciscan Studies*, V, 1945, pp. 37-54.

_____. "The Notitia Intuitiva of Non-existents according to Wm. Ockham," *Traditio*, I, 1943, pp. 223-275.

_____. (ed.) *Ockham. Philosophical Writings.* ("Nelson Philosophical Texts") London: Nelson, 1957.

BIBLIOGRAPHY

_____. "Ockham's Philosophy in the Light of Recent Research," in *Collected Articles on Ockham*. Ed. Eligius Buytaert. ("Franciscan Institute Publications, Philosophy Series," No. 12) St. Bonaventure, N.Y.: Franciscan Institute, 1958, pp. 23-28.

_____. "Ockham's Political Ideas," *Review of Politics*, V, 1943, pp. 462-487.

_____. "The Realistic Conceptualism of William Ockham," *Traditio*, IV, 1946, pp. 307-335.

_____. "A Recent Presentation of Ockham's Philosophy," *Franciscan Studies*, XI, 1951, pp. 305-316.

_____. "The Spirit of Franciscan Philosophy," *Franciscan Studies*, II, 1942, pp. 217-237.

_____. "Der Stand der Ockham-Forschung," *Franziskanische Studien*, XXXIV, 1952, pp. 12-31.

_____. "The Text Tradition of Ockham's Ordinatio," *New Scholasticism*, XVI, 1942, pp. 203-241.

_____. (ed.) *The Tractatus de praedestinatione et de praescientia Dei et de futuris contingentibus of William Ockham*. ("Franciscan Institute Publications, Philosophy Series," No. 2.) St. Bonaventure, N.Y.: Franciscan Institute, 1945.

_____. (ed.) *The Tractatus de successivis Attributed to William Ockham*. ("Franciscan Institute Publications, Philosophy Series," No. 1.) St. Bonaventure, N.Y.: Franciscan Institute, 1945.

Bonke, Elzearius. "Doctrina nominalistica de fundamento ordinis moralis apud Gulielmum de Ockham et Gabrielem Biel," *Collectanea franciscana*, XIV, 1944, pp. 57-83.

Brampton, C. Kenneth. *De imperatorum et pontificum potestate of William of Ockham* Oxford, 1927.

Brehier, Emile. *La philosophie du moyen âge*. Paris: Michel, 1949.

Buescher, Gabriel. *The Eucharistic Teaching of William Ockham*. ("Franciscan Institute Publications, Theology Series," No. 1.) St. Bonaventure, N.Y.: Franciscan Institute, 1950.

Buytaert, Eligius (ed.) *Philotheus Boehner: Collected Articles on Ockham*. ("Franciscan Institute Publications, Philosophy Series," No. 12.) St. Bonaventure, N.Y.: Franciscan Institute, 1958.

BIBLIOGRAPHY

Copleston, Frederick. *A History of Philosophy*. Vol. III: *Ockham to Suarez*. Westminster: Newman, 1953.

Federhofer, Franz. "Die Philosophie des Wilhelm von Occam in Rahmen seiner Zeit," *Franziskanische Studien*, XII, 1925, pp. 273-296.

Fuchs, Oswald. *The Psychology of Habit according to William Ockham*. ("Franciscan Institute Publications, Philosophy Series," No. 8.) St. Bonaventure, N.Y.: Franciscan Institute, 1952.

Garvens, Anita. "Die Grundlagen der Ethik Wilhelms von Ockham," *Franziskanische Studien*, XXI, 1934, pp. 243-273; 360-408.

Gilson, Etienne and Boehner, Philotheus. *Christliche Philosophie*. Paderborn: Schoeningh, 1954.

Gilson, Etienne. *History of Christian Philosophy in the Middle Ages*. New York: Random House, 1955.

_____. *La philosophie au moyen âge*. (Ed. 3.) Paris: Payot, 1947.

Guelluy, Robert. *Philosophie et théologie chez Guillaume d'Ockham*. Paris: Vrin, 1947.

Hamman, Adalbert. *La doctrine de l'Eglise et de l'Etat chez Occam*. ("*Etudes* de Science Religieuse," I.) Paris, 1942.

Heynck, Valens. "Ockham Literatur," *Franziskanische Studien*, XXXII, 1950, pp. 164-183.

Hirschberger, Johannes. *Geschichte der Philosophie*. I: *Altertum und Mittelalter*. Freiburg (Br.): Herder, 1949.

Hochstetter, Erich. "Nominalismus?" *Franciscan Studies*, IX, 1949, pp. 370-403.

_____. "Ockham-Forschung in Italien," *Zeitschrift für philosophische Forschung*, I, 1947, pp. 559-578.

_____. *Studien zur Metaphysik und Erkenntnislehre Wilhelms von Ockham*. Leipzig: W. de Gruyter, 1927.

Iserloh, Erwin. *Gnade und Eucharistie in der philosophischen Theologie des Wilhelm von Ockham*. Wiesbaden: Steiner, 1956.

_____. "Um die Echtheit des Centiloquium," *Gregorianum*, XXX, 1949, pp. 78-103; 309-346.

Kölmel, Wilhelm. "Das Naturrecht bei Wilhelm Ockham," *Franziskanische Studien*, XXXV, 1953, pp. 39-85.

BIBLIOGRAPHY

Lagarde, Georges de. *La naissance de l'esprit laïque au déclin du moyen âge.* IV: *Ockham et son temps.* V: *Ockham: Bases de départ.* VI: *Ockham: La morale et le droit.* Paris: Presses Universitaires de France, 1942-1946.

Maier, Anneliese. "Zu einigen Problemen der Ockhamforschung," *Archivum franciscanum historicum,* XLVI, 1953, pp. 161-194.

Maurer, Armand. "Scotism and Ockhamism," in *History of Philosophical Systems.* Ed. Vergilius Ferm. New York: Philosophical Library, 1950, pp. 212-224.

Menges, Matthew. *The Concept of Univocity regarding the Predication of God and Creature according to William Ockham.* ("Franciscan Institute Publications, Philosophy Series," No. 9.) St. Bonaventure, N.Y.: Franciscan Institute, 1952.

Meyer, Hans. *Geschichte der abendländischen Weltanschauung.* Bd. III: *Die Weltanschauung des Mittelalters.* Paderborn: Schoeningh, 1948.

Moody, Ernest. *The Logic of William of Ockham.* New York: Sheed and Ward, 1935.

_____. "Ockham and Aegidius of Rome," *Franciscan Studies,* IX, 1949, pp. 417-442.

Morrall, John. "Ockham's Political Philosophy," *Franciscan Studies,* IX, 1949, pp. 335-369.

Pegis, Anton. "Concerning William of Ockham," *Traditio,* II, 1944, pp. 465-480.

_____. "Necessity and Liberty: An Historical Note on St. Thomas Aquinas," *New Scholasticism,* XV, 1941, pp. 18-45.

_____. "Some Recent Interpretations of Ockham," *Speculum,* XXIII, 1948, pp. 452-463.

Pelzer, Auguste. "Les 51 articles de Guillaume Occam censures en Avignon en 1326," *Revue d'histoire ecclesiastique,* XVIII, 1922, pp. 240-270.

Rubert y Candáu, José Mariá. "Los principios básicos de la Etica en el Ockhamismo y en la via moderna de los siglos XIV y XV," *Verdad y vida,* XVIII, 1960, pp. 97-116.

Sikes, J.G. et al. (eds.) *Gulielmi de Ockham. Opera Politica.* Vol. I. Manchester: University Press, 1940.

Stöckl, Albert. *Geschichte der Philosophie des Mittelalters.* Mainz, 1864-1866.

BIBLIOGRAPHY

Suk, Othmar. "The Connection of Virtues according to Ockham," *Franciscan Studies*, X, 1950, pp. 9-32; 91-113.

Tornay, Stephen. *Ockham. Studies and Selections*. LaSalle, Ill.: Open Court, 1938.

Ueberweg, Friedrich and Geyer, Bernhard. *Grundriss der Philosophie*. II: *Die patristische und scholastische Philosophie*. Basel, 1951.

Vignaux, Paul. "Nominalisme," in *Dictionnaire de théologie catholique*, t. XIa, col. 733-765. Paris: Letouzey et Ané, 1931.

_____. "Occam," in *Dictionnaire de théologie catholique*, t. XIa, col. 876-889. Paris: Letouzey et Ané, 1931.

Webering, Damascene. *The Theory of Demonstration according to William Ockham*. ("Franciscan Institute Publications, Philosophy Series," No. 10.) St. Bonaventure, N.Y.: Franciscan Institute, 1953.

Wolter, Allan. "Ockham and the Textbooks: On the Origin of Possibility," *Franziskanische Studien*, XXXII, 1950, pp. 70-96.

Wulf, Maurice de. *Histoire de la philosophie médiévale*. (Ed. 5) Louvain: Institut supérieur de philosophie; Paris: Alcan, 1924-1925.

Zuidema, S. U. *De philosophie van Occam in zijn commentaar op de Sententien*. I. Hilversum: Schipper, 1936.

BIBLIOGRAPHY

GENERAL WORKS

Adler, Mortimer. "The Doctrine of Natural Law in Philosophy," in *University of Notre Dame Natural Law Institute Proceedings*, vol. I, pp. 65-84. Notre Dame, Ind.: College of Law, University of Notre Dame, 1949.

Bittle, Celestine. *Man and Morals: Ethics*. Milwaukee: Bruce, 1950.

Buckley, Joseph. *Man's Last End*. St. Louis: Herder, 1949.

Budzik, Gratianus. *De conceptu legis ad mentem Joannis Duns Scoti*. Burlington, Wis., 1954.

Cathrein, Victor. *De bonitate et malitia humanorum actuum doctrina S. Thomae Aquinatis*. Louvain: Museum Lessianum, 1926.

Collins, James. *A History of Modern European Philosophy*. Milwaukee: Bruce, 1954.

Cronin, Michael. *The Science of Ethics*. Vol. I: *General Ethics*. New York: Benziger, 1909.

Davitt, Thomas. *The Nature of Law*. St. Louis: Herder, 1951.

Day, Sebastian. *Intuitive Cognition: A Key to the Significance of the Later Scholastics*. ("Franciscan Institute Publications, Philosophy Series," No. 4.) St. Bonaventure, N.Y.: Franciscan Institute, 1947.

Denifle, Heinrich. *Luther und Luthertum*. Mainz: Verlag von Kirchain, 1904-1909.

D'Entrèves, A.P. *Natural Law: An Introduction to Legal Philosophy*. London: Hutchinson's University Library, 1951.

Donat, J. *Summa philosophiae christianae*. Tom. VII: *Ethica generalis* (Ed. 7.) Barcelona: Herder, 1944.

Grisar, Hartmann. *Luther*. Vol. I: *Luther the Monk*. Trans. E.M. Lamond. Ed. Luigi Cappadelta. St. Louis: Herder, 1913.

Jansen, Bernhard. *Aufstieg zur Metaphysik heute und ehedem*. Freiburg (Br.): Herder, 1933.

Klubertanz, George. "Ethics and Theology," *The Modern Schoolman*, XXVII, 1949, pp. 29-39.

BIBLIOGRAPHY

Lottin, Odon. *Psychologie et morale aux XIIe siècles*. T. II-III: *Problemes de morale*. Louvain: Mont.-César, 1948-1949.

McKinnon, Harold. "Natural Law and Positive Law," in *University of Notre Dame Natural Law Institute Proceedings*, vol. I, pp. 85-103. Notre Dame College of Law, University of Notre Dame, 1949.

Pohle, Josef. *Dogmatic Theology*. Vol. I: *God: His Knowability, Essence, and Attributes*. Ed. Arthur Preuss. St. Louis: Herder, 1942.

Rommen, Heinrich. "The Natural Law in the Renaissance Period," in *University of Notre Dame Natural Law Institute Proceedings*, vol. II, pp. 89-124. Notre Dame, Ind.: College of Law, University of Notre Dame, 1949.

_____. *The State in Catholic Thought. A Treatise in Political Philosophy*. St. Louis: Herder, 1947.

Stratenwerth, Günter. *Die Naturrechtslehre des Joannes Duns Scotus*. Göttingen: Vandenhoeck and Ruprecht, 1951.

Tanquerey, Adolphe. *Synopsis theologiae dogmaticae*. T. II: *De Fide, de Deo uno et trino, de Deo creante et elevante, de Verbo Incarnato*. (Ed. 12.) Rome: Desclée, 1921.

Vignaux, Paul. *Luther, commentateur des Sentences*. ("Etudes de philosophie médiévale," XXI.) Paris: Vrin, 1935.

Wright, William. *A History of Modern Philosophy*. New York: Macmillan, 1941.